SIGNotation

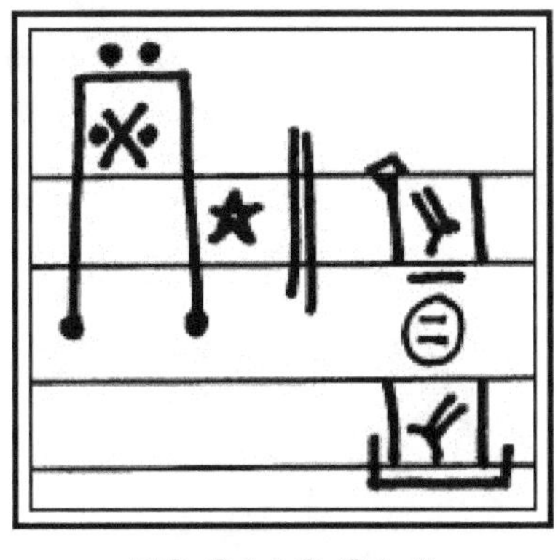

"SCHOOL"

The Musical Architecture of Signed Languages

The Intersection of Signed Languages, Music and Mathematics

S. Hansen CI/CT/SC:L/Ed:K-12

www.signotation.com

ISBN-13:978-0692670187 (ASLiSH)

ISBN-10:0692670181

DEDICATION

To my darling family and the Deaf Community for sharing their language and culture with me each day. And with thanks to God for blessing me and helping me be able to work, have time to think and create and have such a rewarding and challenging career.

I would also like to dedicate this book to the students and staff in the Pasco School district, especially the elementary kids in Ms. Amber Havers' room, who challenge and inspire me and are *so much fun!*

CONTENTS

MUSICAL ARCHITECTURE

"The term **musical form** (or **musical architecture**) refers to the overall structure or plan of a piece of music, and it describes the layout of a composition as divided into sections. In the tenth edition of *The Oxford Companion to Music*, Percy Scholes defines musical form as 'a series of strategies designed to find a successful mean between the opposite extremes of *unrelieved repetition* and *unrelieved alteration*.'"

Source:
https://en.wikipedia.org/wiki/Musical_form
Retrieved 12/28/15

ACKNOWLEDGMENTS

With gratitude to all the D/HH/DB kids I've worked with over the years along with the TOD who have inspired me and challenged me to continually look for new ways to communicate and explore both academic content and interpersonal communication in the collaboration that is interpreting.

A RESEARCH PREMISE & CONCEPTUAL FRAMEWORK FOR USE IN K-12 BILINGUAL EDUCATION

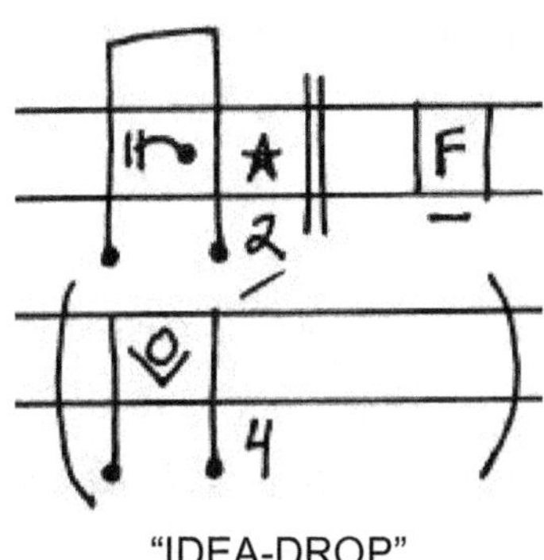

"IDEA-DROP"

My primary objective for this text is to present an option for recording the complexity of ASL or other signed languages in a written format for educational purposes. I offer this as a potential contribution to the efforts in bilingual-bicultural education and increased metalinguistic awareness for Deaf, Hard of Hearing and DeafBlind students. As a community freelance interpreter for over 25 years and an active educational interpreter in public school settings, I have attempted to create something useful for classroom instruction on the relationships between the grammatical structure and complexity of signed languages and the complementary intersection of ASL with musical notation and mathematical and spoken language written conventions. This is to be considered as a proposal, open to feedback and revision based on usefulness for educational purposes in K-12 settings.

This work is not intended to be a linguistics text. It is a pragmatic approach based on functional usage and not strict adherence or conformity to formal linguistic norms, based on my perspective as a community interpreter. Any similarity to another approach is unintentional and coincidental. The impetus for this project, besides my interactions in K-12 Deaf Ed and love for ASL, is a course on linguistics I took a couple of years ago that included a homework assignment to create a written approach to sign language, and a viewer from Youtube asking me to provide feedback on a system for written ASL that used the "qwerty" or standard keyboard exclusively.

My goal has been to present a basic conceptual framework that hopefully has enough versatility and structure to accommodate and respect the unique features of visual language use and signed languages including ASL. This text is intended to be an open-ended starting point for further dialogue, collaboration, experimentation, revision and development within the signing and educational communities.

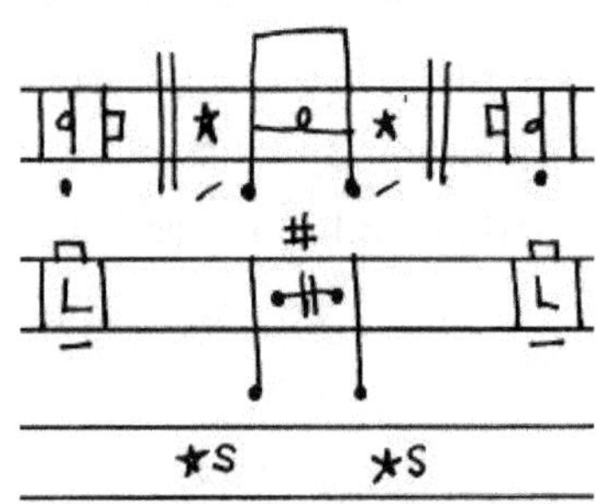

“SIGN LANGUAGE”

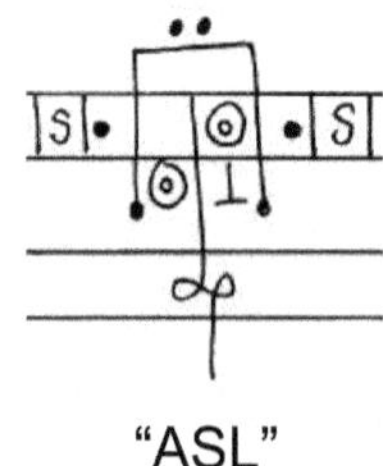

“ASL”

FOUNDATIONS

How can complex, detailed information such as a visual spatial language be put to paper?

If you watch a video of a fluent signer telling a compelling and detailed narrative that includes action, dialogue and reflective response, the task of somehow putting that to paper is daunting. (You can see excellent examples of fluent ASL use on Youtube: ASLized.) ASL is a visual three dimensional language, utilizing movement and symbols interacting in space, and is expressed by the full body and face to convey an endless array of subtle and nuanced meanings. Even the eye lids, nose and tongue contribute grammatically.

Currently we have a variety of effective means to transcribe information for shared exchange for:

- Verbal languages
- Music
- Mathematical relationships
- Chemical properties (ie: The Periodic Table of the Elements)
- Computer programming languages or codes
- Graphs and charts (ie: Growth charts, audiograms, etc...)

For example here is a standard set of musical symbols used internationally:

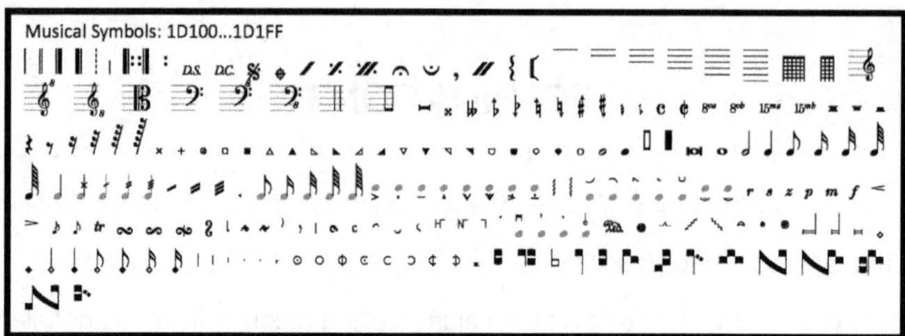

http://luc.devroye.org/GeorgeDouros-MusicalSymbols.png

Retrieved 10/7/15

ASL and signed languages are also capable of being recorded effectively and completely on paper in a way that allows for limitless variance in content, while conserving all grammatical elements of meaning.

CONVENTIONS

Signotation incorporates the standard conventions of:

- alphabetical characters
- numerical characters and symbols
- punctuation marks and symbols
- musical and mathematical symbols

in conjunction with simple sketching and created symbols as needed for grammatically accurate detail.

ASSUMPTIONS

Just as spoken languages are the primary driver and written forms are secondary methods to record those naturally occurring languages, Signotation (SN) presumes the user is fluent and competent in the signed language and the recording of those elements of meaning using shared symbols is merely a representation for a living language. Our focus will be on those elements which are grammatically relevant. Individual variations in expression, tone and affect are brought to the printed text by the user. A written format for signed languages should not be artificially dependent on another written oral language and should be consistently replicable.

THE 5 PARAMETERS OF SIGNOTATION

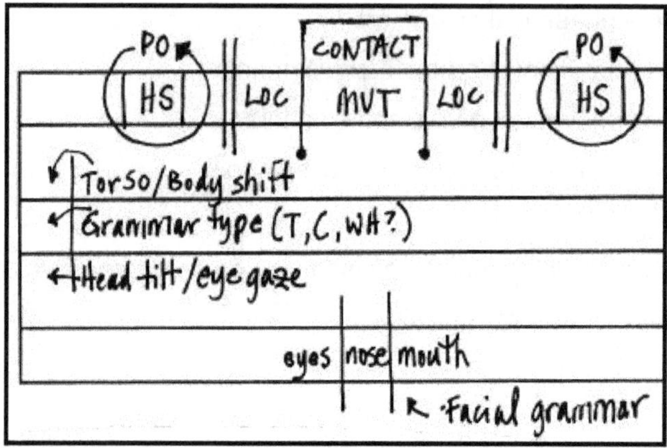

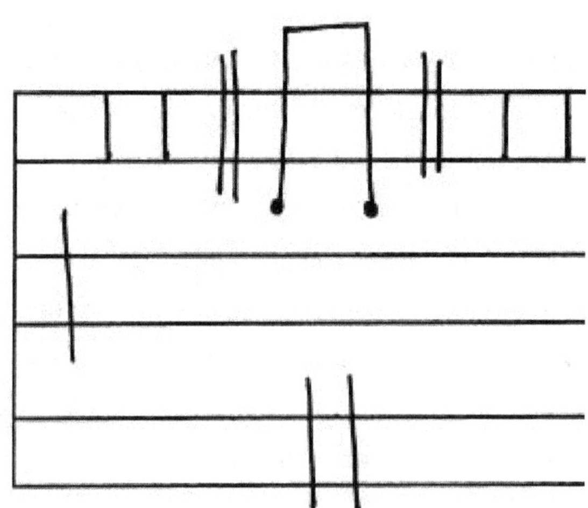

THE 5 PARAMETERS

Linguists recognize five sign language parameters. These parameters are independent of any specific signed language such as LSM (lengua de señas mexicana), FSL (French Sign Language) or ASL (American Sign Language), and are thus foundational for analysis of the structure of signed languages.

The 5 parameters are:

- Handshape (HS)
- Palm Orientation (PO)
- Location (LOC)
- Movement (MVT)
- Facial grammar (FG) or NMGM (Non Manual Grammatical Markers)

Just as spoken languages functions within the oral/auditory mechanisms and therefore observe certain boundaries for expression, so too signed languages function within the manual or physical expressions of the human body and either visual or tactile reception boundaries.

Source:
Linguistics of American Sign Language: An Introduction, Fifth Edition, 2011 by Valli, Lucas, Mulrooney and Villanueva (p. 21) "5 Parameters".

SIGNOTATION STAFF

Signed languages have more in common with music in regards to the experience of producing and receiving messages than to linear spoken languages which proceed one vocal utterance at time. The ability to produce multiple simultaneous and layered elements of meaning along a continuum of complexity is compatible with the norms of recording music on paper.

Below is a sample of the Signotation Staff (SS) used to notate the five parameters of any individual sign, phrase or statement. Each of the five parameters will be applied to this staff:

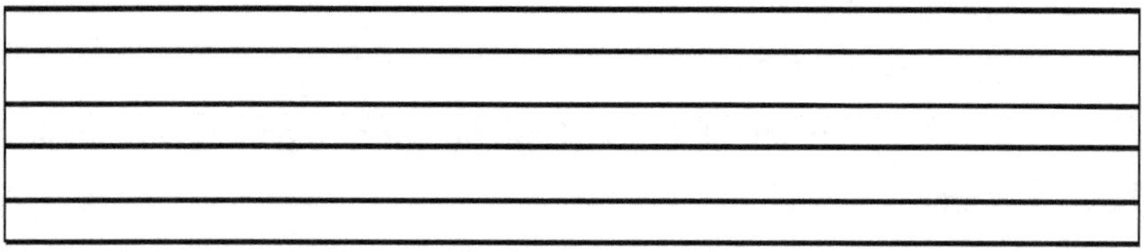

When considering how to arrange the SS, one can analyze the number of typical movements in a single sign. Many signs have only one primary movement or location (ie: school). Other signs have two primary movements or locations (ie: college). And a few signs have a total of three primary movements or locations (ie: house). Later we will look at signs that are compound or have additional movements or locations, but for now, using a SS with three tiers is sufficient for the majority of sign movements.

SAMPLES OF HANDWRITTEN MUSICAL NOTATION

Baude Cordier's chanson "Belle, bonne, sage"

from the Chantilly Manuscript.

Wagner: Wesendonck-Lieder 1

Wagner

Wesendonk Lieder

Der Engel

(Mathilde Wesendonk)

Source:

https://www.google.com/search?q=creative+commons+handwritten+sheet+music&rlz=2C1SAVG_enUS0536US0622&espv=2&biw=1152&bih=763&tbm=isch&tbo=u&source=univ&sa=X&ved=0ahUKEwjvvqmhtNfLAhXHTCYKHRnOBaoQsAQINg#imgrc=p9KtRw3cgmyEJM%3A

Retrieved 3/23/16

SIGNOTATION SAMPLE

ASLized
Signily: American Sign Language Keyboard App

https://www.youtube.com/watch?v=dOMTkit0iXk

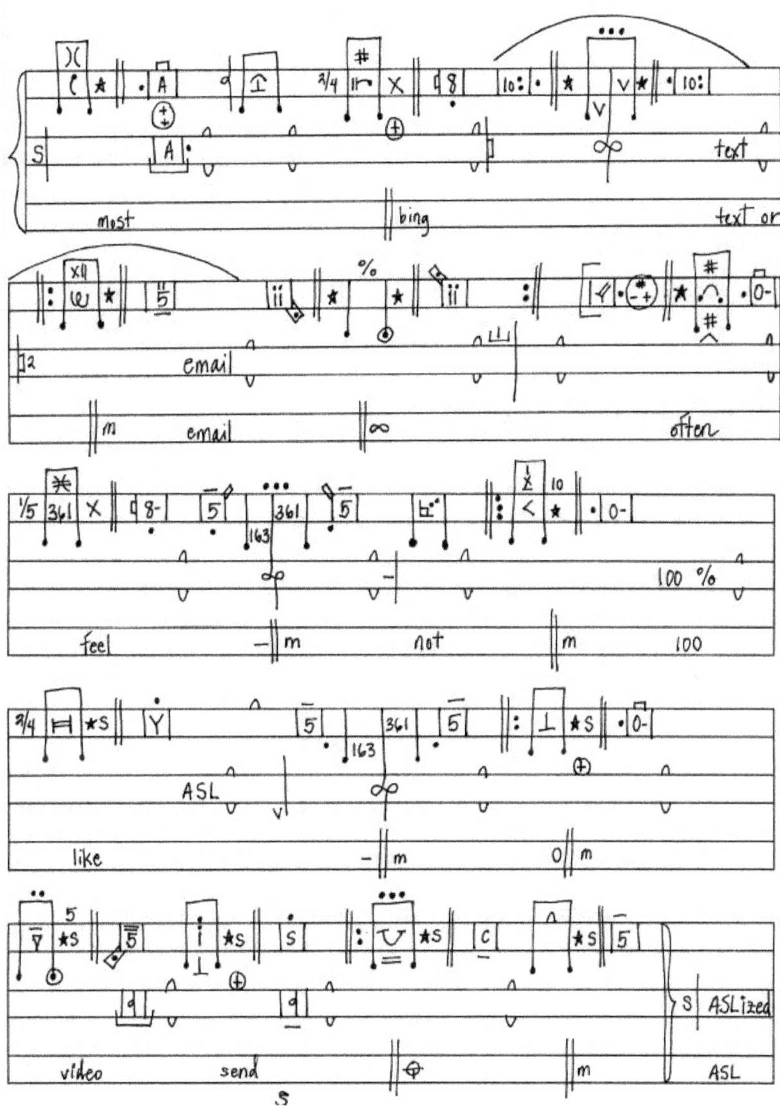

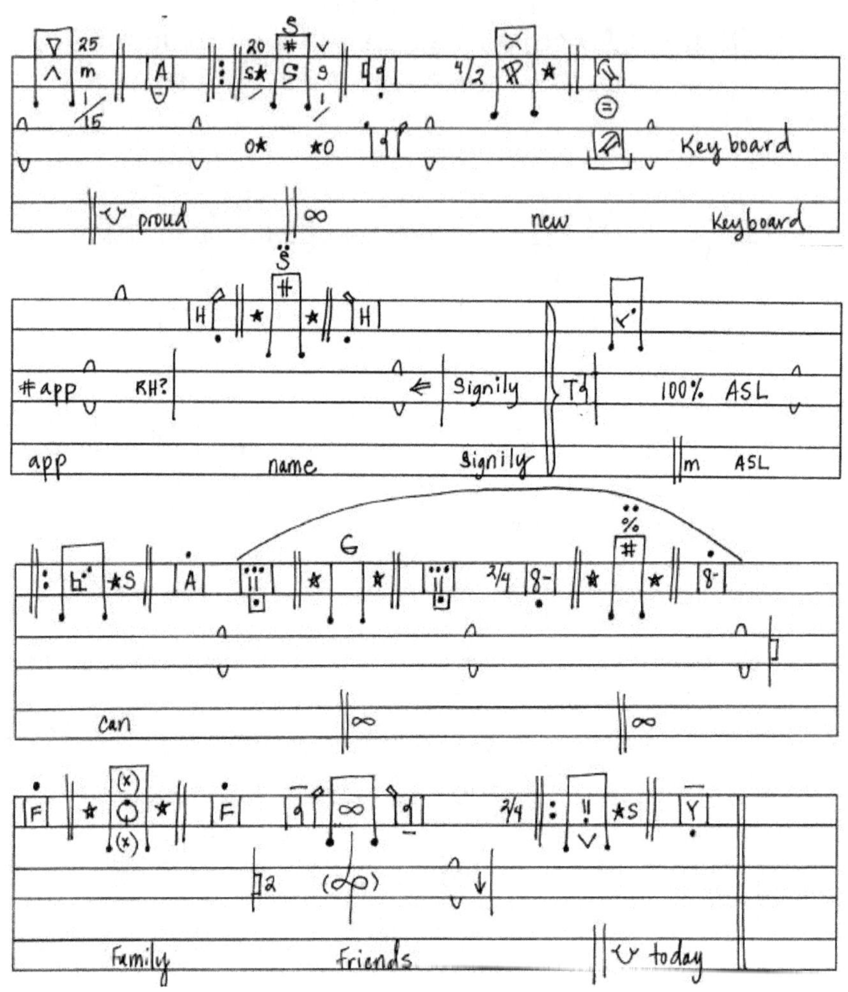

Note: Mouthing was notated on this version.

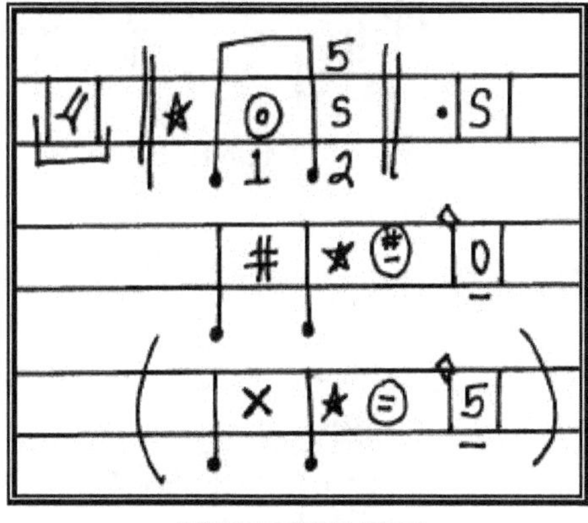

"SIGNOTATE"

BASIC SIGNOTATION

The most basic notation will require 4 parameters: Handshape (HS), Palm Orientation (PO), Location (LOC) and Movement (MVT).

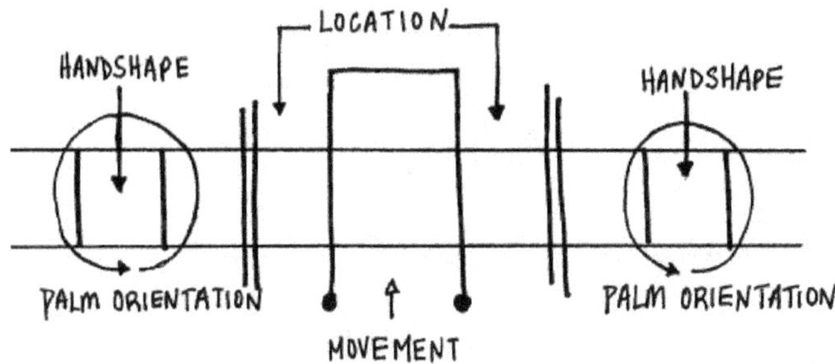

Here is an example of the two-handed sign "more" in SN:

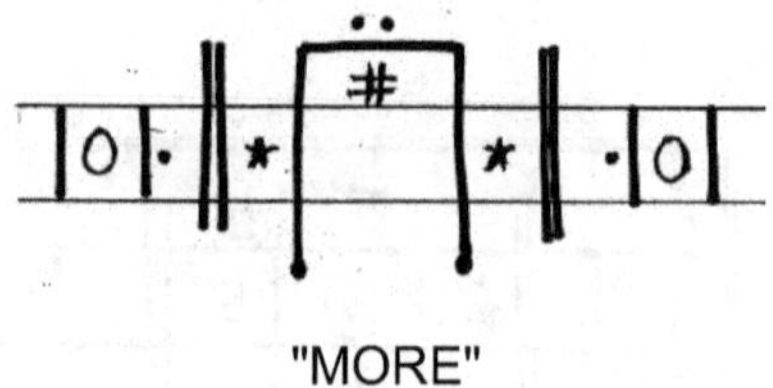

"MORE"

And an example of a one-handed sign "Mother":

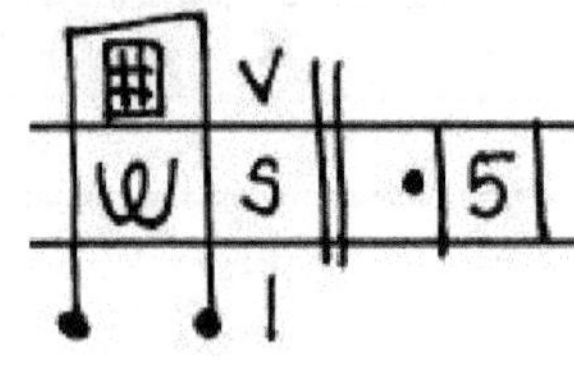

"MOTHER"

A depicting verb:

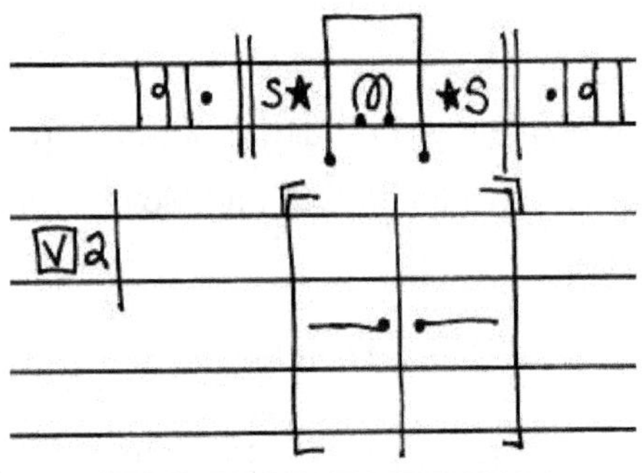

"TWO PEOPLE MEETING"

A lateral alternating movement:

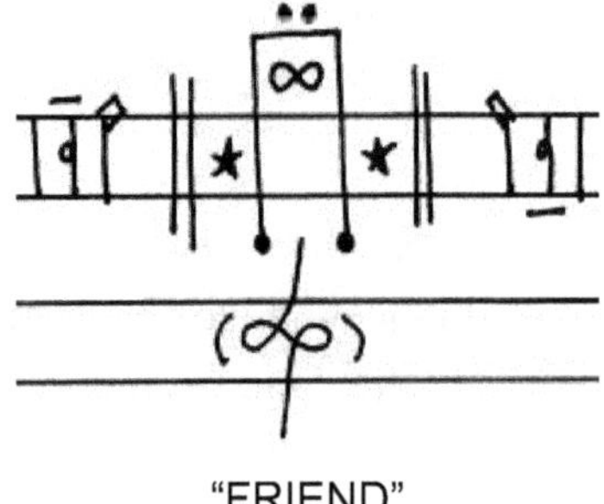

"FRIEND"

DOMINANT AND NON-DOMINANT HANDSHAPES

Each sign is composed of either one or both hands.

The D (dominant) hand is the one typically used to fingerspell words or actively count.

The ND (non-dominant) hand is either inactive, or is used as a base for the actions of the D hand, or can be equally active in conjunction with the D hand.

For example the sign for "mother" utilizes only the D HS and the sign "more" uses both the D and ND handshapes equally.

On the SS, the D HS is on the right of the Movement block, and the ND HS is to the left of the Movement block.

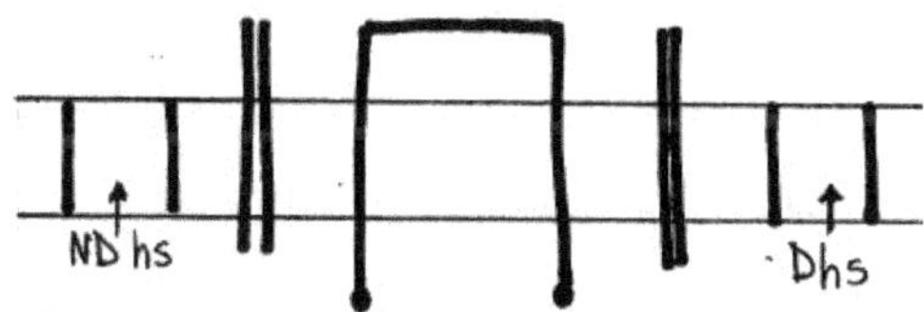

Sources:

Linguistics of American Sign Language an Introduction, 5th Edition, Valli, Lucas, Mulrooney and Villanueva, http://gupress.gallaudet.edu/bookpage/LASL5bookpage.html

PARAMETER #1
HANDSHAPES

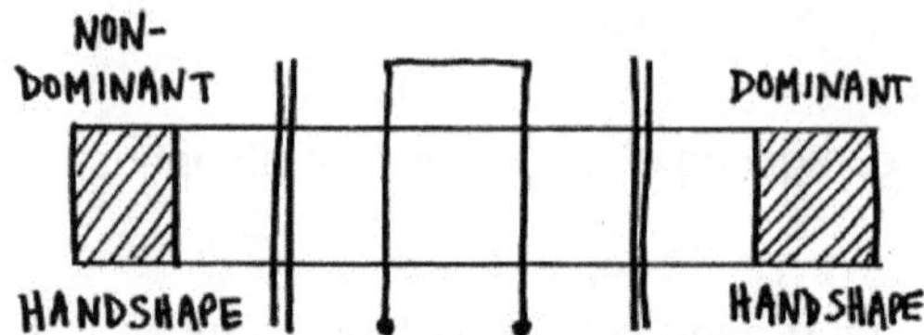

Signotation requires agreement on the symbols used to represent the elements of sign language. This is true for any written form of a language. The users must agree on shared symbols to engage in meaningful exchange that is consistent and transmittable from person to person and generation to generation. Below is a sample of possible symbols to represent various handshapes in ASL. Any symbol could be used for any one particular handshape. The listed HS symbols below are arbitrary and can be modified, replaced, re-created and added to as needed for any unique sign language HS. The country of origin's alphabet would be substituted for the English alphabet.

As I spent time working through a wide range of signs, it became clear that there is more than one way to notate a handshape. For example, these handshapes are nearly identical:

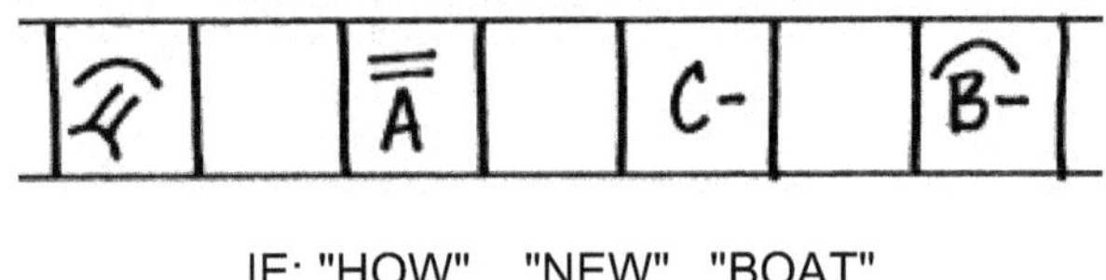

IE: "HOW" "NEW" "BOAT"

And these handshapes are also very similar if not identical:

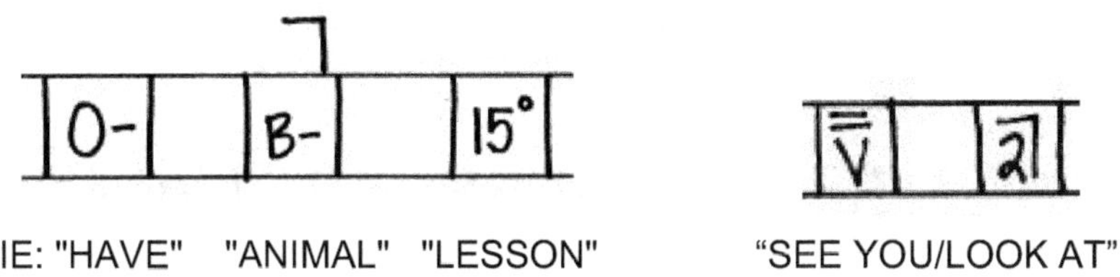

IE: "HAVE" "ANIMAL" "LESSON" "SEE YOU/LOOK AT"

Notations may gravitate towards standardization with time and use.

For the purposes of this text, the following HS are used:

- The standard English alphabet
- Standard "counting" numbers

And the handshapes from the charts below:

HANDSHAPES **SAMPLE SIGN GLOSSES**

⌒	CURVED HS	⌒B-	"how (are you)"
॥	CLAW HS	॥5	"bear",
		॥V	"blind", "doubt"
॥।	COLLAPSED CLAW	॥।5	"desperately want"
॥)	CURVED CLAW	॥5)	"lion", "comb"
=	COLLAPSED AND OPEN	=C	"sandwich"
		=V	"look at"
>	COLLAPSED, FINGERTIPS TOUCH	>3	"NO!" (command)
>‖	COLLAPSED, FINGERTIPS TOUCH REPEATEDLY	>‖3	"duck" "no"
- -	FINGERS SPREAD APART	-X-	"salmon"
⌉	BENT AT KNUCKLES*	B-⌉	"equal"
⌉‖	BENT AT WRIST*	B+⌉‖	"kangaroo"
◡	RELAXED HS	5◡	"what"

NOTE: THESE TWO CAN GO INSIDE OR ABOVE THE HS BLOCK:

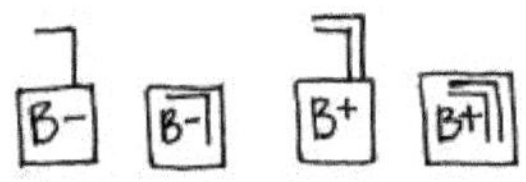

HS: COLLAPSED THUMB

ADD "+" to ANY HS = THUMB COLLAPSED

B+	"baby"
B+	"swim", "forgive"
X+	"turn the channel"

BASE HANDSHAPES (BHS)

		SAMPLE SIGN GLOSSES
	BASE HS	"help" (ND)
	CURVED BHS	"hamburger"
	INDEX BASE HS*	"5 minutes"

NOTE: DEFAULT POSITION FOR BHS IS PALM UP, FINGERTIPS FORWARD OR ANGLED FORWARD ie: "cook"

*DEFAULT POSITION FOR INDEX IS PALM R, FINGERTIP UP TO SKY

NOTE: OTHER HS CAN BE USED AS A BHS

ie: "support" USES "S" BHS

ie: "candle" USES "1" or "index" BHS

HS: EXTENDED THUMB

ADD "-" to ANY HS = THUMB EXTENDED

X-	"who?", "relay operator"
8-	"feel", "why?!"
	"sophomore in HS"
U-	"butter"
A-	"surgery", "Iran"
B-	"cook"
B̑-	"collaborate", "how"
C-	"how", "new"
O-	"equal", "have", "animal"
5-	"senior in HS"
6-	"prep student"
7-	"freshman in HS"
9-	"junior in HS

UNIQUE HS & NUMBERS

		SAMPLE SIGN GLOSSES
3‡	3 "VULCAN SPLIT"*	"escape"
4‡	4 "VULCAN SPLIT"*	"take a break"
78+	7-8 "WRAPPED"	"kids"
78	7-8 "EXTENDED"	"chihuahua"
ILY		"I love you"
Y1	Y with index extended forward	"airplane"
Y3	Y with 3 internal fingers exte forward	"fingerspell" (circular)
⊗	CLOSED "X"	"popsicle"

NUMBERS WITH MOVEMENT: REPS INSIDE HS BLOCK

25	(VIBRATES SO NO REPS)	"why"
•• 11		"understand"
• 12		"goat"
•• 15		"sweet"

NUMBERS WITHOUT MOVEMENT: ADD DEGREE SYMBOL°

REPS ABOVE MOVEMENT BLOCK

15°		"have"

*NOTE: DEFAULT IS FOR CONTACT/MVT TO OCCUR AT SPLIT

YOUR TURN!

HANDSHAPES

Record you own observations!

INDEX HANDSHAPE

An index handshape is very common in ASL and signed languages. This naturally occurring handshape can be noted with either a number "1":

Or with an index handshape symbol:

BASE HANDSHAPE PAIRS (BHSP)

BASE HANDSHAPES (BHS)

		SAMPLE SIGN GLOSSES
	BASE HS	"help" (ND)
	CURVED BHS	"hamburger"

A Base Handshape (BHS) is quite common in ASL. The typical configuration is an **active** D HS and **passive** or supportive ND BHS, occurring in the **same location**, and having **contact** with one another. A BHS provides a spatial foundation for the active HS. Here is a brief sample listing of common English glossed signs that are BHS pairs. There are many many more...

- church
- college
- computer (on the wrist)
- cook
- doctor
- enough
- establish
- evict/kick out/punt
- exaggerate
- iPad
- layoff from employment/waive/dismiss
- list
- medicine
- nurse
- paint
- pay off a bill, debt or account
- put down on paper/note

- terminate/fire from employment
- win

Because a BHS is so common, we can create an iconic symbol for this HS. The standard BHS is an open "B" with the thumb extended out to the side, Palm Orientation upward to the sky and fingertips angled towards the midline, (ie: ND HS: "cook"). Notated alone, the HS: BHS does not need any additional notation and is presumed to have this standard palm up, fingertips angled to the midline relaxed position:

At times it can be useful for the D HS to be notated using the same BHS symbol:

Here are examples of the signs glossed "to cook" and "new" notated with two BHS. The ND BHS is bracketed and directly below the D HS:

"TO COOK"

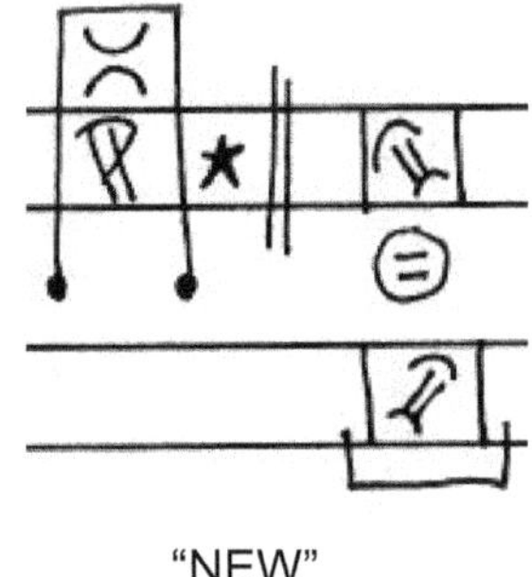

"NEW"

Other HS can be used as a BHS in a BSH Pair, such as the sign glossed "enough" which uses an "S" as a BHS and the sign "candle" that uses an index finger:

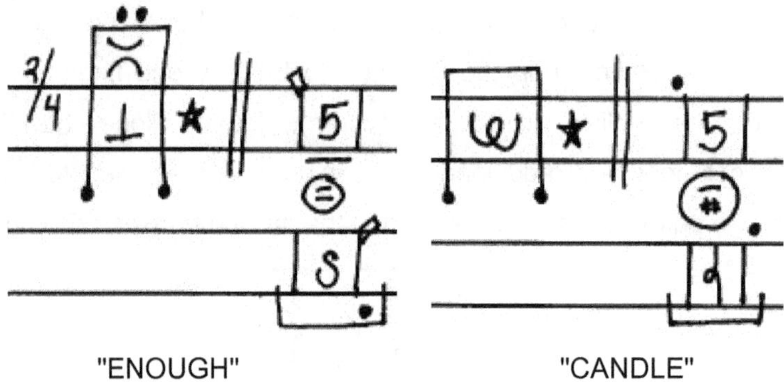

"ENOUGH" "CANDLE"

Some BHSP move together and have contact as a unit such as the verb "help". Other BHSP are also directional verbs, ie: "help someone", "support someone", "pick on someone", "pay someone" etc... A BHSP default is contact, however it may be necessary to include the type of contact. The sign glossed: "I help you" has continuous contact:

BHSP and DIRECTIONAL VERB: TO HELP

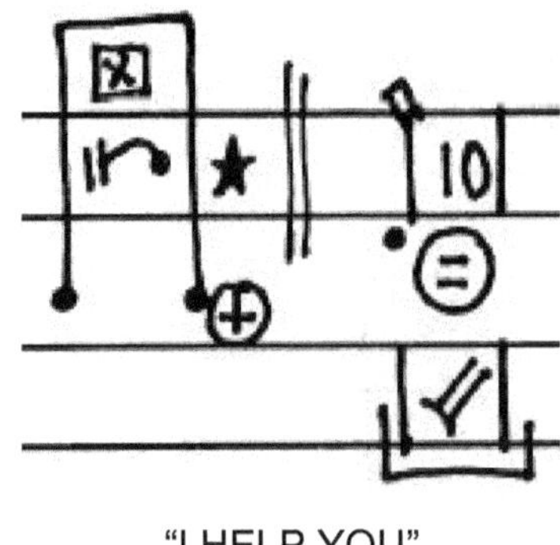

“I HELP YOU”

BHSP MID-TIER +/- CONTACT NOTATIONS

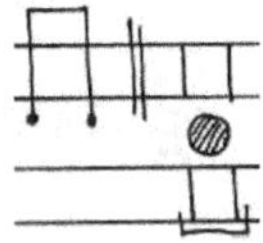

Notice the small circular notation between the two handshapes. This represents a shorthand version of the general location of contact between the handshapes. Here is a set of options for these mid-tier contact notations:

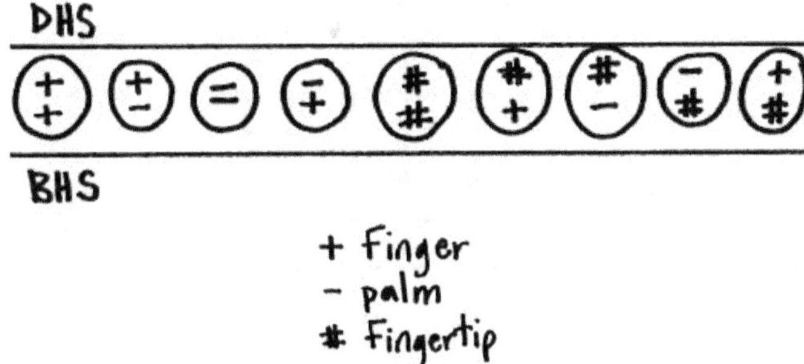

The notations for the signs glossed: "candle" above and "medicine" below are examples of # fingertip to palm or finger contact. The D HS "palm" for an index BHS is the base of the D HS wrist.

Some signs have more than one contact on the BHS. For example, "lesson" and "surgery" have contact on the fingertips and palm of the ND BHS. This will be notated and read left to right:

"LESSON"

"SURGERY"

"WELDING"

NOTE: **Since most index BHS have fingertip contact at the base of the wrist, we can eliminate the mid-tier contact notation and set that as a default position for signs like "candle" and "1 minute", etc…**

VERTICAL BASE HANDSHAPE PAIRS

A Vertical BHS serves as a foundation or support in the up and down or vertical plane. The majority of BHSP are vertical. When using a V BHSP, the initial location is listed for the D HS only, since it applies to both handshapes.

VBHP FORMAT

Here's an example:

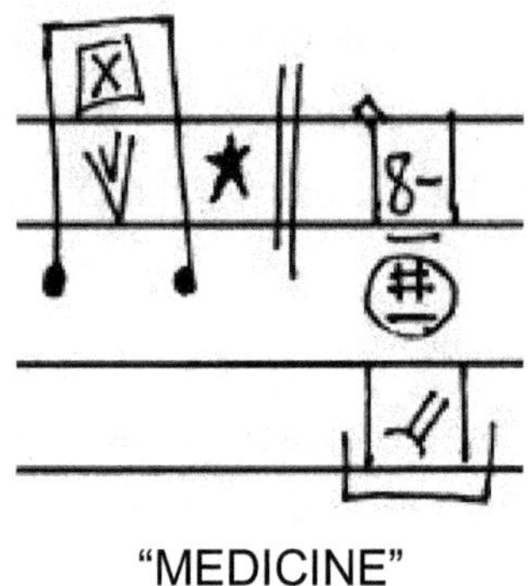

"MEDICINE"

And another example:

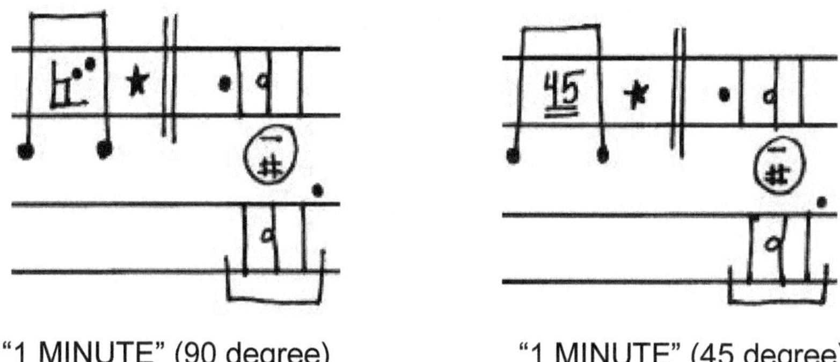

"1 MINUTE" (90 degree) "1 MINUTE" (45 degree)

Two notations are listed for the sign: "1 minute" to demonstrate variations in articulation. Throughout this book, examples are given that reflect a range of articulations.

Here is an example of a sign that has a BHS pair in the second half of the sign and the BHS is in front of rather than under the D HS:

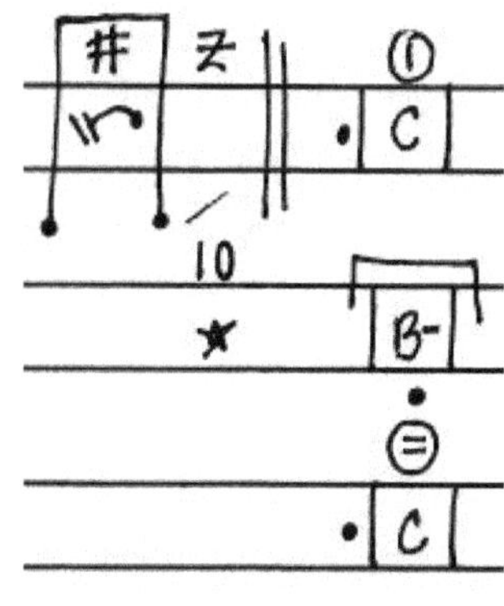

"PICTURE" OR "PHOTO"

Sometimes the D HS will have more than one palm orientation or handshape in conjunction with a single BHS. An example is the sign glossed, "cookie" in which the HS shifts orientation 90 degrees, and is notated on the third tier. This is feasible because the BHSP is "locked" together by the original mid-tier +/- contact notation:

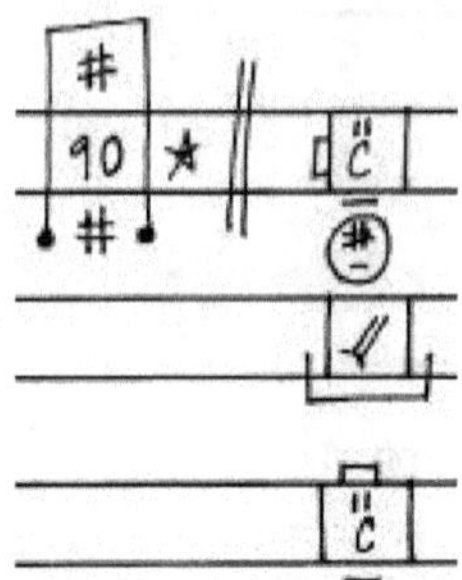

"COOKIE" NOTATION APPROACH (1)

Here are a couple more options of possible ways to notate this type of VBHSP. Which do you prefer?

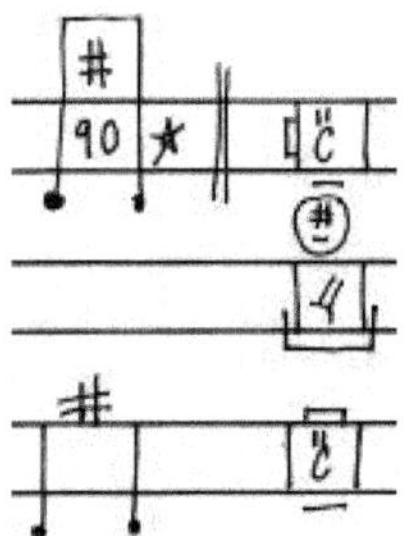

“COOKIE” NOTATION APPROACH (2)

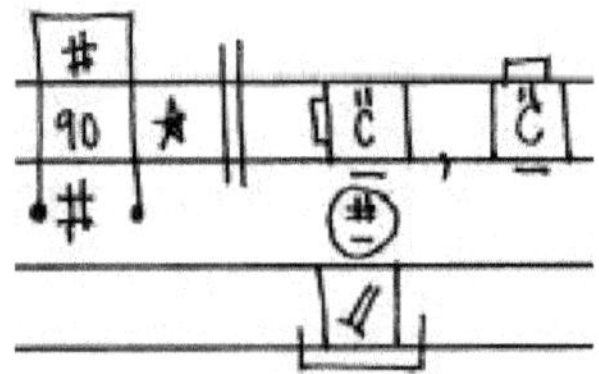

“COOKIE” NOTATION APPROACH (3)

BHS MULTIPLE-TIER

Another variation on a vertical BHSP is an extended set. For example the compound sign of "ASL" + "to put down on paper" or "make a note" has the BHS interacting on all three tiers. In the first tier, the BHS provides the framing for the subsequent BHSPs. The second and third tier have the interactive D HS along with the mid-tier contact notations, contact movement, and the stress notated on the final articulation:

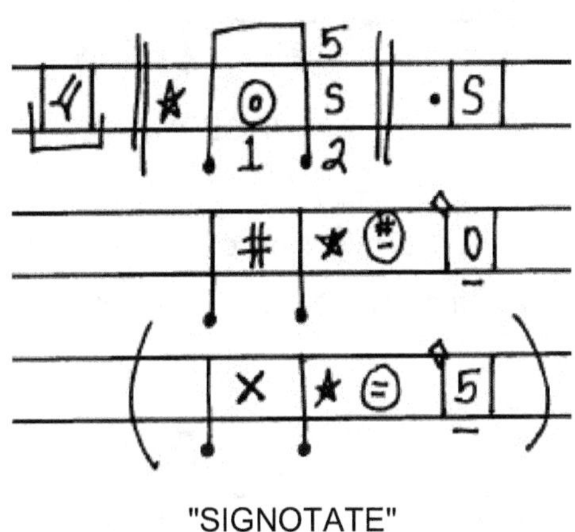

"SIGNOTATE"

LATERAL BASE HANDSHAPE PAIRS

A lateral base handshape serves as a foundation or support on the side-to-side or horizontal plane. When using a lateral BHS, the initial location is listed for the ND HS only, since it applies to both handshapes.

LBHP FORMAT

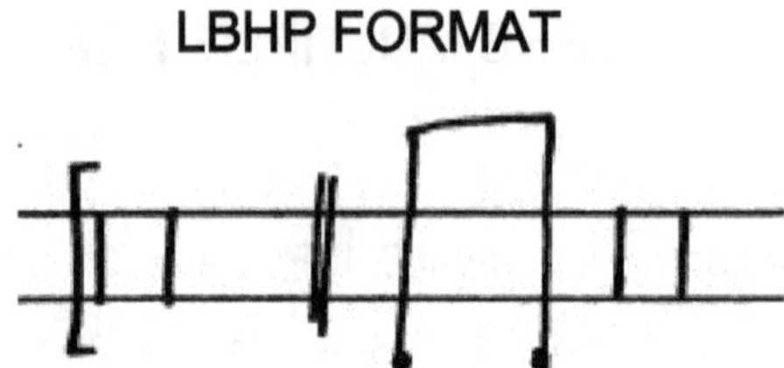

Here's an example:

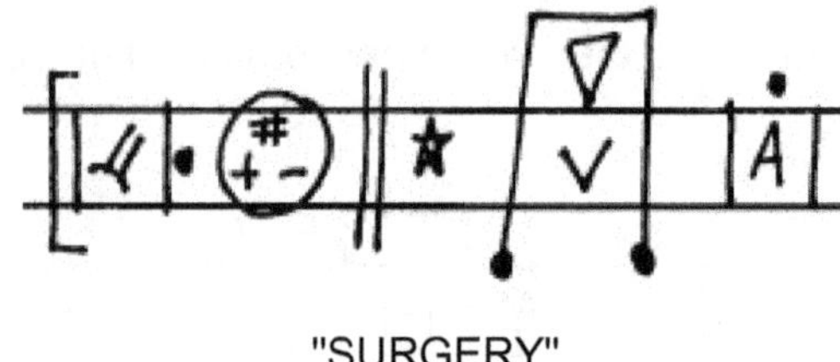

"SURGERY"

Here is another fun example: Notice that the location for lateral BHSP is on the ND side of the MVT block. The original location is tied to the BHS.

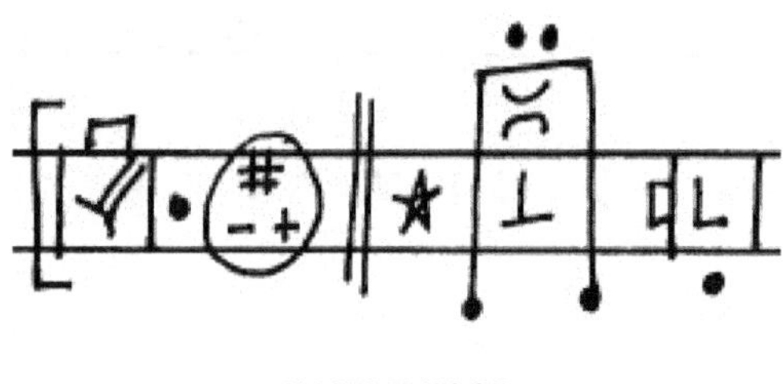

"WELDING"

An extra bit of space is needed between the lateral BHS on the far left, and the location. This allows for the insertion of the contact details, read top to bottom. The notation above records the movement from palm to fingers of the ND BHS, by the fingertips of the D HS.

MULTIPLE MOVEMENT OR HANDSHAPE LBHSP

When a lateral BHSP has more than one movement, notate by placing the mid-tier contact notation on the second tier. “Palm” for a “C” HS in this orientation is the cross-section that encompasses the palm:

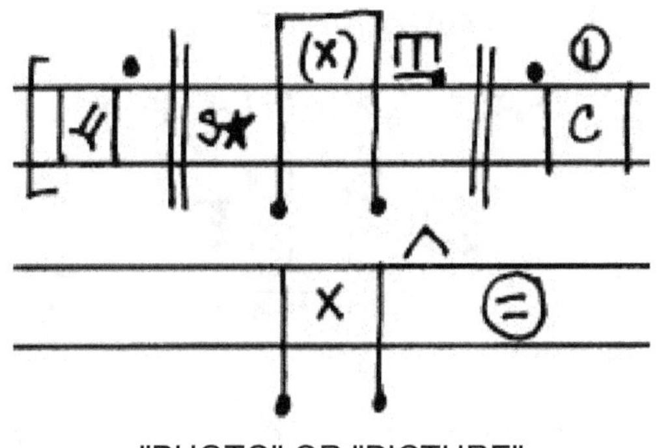

"PHOTO" OR "PICTURE"

YOUR TURN!

Insert the initial HS notation for the ASL sign glossed: "snake"! Check your answer in the back section under "YOUR TURN! ANSWERS" (#1)

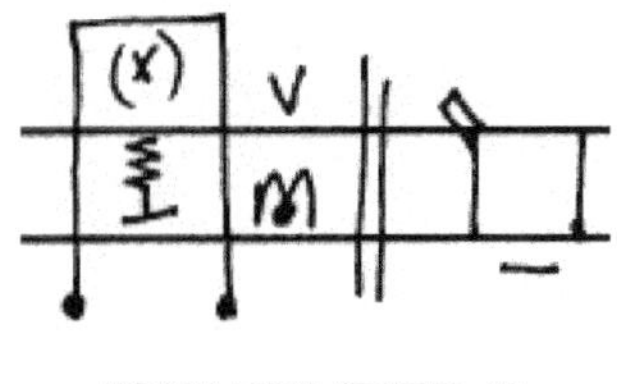

"SNAKE" (TIER 1)

PARAMETER #2

PALM ORIENTATION

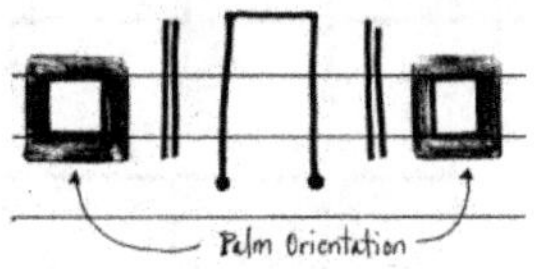

The orientation of the palm is a differentiator between signs and changes the meaning of any particular handshape. For example, the same basic HS of the open 5 palm facing forward can mean "stop" or "your" and when turned toward the signer can mean "mine" or "my".

This can get tricky because we are dealing with a joint of the body (the wrist) and it has a wide range of motion. We will have to adopt agreed conventions on labeling the various positions of the palm.

VERTICAL PALM ORIENTATION (VPO)

VPO is marked by a dot on the outside perimeter of the HS block:

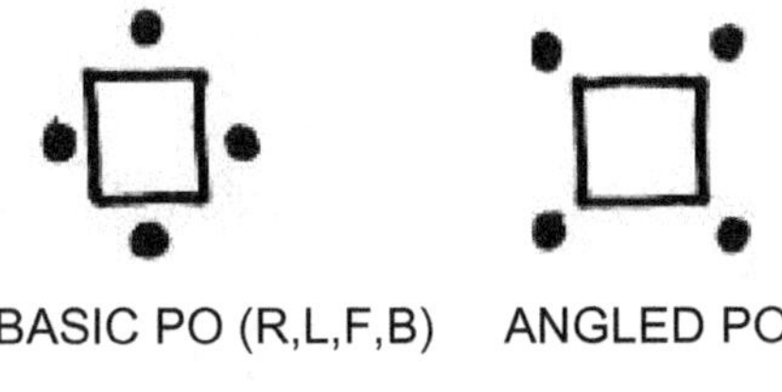

BASIC PO (R,L,F,B)   ANGLED PO

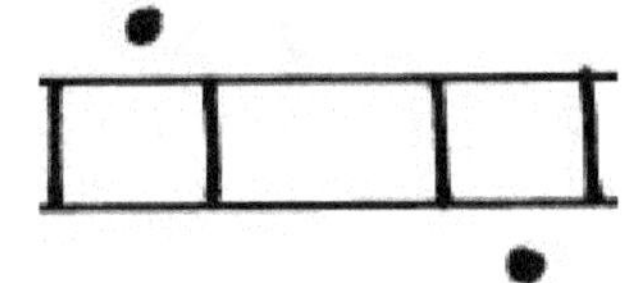

PO FORWARD: "YOUR"   PO BACK: "MY"

PO LEFT: "MOTHER"   PO RIGHT: "THEIR"

NOTE: VPO Default position is upward with fingertips upward pointing at the sky. One way to check this is to open the fingers of a closed handshape to determine which direction the fingertips are pointing. For example the standard ASL signs "more" or "equal" are made with fingertips in the VP.

FINGERTIP TABS

Any handshape that has a palm orientation (PO) placing the fingertips on the HORIZONTAL plane (HP) such as the sign "name" will be marked using small tabs:

BASIC (R,L,F,B) FINGERTIP TABS

ANGLED FINGERTIP TABS

The sign for "name" would have the following tabs:

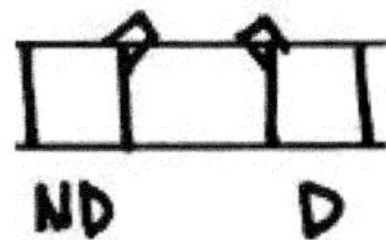

"NAME" FINGERTIP TABS

If you want to clarify, you can add a second layer tab to emphasize that the fingertip orientation stays same thru subsequent tiers of the SS:

Rounded tabs are used if fingertips are pointed to the ground:

Note: Tabs can be marked on any side of the HS block.

90 DEGREE RULE

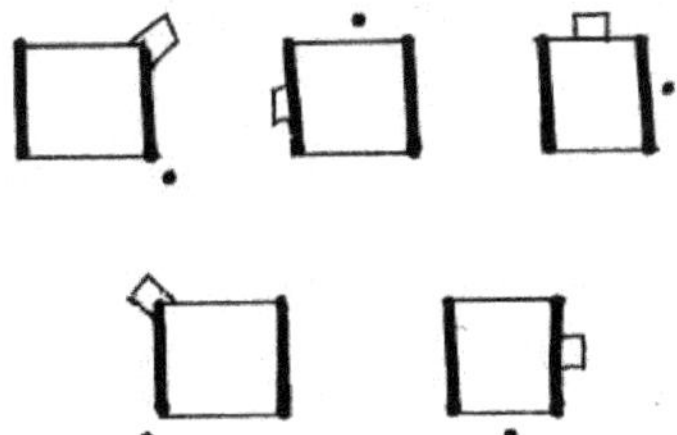

There is a simple way to remember the notations for fingertip tabs with HPO...they are usually at a 90 degree angle with the palm.

HORIZONTAL PALM ORIENTATION (HPO)

HPO is marked by a solid line below or above the HS block:

PO DOWN TO GROUND PO UP TO SKY

The sign for "school" would have the following HPO.

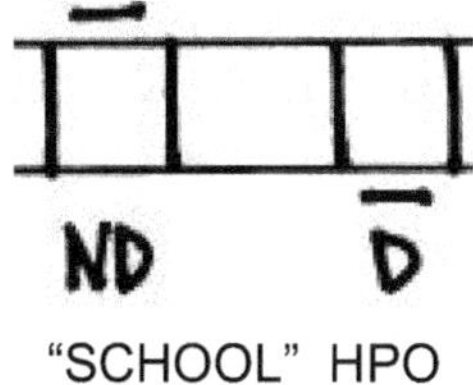

"SCHOOL" HPO

NOTE: HPO Default position is forward with fingertips pointing to the front or away from the signer forward. An example is the sign for "maybe", which would not need any additional fingertip tabs. Tabs are only required if the fingertips are shifted to either side or towards the signer. We will see more examples later of this notation.

Many signs have a change in orientation that creates a unique morpheme or unit of meaning. An example is the sign for "pay attention" which starts out on the HP and ends on the VP. Version (1) has a single, arching movement towards the signer and version (2) has a short horizontal, repeated movement near the temple. I have included the mirror notation for each, which we will explore later in the movement section.

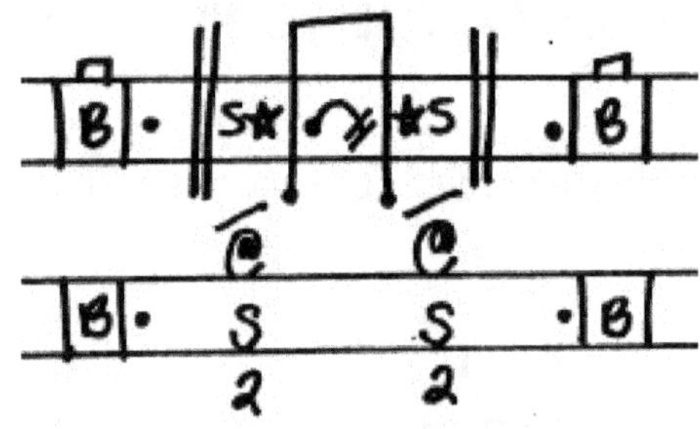

"PAY ATTENTION" (1)

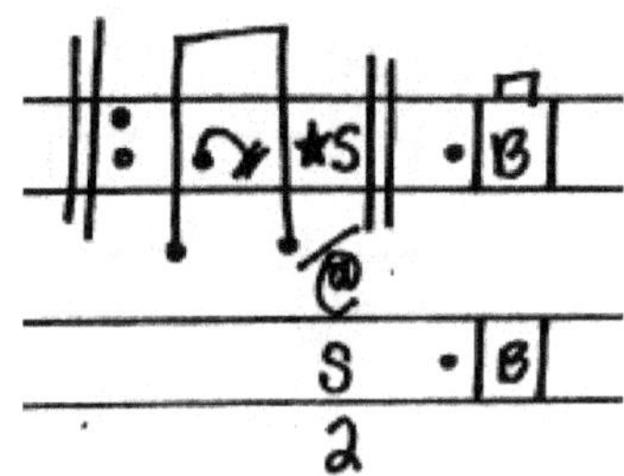

"PAY ATTENTION" (1) MIRROR NOTATION

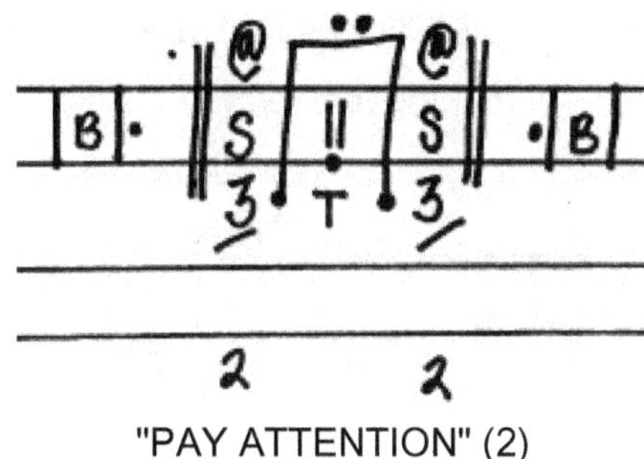

"PAY ATTENTION" (2)

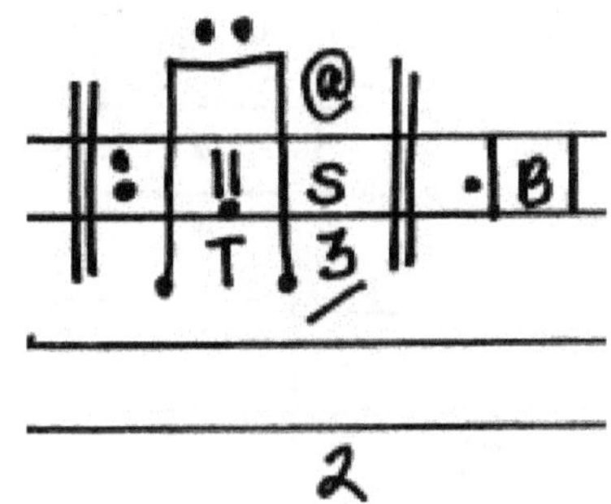

"PAY ATTENTION" (2) MIRROR NOTATION

45 DEGREE TILT

Some signs have a slanted PO. An upward or downward tilt in fingertip orientation from the “sky” or “ground” PO is notated using a combination of dots and underlines:

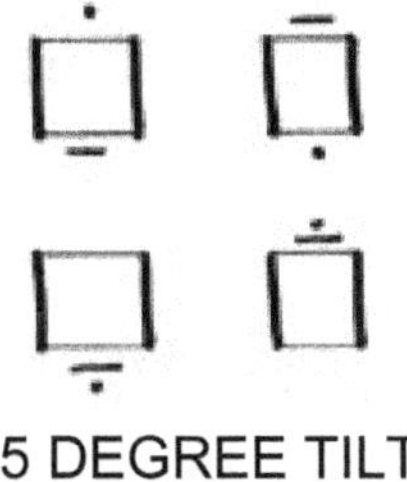

45 DEGREE TILT

Here are some samples of possible uses for a 45 degree tilt PO. From left to right: “pump the brakes”, “look in the mirror”, “downhill incline”, “lift weights” :

For example the sign glossed, "certified" has a PO angled toward the midline, with an upward tilt such as the sign glossed, "certified":

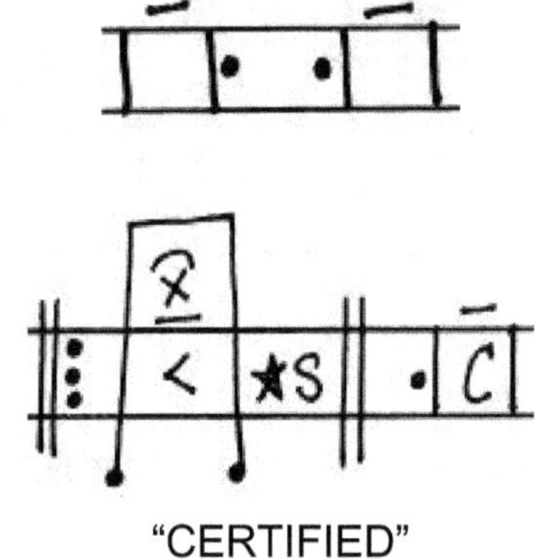

“CERTIFIED”

Another example is the sign glossed: "prevent, block, barrier" which has both palms oriented to the ground, fingertips toward the midline, tilting upward 45 degrees:

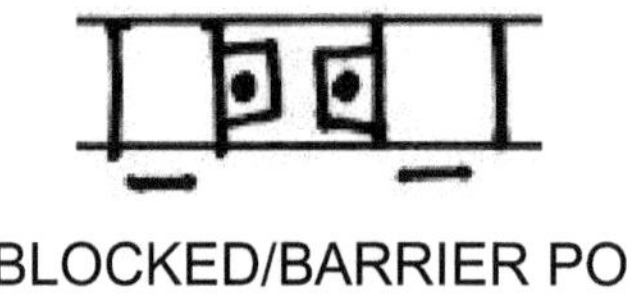

BLOCKED/BARRIER PO

YOUR TURN!

See if you can correctly mark the PO of the following English glossed signs. Check your answers in the back section under "YOUR TURN!

ANSWERS" (#2)

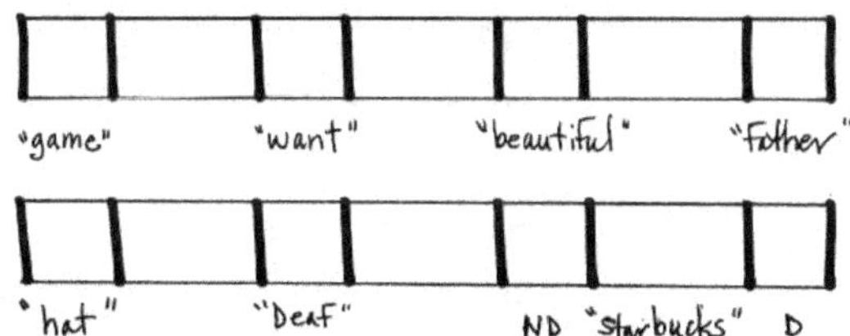

PARAMETER 2
FUN SURPRISES

I love seeing signs in a new way…Compare the signs: "pay" and "smooth" or "efficient". Both use the same HS and MVT but the PO changes the meaning.

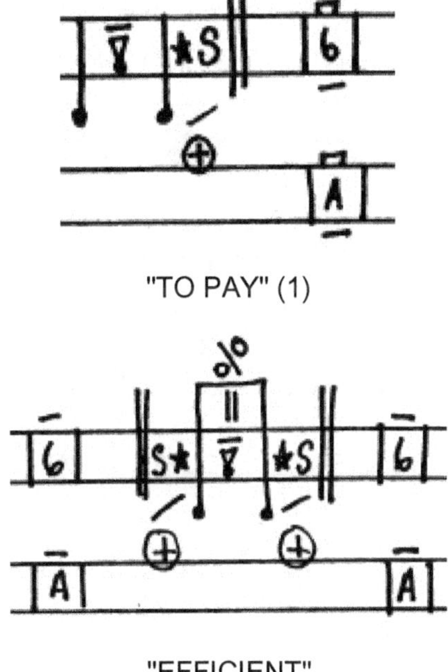

"TO PAY" (1)

"EFFICIENT"

Additionally, with shifts in the PO, unique meanings are conveyed:

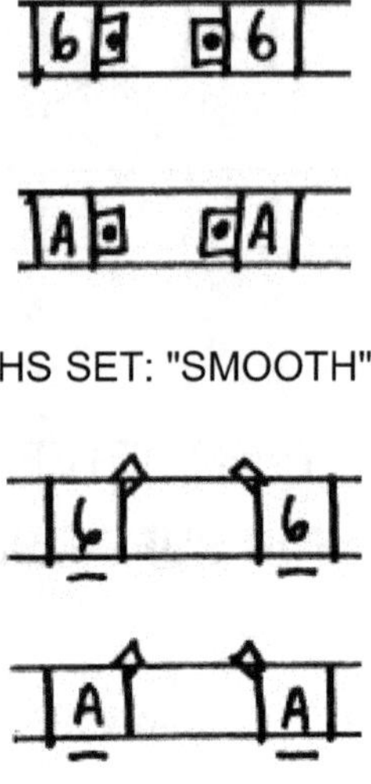

HS SET: "SMOOTH"

HS SET: "TO PLANT"

Here is a complex sign to execute that involves an entry movement, begins on the ND side and ends on the D side:

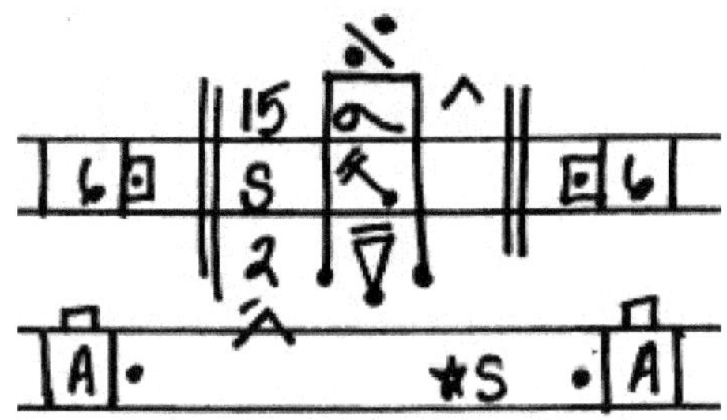

"TO EXPEND RESOURCES/MONEY/TIME"

NOTE: The palm orientation for the “A” handshape is based on where the fingertips are if the handshape is opened.

PARAMETER #3

LOCATION

v

m

h

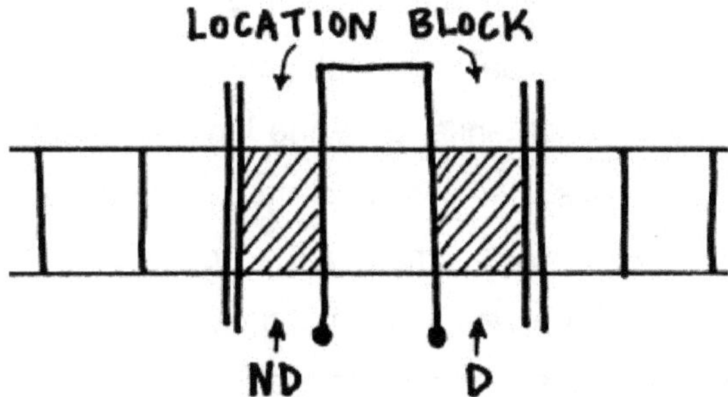

So far, we have looked at Handshape and Palm Orientation. The third parameter is Location. Because the signer has a large signing space with which to work, and what seems like an infinite number of positions in space and on the body that can be tagged as a unique locative for a particular handshape, we will have to create working grids to identify primary locations.

HH (HANDS HIGH)

What should our unit of measurement be based upon? When dividing up our working space, what tends to be the logical dividing line spatially? Several measurement systems incorporate parts of the body, such as an "inch" based upon a finger segment and a "foot" paced out by an adult. Hands are used in the equestrian community to measure horses. Each hand is equal to 4 inches, and a horse that is 15 hands high is 60 inches tall from the ground to the base of the mane. In ancient times, a "handbreadth" was used for measurements by Egyptians and in the Bible. For our purposes, it makes sense to use a handbreadth, which coincides with a visual language that manually manipulates symbols in spaces differentiated by a common denominator of a base unit: the hand.

Source:
https://en.wikipedia.org/wiki/Hand_(unit)
Retrieved 2/15/16

DIMENSION #1
THE VERTICAL PLANE

The first dimension the signer has as an available platform is the **vertical plane**. The V plane can be segmented into multiple regions. Let's reinforce an educational concept and count by fives:

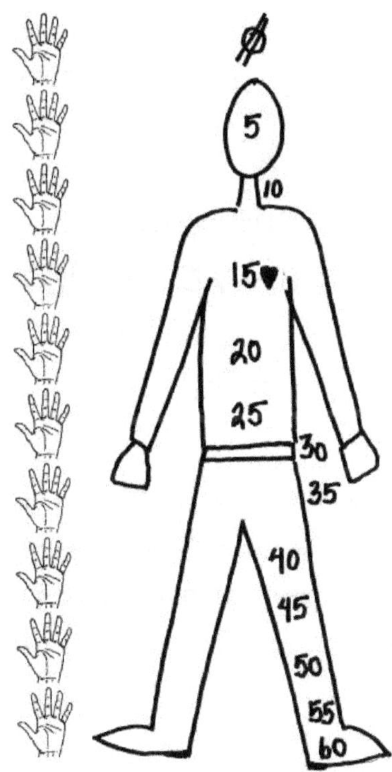

VERTICAL PLANE

		SAMPLE SIGN GLOSSES
0	OVERHEAD	"heaven"
5	HEAD/FACE	"beautiful"
10	NECK	"thirsty"
15	UPPER ABDOMEN	"feel", "heart"
20	MID ABDOMEN	"stomach", "gut-feel"
25	LOWER ABDOMEN	"ovaries"
30	WAIST	"Russian" (older sign)
35	HIPS	"tail wag"
40	THIGH	"dog"
45	KNEE	"kneecap"
50	LOWER LEG	"lower leg"
55	ANLE	"ankle"
60	FOOT	"foot"

DIMENSION #1A
THE HEAD AND NECK

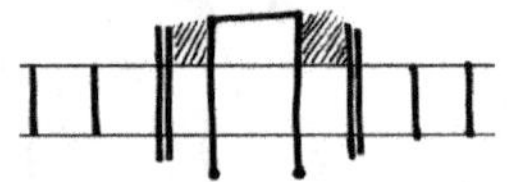

Another area we need to map further is the face and neck. The signs "onion" and "apple" for example only differ by the small distance between the eye and the cheek. Using a simple labeling system that starts at the top of the head we can clearly identify these distinct differences in location:

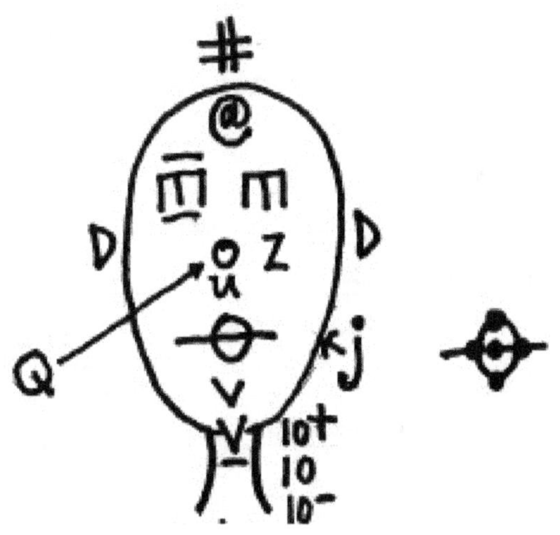
#
@
D
Z
D
Q
kj
10+
10
10-

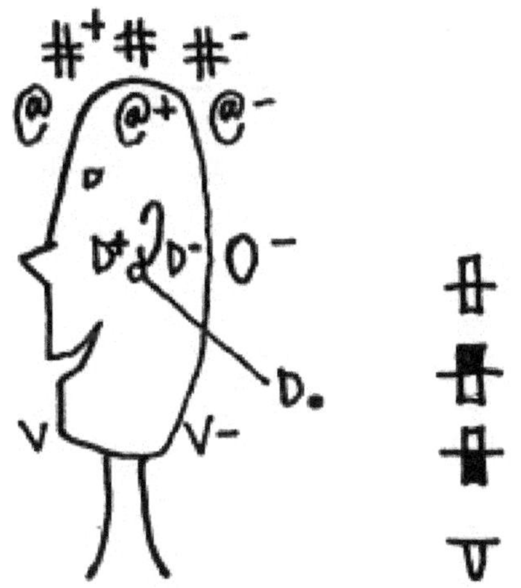
#+ # #-
@ @+ @-
O-
D.
V
V-

	FACE AND NECK LOCATIONS	SAMPLE SIGN GLOSSES
#	TOP OF HEAD/CROWN	"hat"
#+	IN FRONT OF THE CROWN	"lion" part 1
#-	REAR OF THE CROWN	"lion" part 2
@	FOREHEAD	"stupid"
@	TEMPLE ("S" in Midline block)	"for-for?"
@+	SIDE OF THE UPPER HEAD	"Seahawks"
@-	REAR OF THE UPPER HEAD	"hit from behind"
ΓΠ	EYE	"contacts"
‾ΓΠ	ABOVE THE EYE/EYEBROW	"black"
ΓΠ_	BELOW THE EYE	"witness"
o	NOSE	"fox", "mouse"
ʌ	UNDER THE NOSE	"kid"
Q	NOSTRIL	"bored"
O-	MIDDLE BACK OF THE HEAD	"Put in back of mind"
-θ-	MOUTH/LIPS	"tomato" part 1
-⊕-	DOTS = AREAS ON MOUTH/LIPS	"red", "color", "talk"
Ʊ	TONGUE	"medicine under tongue"
-ᗺ-	TEETH	"brush teeth"
-ᗺ-	UPPER TEETH	"glass", "nut"
-ᗺ-	LOWER TEETH	"lower molar cavity"
V	CHIN	"metal"
V_	LOWER EDGE OF THE CHIN	"not"
V-	LOWER BACK OF THE HEAD	"keep in mind"
10+	TOP OF THE NECK	"thirsty" part 1

10	MID-NECK	"put me in my place"
10^-	BASE OF THE NECK	"thirsty" part 2
D	EAR	"listen" with ears
D^-	BEHIND THE EAR	"hearing aid"
D^+	IN FRONT OF THE EAR	"listen" (initialized)
D•	EAR LOBE	"deaf" part 1, "foul"
Z	CHEEK	"apple"
j	JAWLINE	"girl"
|||	HAIR	"hair"
◊	CLOTHING	"shirt", "volunteer"

When recording on the SS staff, these locations will be listed in the **Vertical Plane** section of V/M/H.

DIMENSION #2
THE MIDLINE PLANE

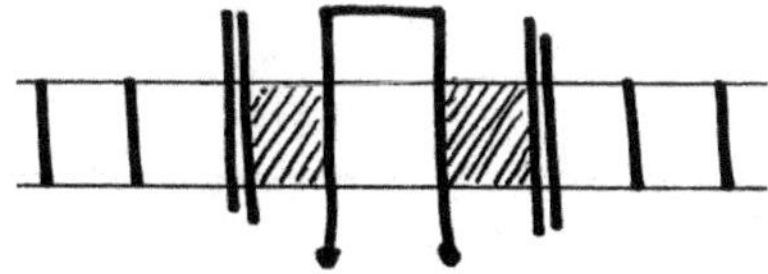

The second dimension is the **midline or lateral plane**. There are three main sections or zones that exist for the signer symmetrically based on the midline:

- **M** The midline
- **S** The side or arm section
- **O** The outer region, beyond the perimeter of the body

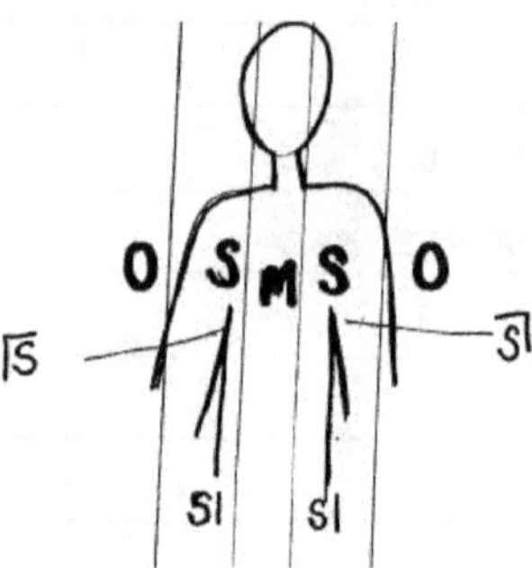

Some signs are along the side of the torso and the location is **S1** (ie: "monkey"). Others are in the armpit area and are labeled:

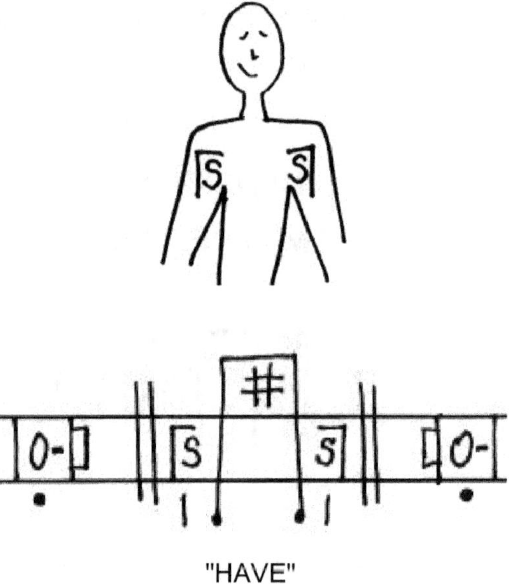

"HAVE"

In ASL, the area above the heart is a unique location used for name signs, references to emotions such as love and grief and making promises. We will use an **X** as in "cross your heart" for this location:

Some signs occur on the ND side in the same location so for simplicity we will use this for both sides:

Below is the location for the sign glossed: “bear”:

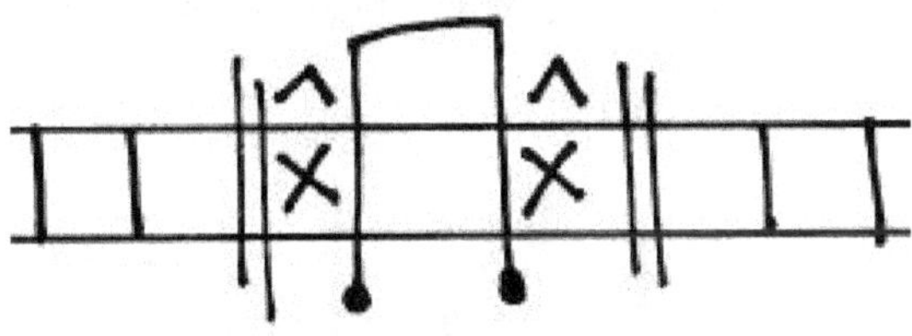

LOCATION FOR “BEAR”

Directly center such as the sign glossed: "birthday" can be notated using the midline center notation:

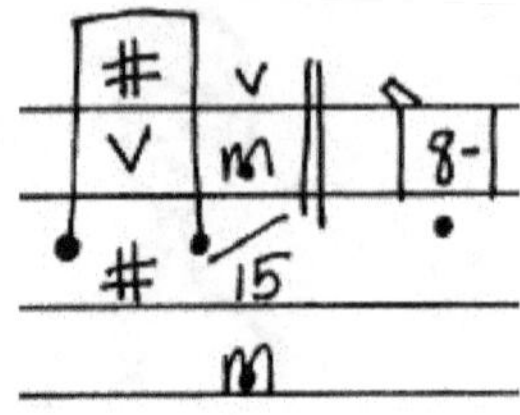

"BIRTHDAY"

The repeated midline notation could be eliminated in the second tier based on the straight down vertical movement:

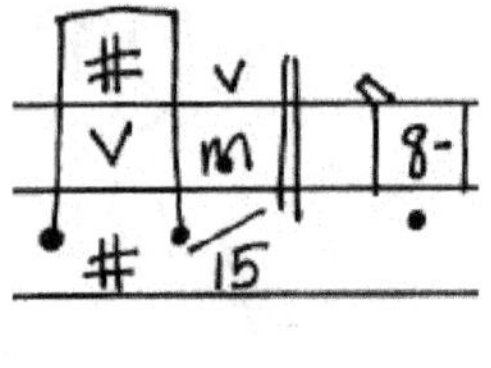

"BIRTHDAY"

When recording on the SS staff, these locations will be listed in the **Midline Plane** section of **V/M/H**.

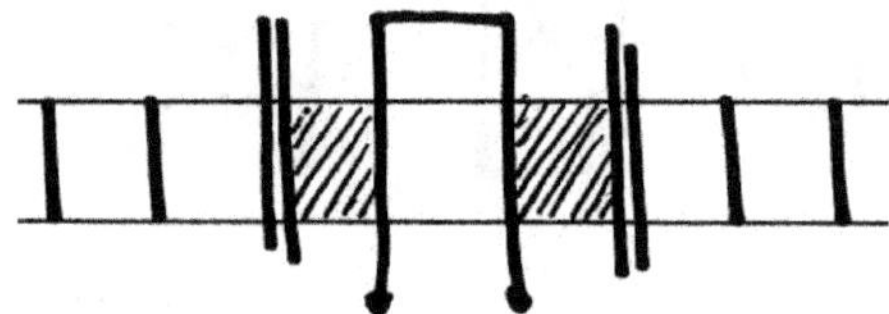

NOTE: Locations on the face also have a M, S, O aspect and can be identified in conjunction with the facial locations.(ie: "idea" is to the side (S) of the forehead = the temple).

DIMENSION #3

THE HORIZONTAL PLANE

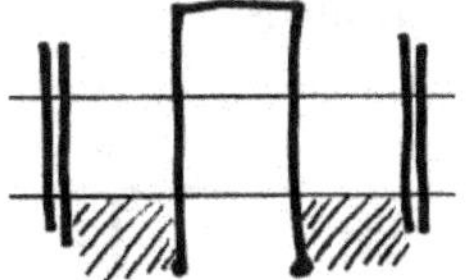

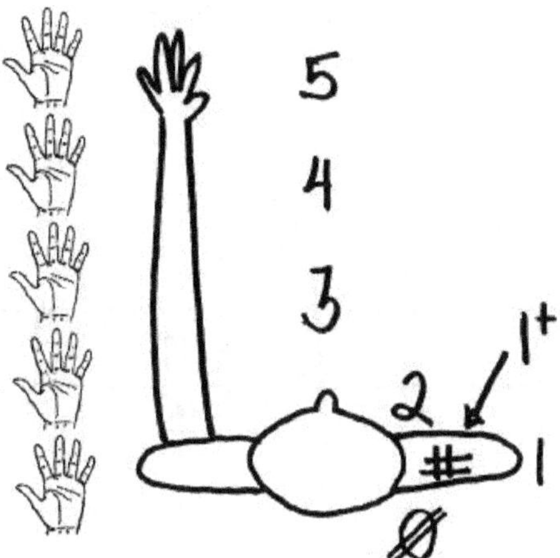

The third dimension is the horizontal plane that stretches forward when the signer's arms are extended. There are several sections in the horizontal plane.

- **5** The region available to the outstretched arm
- **4, 3, 2** The neutral zone directly in front of the signer where the majority of signs occur
- **1** The region filled by the body. Signs in this region touch the body or torso.
- **1+** Signs which "pull" or touch the clothing, skin or hair (ie: "curious", "shirt")
- **#** The top of the shoulders (ie: "responsibility")
- **0** The region behind the body

When recording on the SS staff, these locations will be listed in the **Horizontal Plane** section of **V/M/H**.

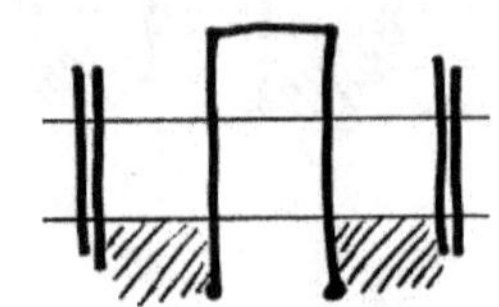

"RESPONSIBILITY"

Notice that there is no vertical notation because there is only one **"#"** horizontal location.

There are at least two areas that need further, secondary detail: The ARM and HAND locations and FINGER ID.

Many signs differ based on the specific location on the hands and arms. For example, the only difference between the location for the signs "what" and "can't" is the location on the hand or fingers. In the next section on movement we will consider the concept of lines and wheels. For now, let's label the areas running along the arm starting at the shoulder and moving down to the ends of the fingers.

DIMENSION #3A
(THE ARM AND HAND)

The arm and hands are composed of joints and bones. Starting at the shoulder, each **joint** is labeled using **odd numbers,** (written within a set of parenthesis). Beginning with the upper arm, each **bone** segment is labeled with an **even number,** (also written within a set of parenthesis):

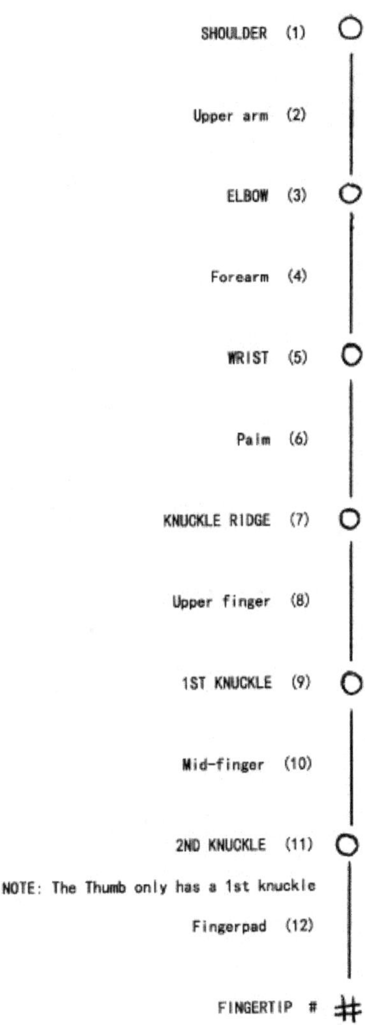

FINGER IDENTIFICATION

We need to have a solid way to identify which finger(s) are involved to accurately notate some signs.

NOTE: In order to keep things straight, finger ID is circled.

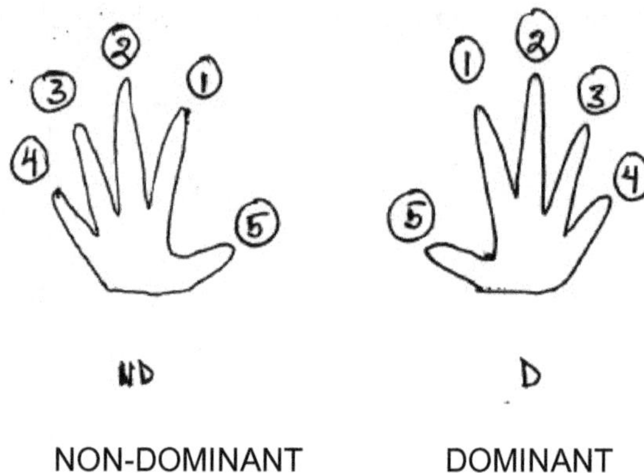

NON-DOMINANT DOMINANT

Here is sample using Finger ID:

"SENIOR, JUNIOR, SOPHOMORE, FRESHMAN, PREP"

Notice the use of repetition marks to notate that the finger locations are to be taken as a series with the movement and palm orientation repeated for fingers 1-4.

When recording on the SS staff, the ARM, HAND and FINGER locations critical for clear articulation will be listed **above** the applicable **HS block.**

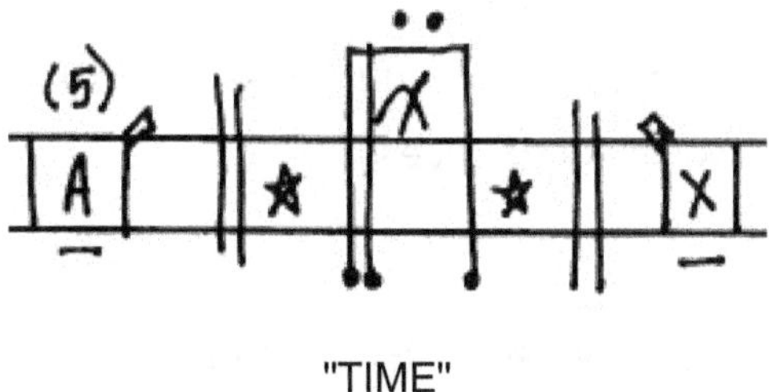

"TIME"

The location of the D "X" hand contact is on the wrist or (5) of the ND hand.

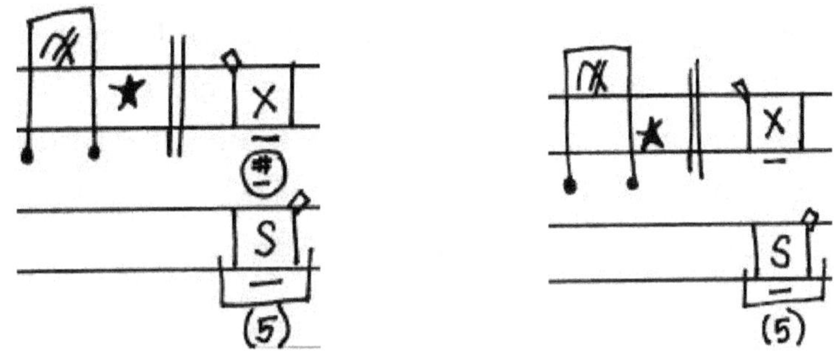

"TIME" with BHSP notation "TIME" without contact tab (redundant)

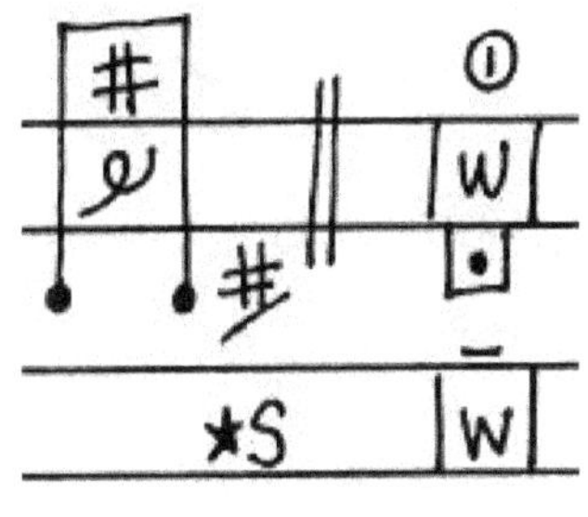

"WASHINGTON"

The location of the D "W" hand contact is on the upper side surface of the shoulder using only the index finger of the D HS.

NOTE: Washington is a good example of a sign MVT that could be standardized to occupy or extend for a specific spatial range and then the second tier would not be necessary.

STANDARD SIGNING SPACE *

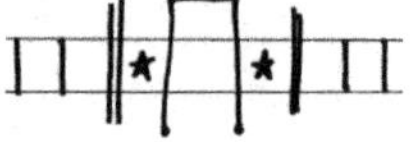

After a bit of practice writing the locations for many different signs, it will become obvious that this can be cumbersome for many common signs. This is because a large percentage of signs are done in what would be considered the standard signing space in the intersection of locations **20/M/3.** This is not an exact science...but in general, people sign in the ergonomically comfortable space directly in front of the torso:

STANDARD SIGNING SPACE *

(Overhead view)

Shorthand for this is:

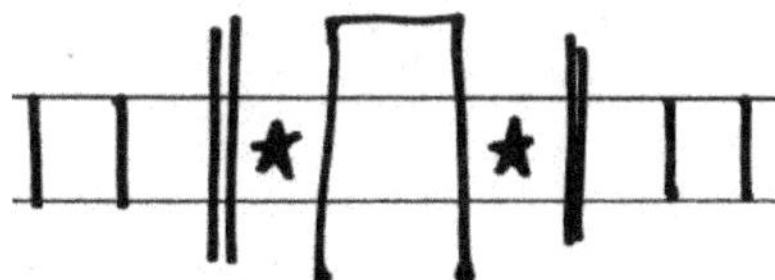

Here is one version of the sign "school" using SSS* notation. In the MVT section we will explore another way to notate this sign, but for now it is a good example:

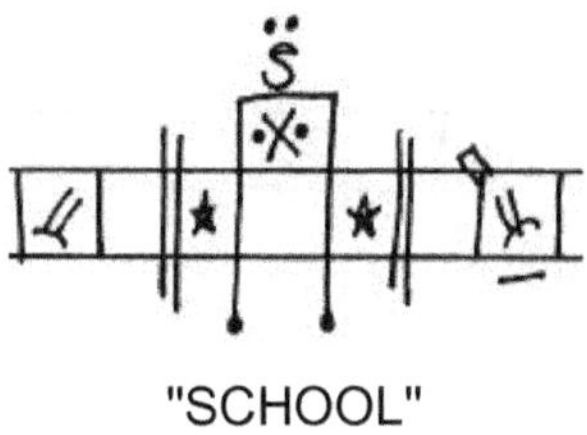

"SCHOOL"

The notation can be more specific if desired or grammatically necessary and include the V or H. Here is a sample using the sign glossed: "terrible, awful" with two different vertical locations:

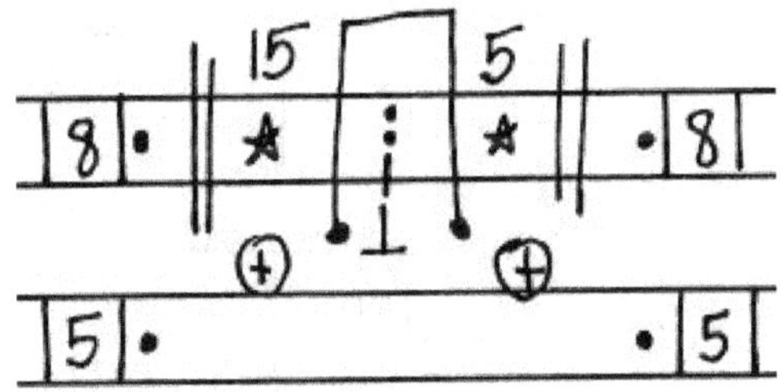

"TERRIBLE/AWFUL"

Below is another sample location for the sign glossed: "Sunday":

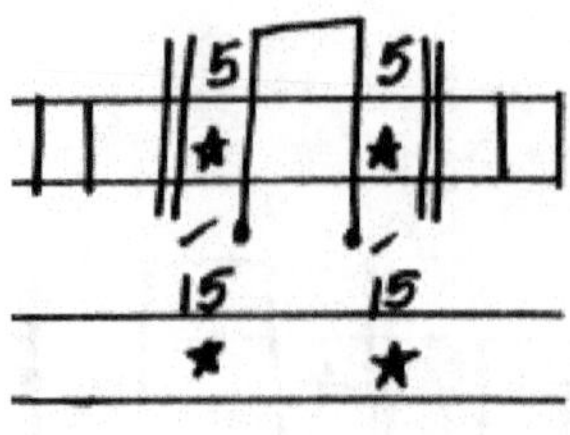

"SUNDAY"

Once the first tier location is established, the subsequent tiers can be + or - (approx. one level above or below * vertically) or + or - (approx. one level forward or back from * horizontally):

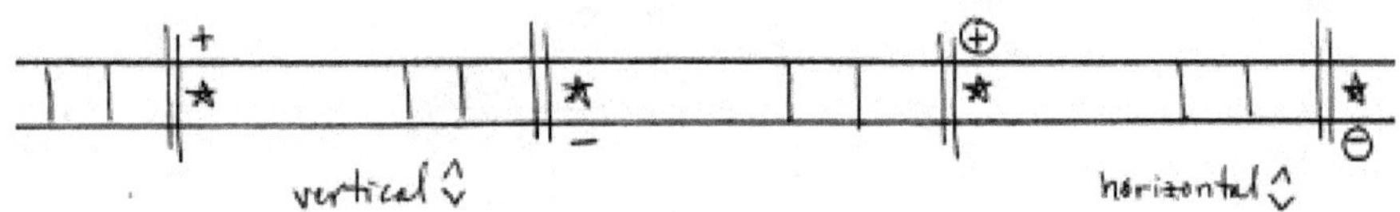

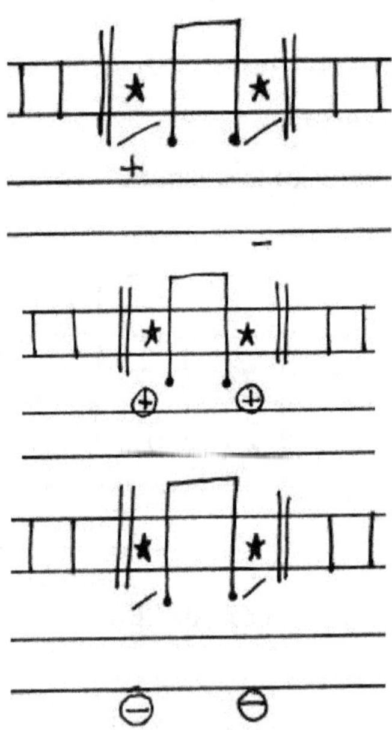

The Midline Plane (M,S,O) can also be incorporated with the SSS:

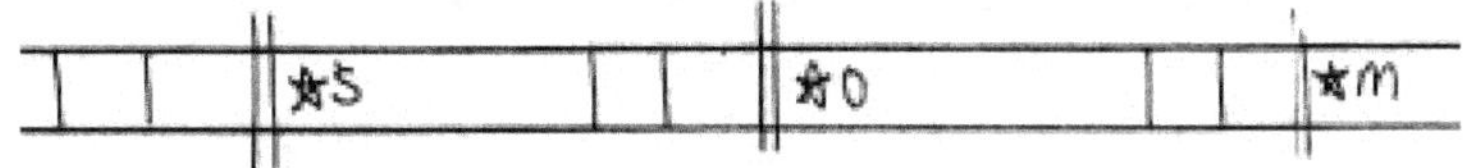

Usually the *S is the most useful of these three, but they are options as needed.

IN SUMMARY

One can always opt to go for the full or longhand version of the location, but this shorthand method for the SSS* (Standard Signing Space) is more efficient.

YOUR TURN!

See if you can correctly mark the LOC of the following English glossed signs. Check your answers in the back section under "YOUR TURN! ANSWERS" (#3)

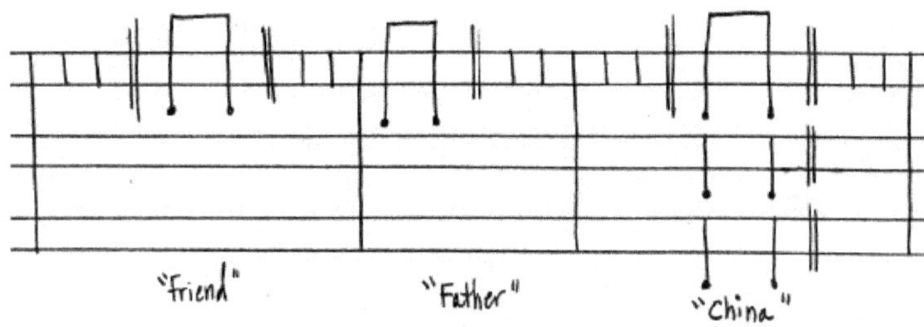

PARAMETER #4
MOVEMENT...LINES AND WHEELS

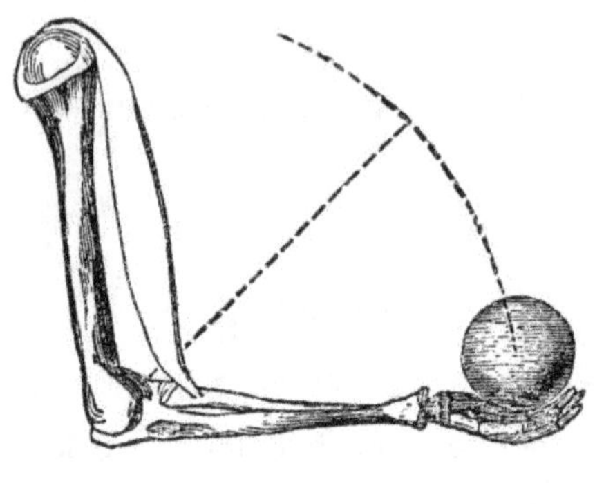

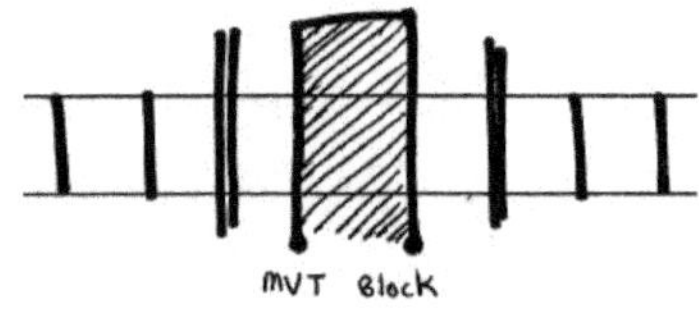

Now that we have established the three parameters of Handshape, Palm Orientation, and Location, we can add the crucial fourth parameter of movement!

I think of ASL as being composed of Lines and Wheels. Each joint of the hand, wrist, elbow or shoulder provides a rotational range of motion or "wheel" and each linear bone of the finger or arm contributes the "lines" of ASL. While we are focusing on the standard signing space in front of the torso, it is also important to note the waist, hips, legs, knees and feet also contribute to the meaning of a message as the signer increases the range and type of motion via body positioning and movement. Think Dak Virnig (https://www.youtube.com/channel/UCNgZ RS5HFALSvLs7Me_I7qg). A signer seated can convey a full message, but a signer who is standing has an additional repertoire of options to convey meaning.

There are a nearly infinite number of different movements possible...Here is sample of Stokoe's circa 1960 list of movements (SIG of the DEZ, TAB, SIG):

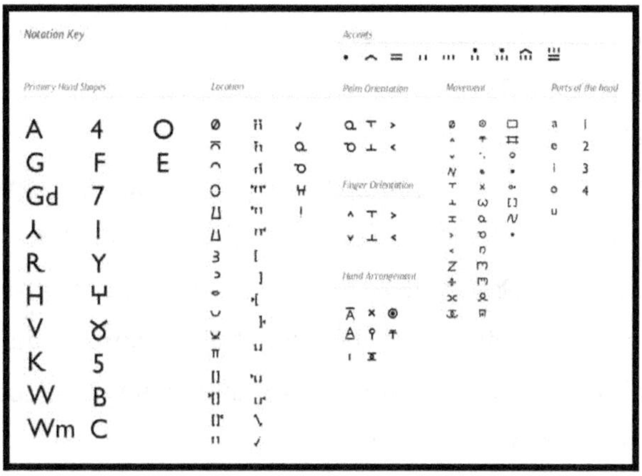

Source:
http://i65.photobucket.com/albums/h226/Julia18_2006/pg1.jpg
Retrieved 10/7/15

This to me is the most challenging of the parameters because there are so many different movements possible with a seemingly unlimited number of articulation modifications. These are the primary distinguishing characteristics of fluent native signers and non-native signers (along with facial grammar). The angle, force, speed, direction of each motion is like the accent in people's voices. You can immediately get a sense of the signer's language background from his/her articulation as conveyed through movement. Fluent signers conserve and expend energy very specifically. When I consider creating a notation for the parameter of motion, I imagine this being an area where each signed language community would create its own sets of agreed movement notations to represent specifically identified distinguishable movements based on specific signs.

The following list is a preliminary attempt to provide examples of common movements in ASL. This is not a comprehensive or concrete list of movement notations. It is offered as a *sampling of movements*...these notation symbols can be completely re-worked, revised or replaced by the signing community.

The fourth parameter also invokes the principles of mathematics and physics. Concepts of symmetry, degree, speed, slope, order of operations etc... will be incorporated throughout this chapter on movement and the Grammatical Notes section. After compiling all these movements, the notations remind me of Chinese...(Aside: Apparently there are about 50,000 written Chinese characters! and about 3,000 to 4,000 are required for functional literacy.)

Source:
https://en.wikipedia.org/wiki/Chinese_characters
Retrieved 1/17/16

到了呵 名 怕著 快 黃馬 有來
古兒恢魯額 赤列都 阿余周 古兒敦忽必圖 阿主兀
黃馬自的 腿 他的 打著 岡 越過 躲 了呵
忽必余安 忽牙亦訥 迭列抽 忽不里南巴里思 不魯恢魯阿
後頭自 他的 三箇 隨即 趕了 人名 山背
豁亦訥察亦訥 忽兒巴兀剌 兀荅阿剌都罷 赤列都豁失溫
畏過 同著 車子 自的行 來了呵
忽赤里思 合里周 帖兒堅 都里顏 亦列恢魯額
那裏 婦人名 說 那 三箇 人行 覺麼你
田迭阿額侖兀真 嗚詰列論 帖迭 忽兒班 合喇泥 兀合巴兀赤

The Secret History of the Mongols

Source:

https://en.wikipedia.org/wiki/Chinese_characters#/media/File:Secret_history.jpg

Retrieved 1/17/16)

MVTS: VERTICAL PLANE

SAMPLE SIGN GLOSSES

	UP	"rocket lift-off"
		"proud", "tall"
	DOWN	"snow", "surgery"
		"thirsty"
	DOWNWARD: EXTRA FORCE	"bomb dropping"
	UPWARD: EXTRA FORCE	"stroke"
	UP AND DOWN REPEATED MVT	"elevator", "child"
	RIGHT	"car drives right"
	LEFT	"car drives left"
	DIAGONAL UPPER RIGHT	"increasing graph line"
	DIAGONAL UPPER LEFT	"path of an insect"
	DIAGONAL LOWER RIGHT	"ugly"
	DIAGONAL LOWER LEFT	"ugly"
	SIDE SWOOP RIGHT	"take off"
	BOUNCING MOTION*	"now!" "eat"
	CURVES UPWARD TO RIGHT AND THEN ABOVE	"College", "University"
	ARCS (R) UP	"rainbow"
	ARCS (L) UP	ND: "sky"
	ARCS (R) DOWN	"divide"
	ARCS (L) DOWN	"divide"
	DEEPER ARCS	

*NEEDS DIRECTION

MVTS: ADVERBIAL

SAMPLE SIGN GLOSSES

	WAVING PATTERN	"snowing", "meth"
	INCREMENTAL MVTS	"improving grades",
		"declining skills"
( )	ADDS A "ROLL" TO TRANSITION	"how"
	OR MOVEMENT	"become"

MVTS: HORIZONTAL

		SAMPLE SIGN GLOSSES
	AWAY FROM SIGNER'S BODY	"meet-you"
	TOWARDS SIGNER'S BODY	"person comes up to me"
	ANGLED (R) AWAY	"car veers to the R"
	ANGLED (L) AWAY	"car veers to the L"
	ANGLED (R) TOWARDS	"person approaches from R"
	ANGLED (L) TOWARDS	"person approaches from L"
	REPEATED SIDE TO SIDE MVT	"what?", "where?", "animal"
	REPEATED FRONT TO BACK MVT	"commute back and forth"
	REPEATED ANGLED BACK AND FORTH (R)	"train"
	REPEATED ANGLED BACK AND FORTH (L)	"negotiate"
	MOVES AWAY FROM CENTER CONTACT (R)	"reflection"
	MOVES AWAY FROM CENTER CONTACT (L)	"echo"
	HS SEPARATE FROM EACH OTHER	"vlog", "separate", "break-up"
	HORIZ. ARC TO RIGHT	"trees in a row"
	HORIZ. ARC TO LEFT	"trees in a row"
	CIRCLES TOWARDS SIGNER'S BODY	"kids sitting in circle"
		"place"
	CIRCLES AWAY FROM SIGNER'S BODY	"family"
	MOVES FORWARD INCREMENTALY	"happens frequently"
	MOVES BACK INCREMENTALLY*	"past occurances on timeline"
	ZIG ZAG (CAN ROTATE TO CHANGE DIRECTION)	"snake"

NOTE: INCREMENTAL MARKS CAN BE ADDED TO ANY HORIZONTAL MVT EXCEPT FOR BACK AND FORTH MVTS

*NOTE: FINAL POSITION DOES NOT NEED TO BE NOTATED, DEFAULT CIRCLE

NOTE: CONTACT MAY BE NEEDED FOR CIRCULAR MOVEMENTS ie: "family"

MVTS: PUSH-PULL

SAMPLE SIGN GLOSSES

↑	PUSHES	"mortgage"
↓	PULLS	"draw arrow back"

MVTS: INTO, OUT, UNDER, THROUGH, ONTO

SAMPLE SIGN GLOSSES

	D GOES UNDER ND HS	"hide"
	D GOES THROUGH ND HS	"email"
	ONTO	"put on a character"
	D GOES INTO ND	"make a basket"
	D COMES OUT OF ND (REVERSAL)	"out"
	OPENS AND CLOSES	"milk"
	OPENS AND CLOSES ON ONE SIDE	"book"
	LAYERING	"tease one another"

NOTE: MAY REQUIRE DIRECTION (R, L, etc...)

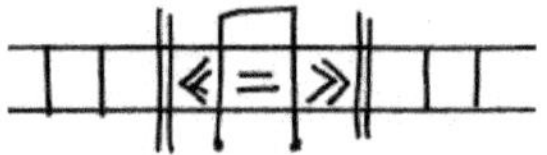

ARMS CROSSED MVT NOTATION

MVTS: TYING

SAMPLE SIGN GLOSSES

	CLOCKWISE TIE	"tied score", "tie a shoe"
	COUNTERCLOCKWISE TIE	"sign language"

MVTS: FINGER

SAMPLE SIGN GLOSSES

	FINGERS WIGGLE	"color", "snow"
	WALKING FINGERS	"walk along"
	WALKING FINGERS CLIMB	"go upstairs"
	SCISSORING	"cut hair", "sheep"
	FLICKS OPEN	"hate", "feedback"
	FINGER BOBS UP AND DOWN	"mouse", "rabbit"
	AT THE KNUCKLES	"bye bye"
	LATERAL BOB	"no-no" gesture
	VIBRATES	"medicine", "how"
	FINGER BENDS AND EXTENDS 1X*	"take a picture"
	LAYERING	"tease one another"
	SNAP	"dog"
	PINCH	"trim nails", "skin"

NOTE: MAY REQUIRE DIRECTION (R,L)

NOTE: THIS NOTATION GOES INSIDE THE HS BLOCK

ie: "take a picture"

MVTS: ROCKING

SAMPLE SIGN GLOSSES

	ROCKS BACK AND FORTH (above)	"earth"
	ROCKS BACK AND FORTH (below)	"baby"
	ROCKS BACK AND FORTH (lateral)	"do", "action"
	ROCKS BACK AND FORTH (tight)	"business"
		"tru biz", "ambivalent"

MVTS: CIRCULAR

		SAMPLE SIGN GLOSSES
360	CIRCLES CLOCKWISE	"1 hour"
063	CIRCLES COUNTER-CLOCKWISE	"signing"
36○	CIRCLES IN AN ELIPSE	emphatic silly "unbelievable"
↑ ○	SPIRALS UPWARD NOTE: ADD DIRECTION: CW, CCW	"celebrate"
○ ↓	SPIRALS DOWNWARD NOTE: ADD DIRECTION: CW, CCW	"listing" spiral
[illegible]	90 DEGREE MVT	"later"
[illegible]	90 DEGREE MVT (EMPHASIS DOWNWARD)	"5 minutes"
[illegible]	90 DEGREE MVT (EMPHASIS UPWARD)	"morning"
90	90 DEGREE MVT CLOCKWISE	"15 min", "later"
09	90 DEGREE MVT COUNTERCLOCKWISE	"review"
180	180 DEGREES CW	"half-hour"
081	180 DEGREES CCW	"radius"
○	ND SUPPORT ROLL [○ | 360]	ND HS "world"
S	SERPENTINE UPWARDS	"spirit"
36△	FLATTENED 360	"carpenter"

NOTE: ROTATION DETERMINED BY VIEWING FROM TOP OR RIGHT SIDE PERSPECTIVE

NOTE: CIRCULAR DEFAULT IS HORIZONTAL ie: "here"

USE DIRECTION NOTATION FOR VERTICAL ie: "happy" ^360v

NOTE: CONTACT MAY NEED TO BE NOTATED ie: "curious" [X] 063

NOTE: USE DIRECTION NOTATION FOR LATERAL ie: "computer" <360>

***CAN ALSO USE 360 (HORIZONTAL), 361 (VERTICAL), 362 (LATERAL) FOR CLOCKWISE AND 063 (HORIZONTAL), 163 (VERTICAL), 263 (LATERAL) FOR COUNTERCLOCKWISE ROTATIONS**

MVTS: HORIZ & VERT

SAMPLE SIGN GLOSSES

	ARCS UP AND AWAY FROM SIGNER	"drive over the hill"
	ARCS UP AND TOWARDS SIGNER	"come back over hill"
		"put on a hat"
	ARCS DOWN AND AWAY FROM SIGNER	"swing on swings"
	ARCS DOWN AND TOWARDS SIGNER	""insult"
	STRAIGHT UP AND AWAY	"volleyball"
	STRAIGHT DOWN AND AWAY	"stay"
	STRAIGHT UP AND TOWARDS	"look at paper closely"
	STRAIGHT DOWN AND TOWARDS	"got in my face"
	CIRCULAR ARC DOWN AND TOWARDS	"daughter", "son"

MVTS: BOUNCING

SAMPLE SIGN GLOSSES

	WRIST VERTICAL: UP AND DOWN	"Yes", "hat" "have to"
	WRIST LATERAL: LEFT TO RIGHT	"where", "movie" "same" (one hand) "wave bye!"
	BOUNCING IN A ROW: HOPPING	"dolphin", "Hard of Hrg" "tip-toe"
	BOUNCING IN STRAIGHT LINE	"Hollywood", "great!" "child"
	ENTIRE SIGN BOBS 1X	Japanese: "greeting" "take a picture w/camera"
	ANNOUNCEMENT	"proclaim", "announce"

NOTE: DIRECTION MAY BE REQUIRED

NOTE: SEE CONTACT MVTS FOR CONTACT + BOUNCE

MVTS: THROWING, CATCHING, DROPPING, FALLING

		SAMPLE SIGN GLOSSES
	THROW (DEFAULT IS TO OPEN 5)	"ASL", "throw a ball"
	CATCH, ABSORB	"learn"
	DROP	"dismiss court case"
	FALL	"bankrupt",
		"tree falling down"
	DOWNWARD THRUSTING THROW	"many, many"
	UPWARD THROW	"how many?"

MVTS: ARTICULATING

		SAMPLE SIGN GLOSSES
	UP AND DOWN ARTICULATION	"machine"
	ROTATING ARTICULATION	"things falling into
		place" "syncing"
	NOTE: NEEDS DIRECTION UP, DOWN	

MVTS: PUNCH, STAB HIT

		SAMPLE SIGN GLOSSES
	STRONG PUNCH	"heart attack",
		"stroke"
		"impact"
	STABBING	"crucified"
		"betrayed"
	HIT/SLAP	"warn"
		"dog" (on thigh)
	POKE	"get attention"
		"airplane"

MVTS: WRIST/ELBOW

	MVTS: WRIST/ELBOW	SAMPLE SIGN GLOSSES
	VIBRATES	"silly", "finish"
		"for-for?", "play"
	TWISTS (Note: SINGLE MVT)	"turn key", "neat/cool"
÷	WRIST FLIP (180 DEGREES)	"cook", "hamburger"
(÷)	WRIST FLIP AND ROLL (+ DIRECTION)	"happen", "how"
•|•	WRIST "DOOR" HINGE SWING (180 DEGREES)	"email", "simple"
	or SHAKE	"dance", "noisy"
•|•>	WRIST HINGE 1X TO OUTSIDE	"finish-done"
√	GRAB	"take advantage", "butter"
		"learn", "galloping animal"
7	"7" SHAPE	"Chicago", "banana", "fun"
PP	PAGE TURN	"Ipad", "dictionary"
PP°	PAGE TURN (REVERSAL)	"investigate"
	HARD SCOOP	"new"*, "what's up"
	WRIST FLICK (90 DEGREES CW)	"not", "nut", "can"
	NOTE: FINAL POSITION NOT NEEDED, NATURAL MVT	
	WRIST FLICK (90 DEGREES CCW)	"reject"
	NOTE: FINAL POSITION NOT NEEDED, NATURAL MVT	
	BREAK	"broke"
≠	CUT	"what", "can't", "absent"
	CHOP	"chop veggies", "convice"
	WAVE	"flag", "windy"
	UNDULATE	"ocean waves", "Hawaii"
	CURLY	"WA state", "famous"

NOTE: MAY NEED TO ADD CONTACT OR DIRECTION, ie: "new"

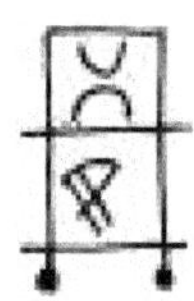

MVTS: OTHER

SAMPLE SIGN GLOSSES

∇	**FINGER RUB**	gestural: "$", "material", "to pester"
∇̄	**SINGLE SMOOTH FINGER RUB**	"pay", "smooth"
?	**QUESTION**	used for "government", and "?"
45	**45 DEGREE SHIFT CLOCKWISE**	"pump the brake"
54	**45 DEGREE SHIFT COUNTERCLOCKWISE**	"last minute"
45	**45 DEGREE (EMPHASIS DOWNWARD)**	"1 minute"
54	**45 DEGREE (EMPHASIS UPWARD)**	"immediately"

On the SS, MVTs are recorded in the MVT block either as a joint movement

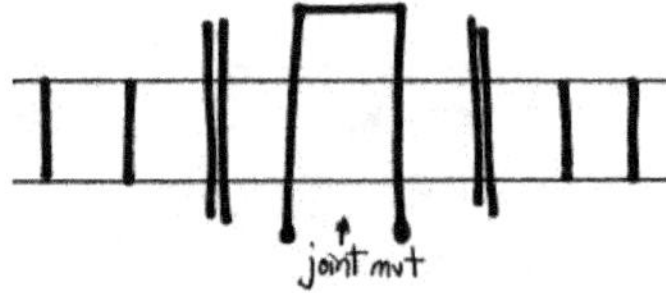

or individual movements of the ND and D HS:

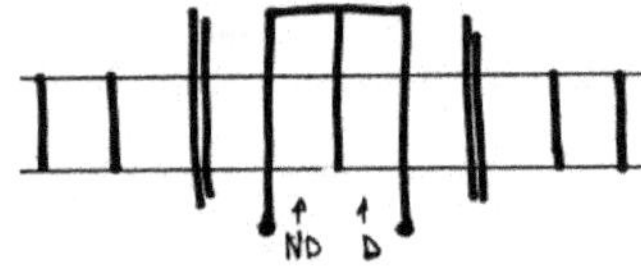

Here is an example of the MVT for the sign glossed: "to continue":

And an example of separate ND and D HS movements for the sign showing weighted scales shifting down on the right and up on the left:

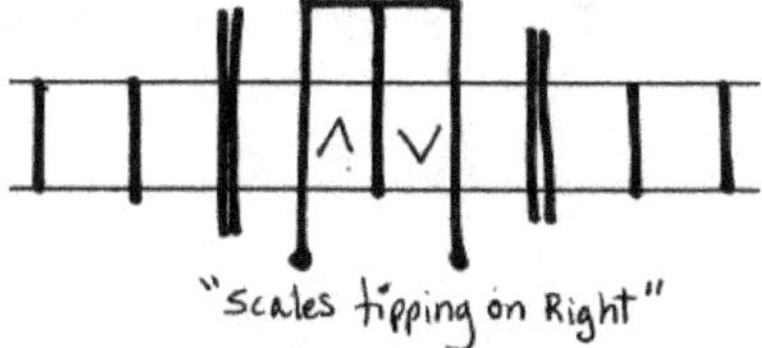

The MVT block can be notated differently for Contact and Non-Contact movements. The upper section is necessary to notate contact. If there is no contact, you can use a shorter notation for the MVT block while still preserving the double sections required for noting directionality of movements:

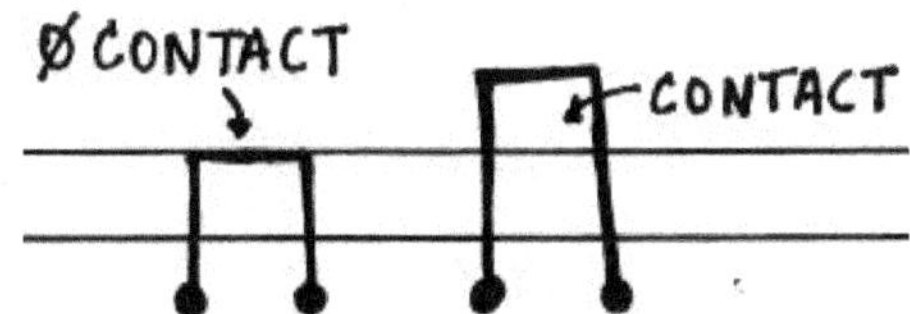

Here are a few examples of these MVT notations:

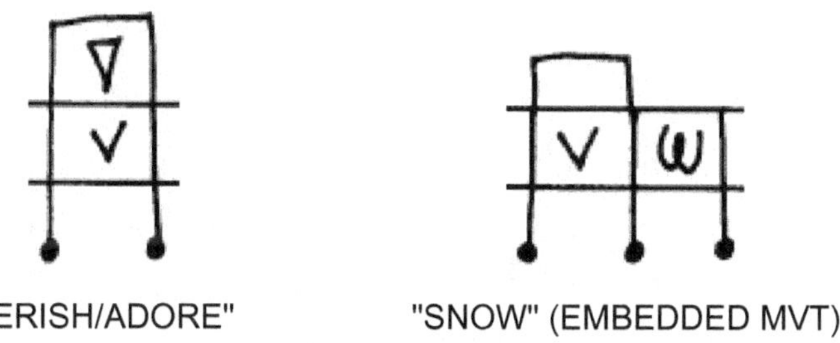

"CHERISH/ADORE" "SNOW" (EMBEDDED MVT)

COMPOUND MVTS: ADVERBIAL

You will notice that some signs have a compound MVT that incorporates a type of adverb such as directionality or the "how" of the

MVT. These can either be notated vertically or together horizontally, but are to be considered a MVT unit performed simultaneously:

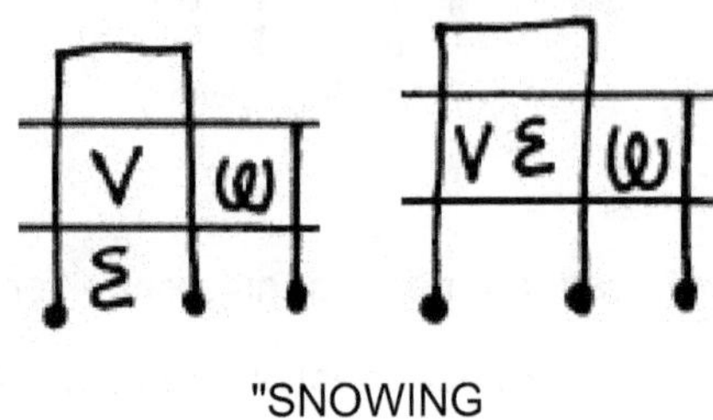

"SNOWING

CONTACT AS MVT

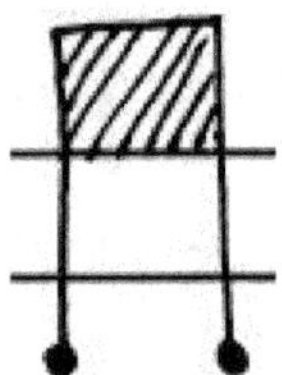

There is an extensive repertoire of possible contacts that can stand alone as an independent MVT or function as part of a MVT set. As additional contacts are identified, it is helpful to provide an example with each to clarify the particular type of contact intended. Each representation in the form of notation is only useful in the context of actual language usage.

MVTS: CONTACT

	SAMPLE SIGN GLOSSES
PARALLEL (NON-CONTACT POSITION)	"hallway"
APPROACHES BUT DOES NOT CONTACT	"reduces" (using indexes)
CONTACT	"China", "bus"
TAPPING CONTACT	"warning"
FINGERTIP CONTACT	"justice", "smart"
TAPPING FINGERTIP CONTACT	"calculator", mobile home"
	"favorite"
CONTINUOUS CONTACT	"art", "romance"
CONTINUOUS FINGERTIP CONTACT	"medicine", "animal"
CONTACT DRAGS	"girl"
CONTACT DRAGS IN WAVING PATTERN	"meth"
INTERSECTING FINGERS AT BASE	"football", "bother"
INTERSECTING FINGERS	"America"
INTERTWINING FINGERS	"friend"
CONTACT ON FINGERS	"name"
CLAPPING CONTACT	"school"
SWEEPING/BRUSHING OFF CONTACT	"clean", "forgive", "rough"
MAGNETIC OR "STICKING" CONTACT	"government", "post-it"
PINCHING THE SKIN OR CLOTHING	"meat", "volunteer"
CLASP	"married", resting hands
STRONG CONTACT	"illegal"
BOUNCES OFF AFTER STRONG CONTACT	"forbidden"
BOUNCES OFF IN STRAIGHT LINE	"kiss-fist", "equal"
CONTACT, BOUNCE, CONTACT*	"deaf", "birthday"

NOTE: DEFAULT FOR CONTACT ON FINGERS (ie: "name") is mid-finger.

(x)	VERY LIGHT CONTACT	"color"
(#)	VERY LIGHT FINGERTIP CONTACT	"braille"
)(	GLANCING OFF (VERTICAL)	"star"
	GLANCING OFF (HORIZONTAL)	"paper"
))•((	STRONG GLANCING OFF	"blame", "new"
	FINGERTIPS GLANCE OFF	"best", "cat", "simple"
	GLANCES OFF BODY	"drama", not my problem"
	SCRATCHING	"bear"
	PUT ONTO/CAP/LID	"canning"
	TO SET ON TOP OF	"establish"
O-O	CONTACT + PULL APART	"marshmallow", "story"
	LAYERED CONTACT	"build"
♡	KISS	"kiss-fist"
	PAINTING	"paint"
HS	BASE HS: DEFAULT IS CONTACT	"help"

NOTE: CONTACT IS PRESUMED AT OUTERMOST EXTENDED PORTION OF HS UNLESS OTHERWISE NOTED

NOTE: GLANCING AND LAYERED MVTS REQUIRE DIRECTION

*NOTE: CAN ADD TYPE OF CONTACT ie: "Deaf" 

YOUR TURN!

	MOVEMENTS	SAMPLE SIGN GLOSSES

Record your own observations!

ALTERNATING MVTS

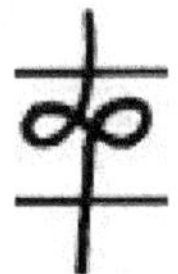

There is a set of signs which utilize an alternating movement pattern. Examples include:

- ASL
- balance
- bicycle/ride a bike
- court
- drama
- maybe
- popcorn
- roller skating
- science
- sports
- which

These signs utilize the same handshape, and the spacing between the hands is comfortably in line with the sides of the SSS*. We will use the notation below for alternating movement signs:

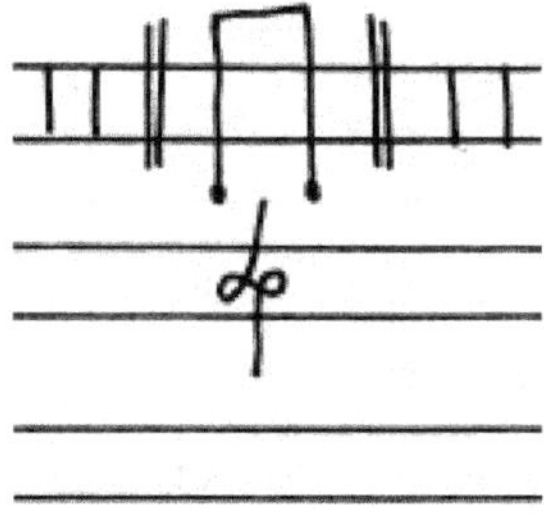

In the notation below, the location is recorded **(S*)...**however since this is the **default location for alternating mvts**...

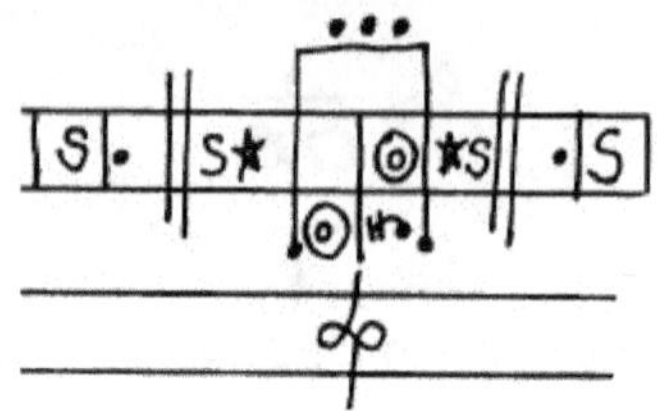

"ASL"

...we can leave the location blank, or delete it altogether:

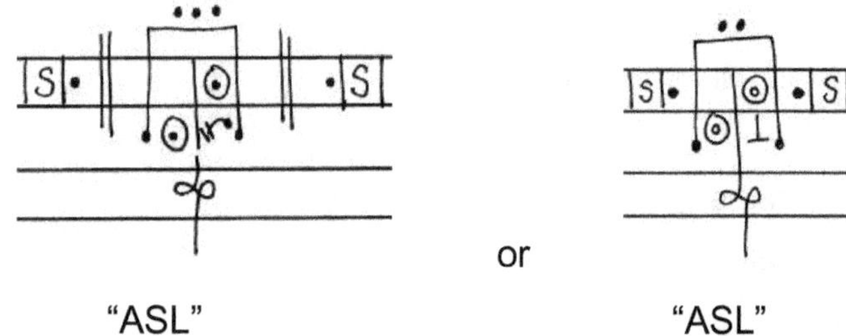

"ASL" or "ASL"

Another possibility is that an alternating movement will occur as a mirrored movement. For example the sign glossed: "color" can be articulated in an alternating D, ND, D pattern with a mirrored movement to the right, left and right. Here is the notation:

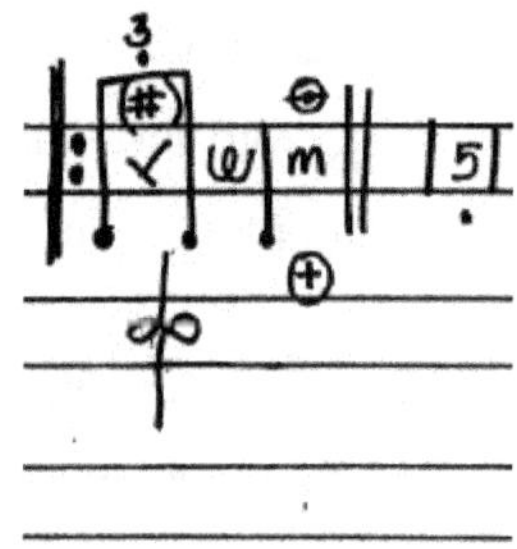

"COLOR, COLOR, COLOR"

To see a great example of this sign watch Tar2006's vlog on Youtube: "Black Deaf Person"

https://www.youtube.com/watch?v=LV8nF3TUuws

The MVT notations are listed on the mid and lower sections to emphasize the alternating pattern, and the repetition marks/dots above the MVT block represent cycles of alternating movements. For the sign glossed: "ASL", the movement would be initiated by the D HS, repeated by the ND HS, and completed by a final cycle with the D HS. The direction of the MVT is established by the initial MVT (forward arcing away from the signer). Alternating movements require a minimum of two movements which represent one full cycle.

LATERAL ALTERNATING MOVEMENTS

Some movements alternate laterally. An example is the sign glossed: "Jesus" which has an alternating pattern:

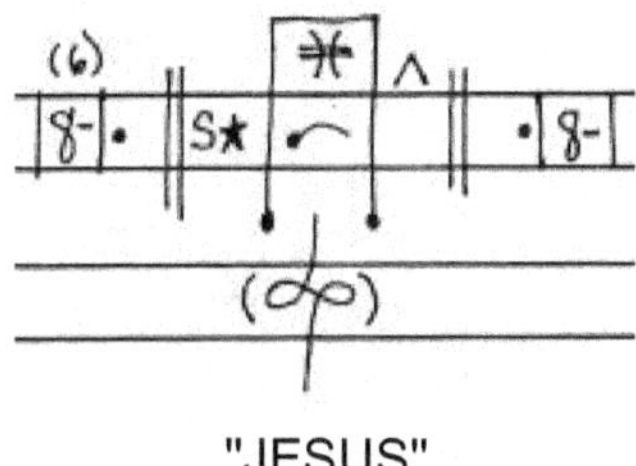

"JESUS"

Default location for lateral alternating movements is **"*"**. For example, the sign glossed: "friend" can be written shorthand:

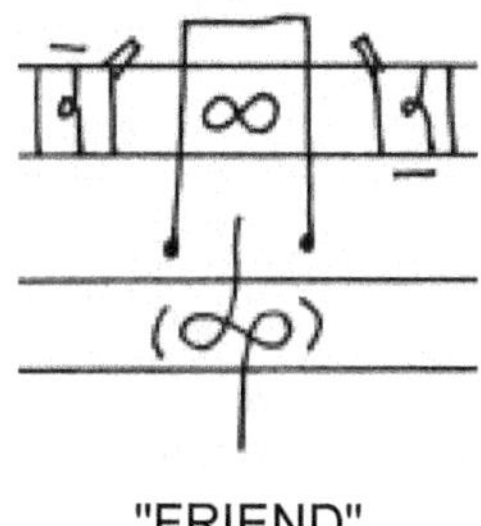

"FRIEND"

YOUR TURN!

Which movement notation fits this sign glossed "Deaf" using indexes along the side of the face? Check your answer in the back section under "YOUR TURN! ANSWERS" (#4)

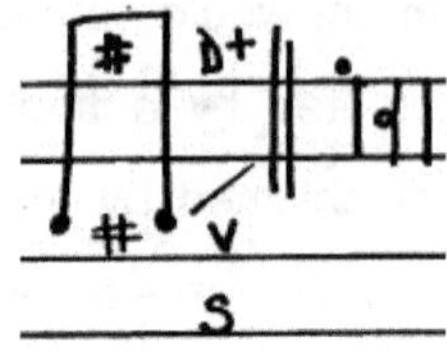

"DEAF"

MIRROR MVTS

Many signs are made with identical handshapes doing the same exact movement in the same relative location along the Midline Plane simultaneously. For example the sign for "parallel lines" is symmetrical:

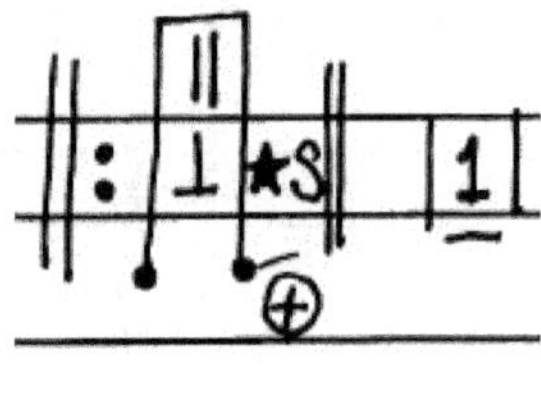

"PARALLEL LINES"

We will use this notation at the beginning of a symmetrical MVT sign to indicate that this sign is done using both ND and D HS in the same relative location:

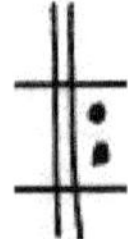

IDENTICAL MIRROR MVTS NOTATION

An example is the sign for "vacation":

"VACATION"

Mirror movements which are symmetrically divergent/convergent are notated:

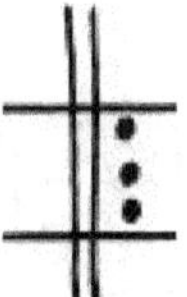

CONVERGENT/DIVERGENT MIRROR MOVEMENTS

An example is the sign glossed: “here”. The D HS circles clockwise and the ND HS circles counterclockwise simultaneously:

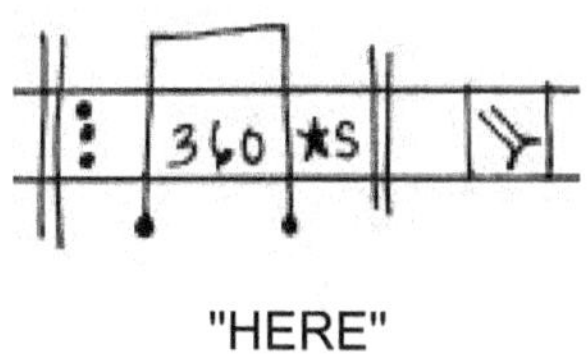

"HERE"

Other examples include the signs for "roommate" and “computer”:

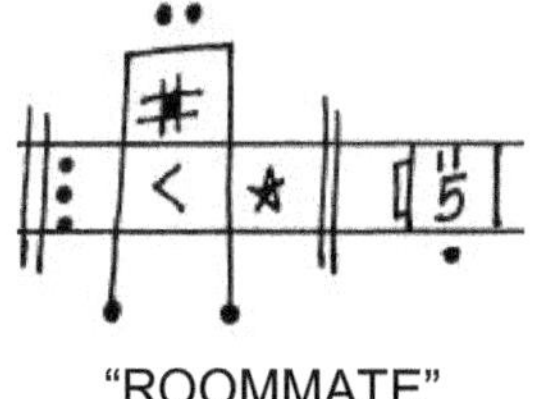

“ROOMMATE”

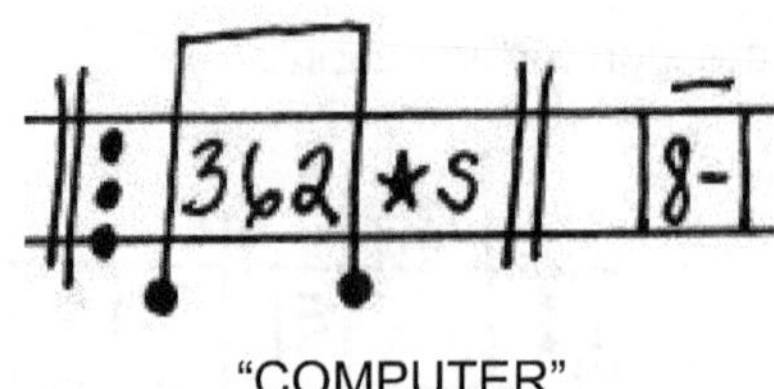

"COMPUTER"

Notice that the horizontal direction is default and to notate a vertical rotation would require direction marks (or use of 361) as in this articulation of the sign glossed "happy":

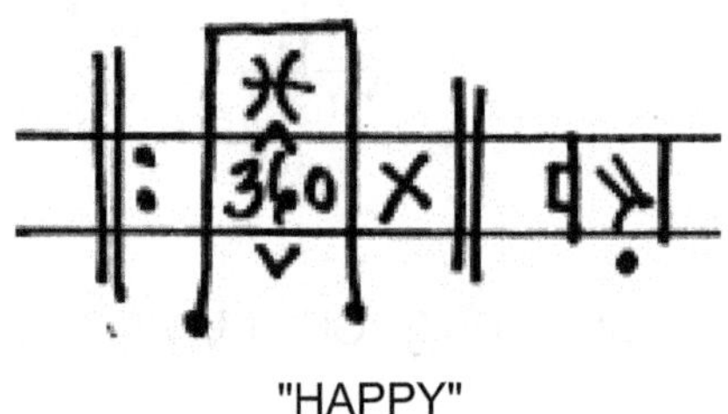

"HAPPY"

YOUR TURN!

See if you can identify which English glossed sign this notation represents. Check your answer in the back section under "YOUR TURN! ANSWERS" (#5)

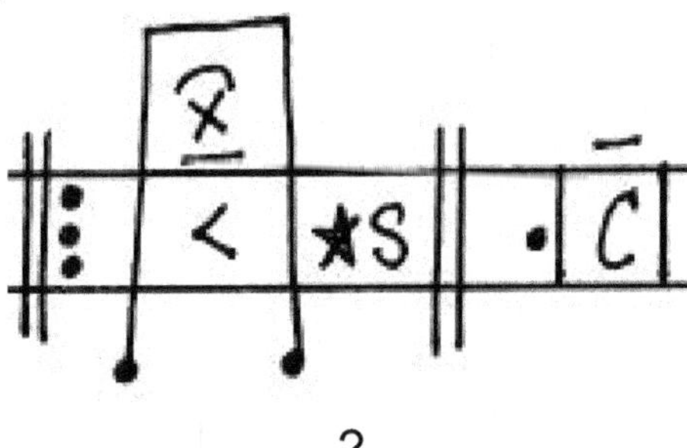

?

EMBEDDED MOVEMENTS

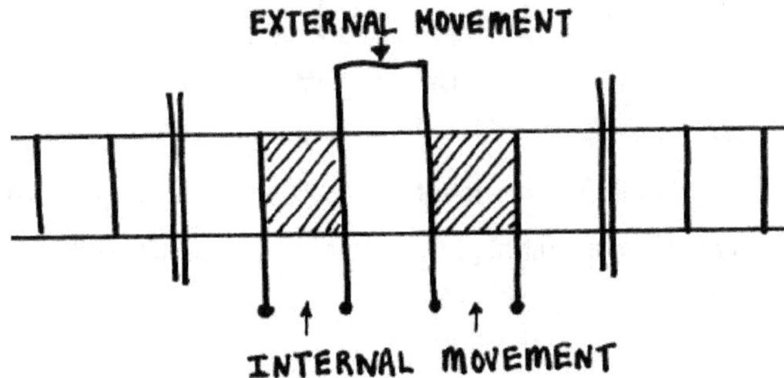

Usually we think of a sign as having a single primary movement per tier. For example, the sign for "microwave" has two consecutive movements and requires two tiers:

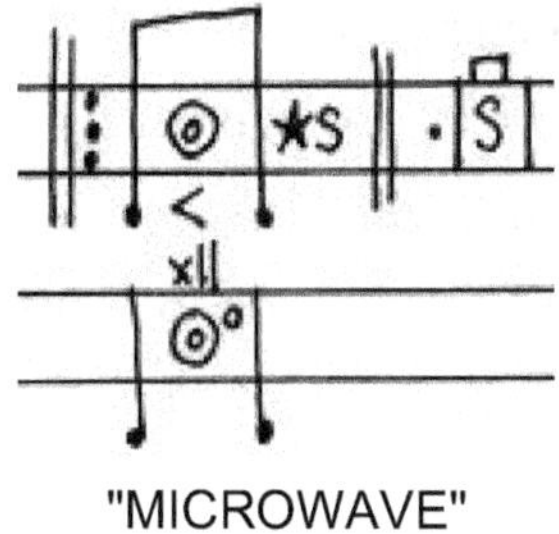

"MICROWAVE"

Some signs are unique and are comprised of an external movement (often the path of travel) and an internal or **embedded movement**. For example the sign "hurricane" is a complex sign that includes a path of travel for the hurricane as well as the internal, embedded movement of the motion of the hurricane itself:

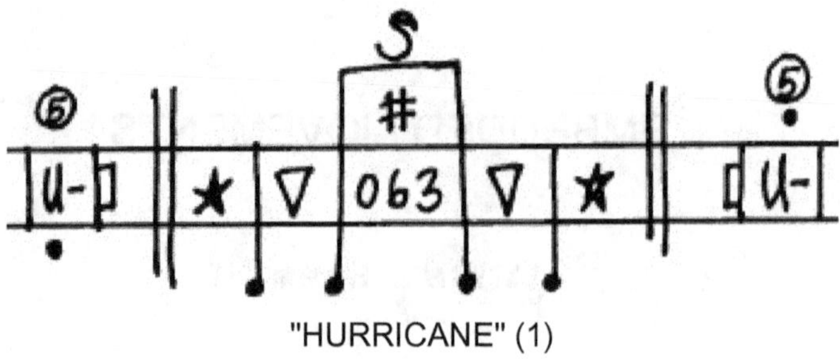

"HURRICANE" (1)

Default is continuous movement of the embedded movement, however if you'd like to highlight for clarity, you can use the continuous reps symbol (:)

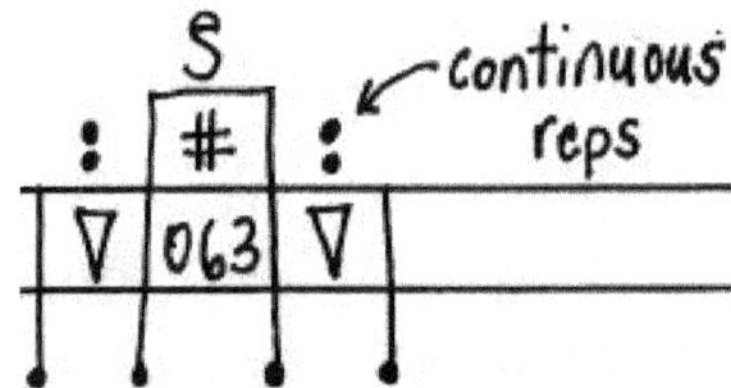

A variation on this sign is to arc the entire sign from the dominant side to the non-dominant side of the standard signing space. You will note the finger identification is omitted...this notation is optional as the handshapes are positioned on top of each other vertically and the thumbs of the handshapes are extended, leaving only one point of mutual contact.

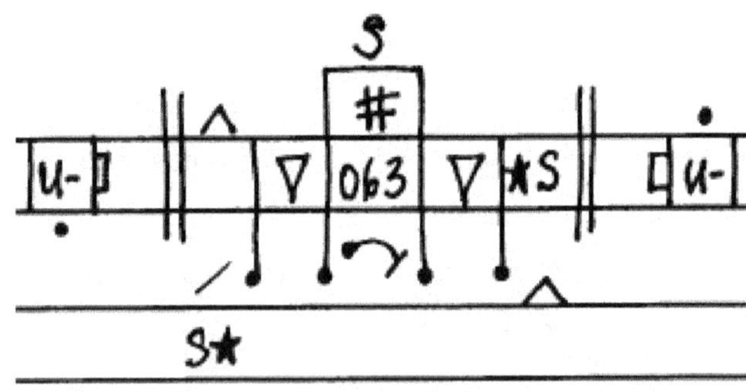

"HURRICANE" (2)

Let's look at some examples. In this version, the sign is moving laterally as the fingers flutter:

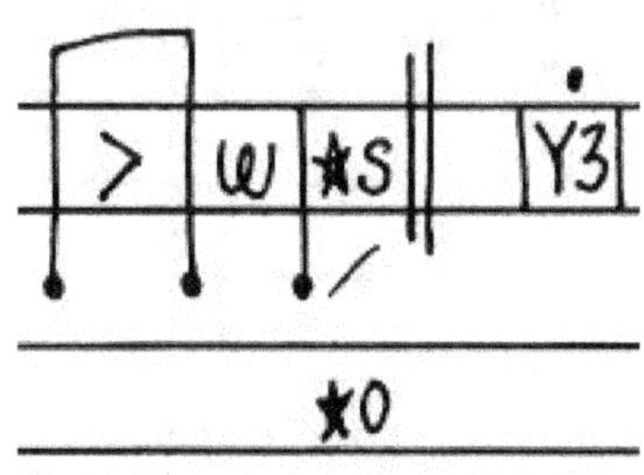

"FINGERSPELLING"

In this version, an alternative articulation is notated:

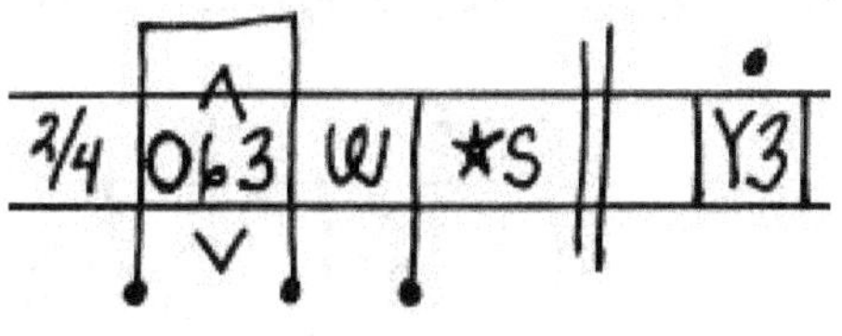

"FINGERSPELLING" (2)

In this sign, I decided to add a side of the movement block on the second tier for clarity.

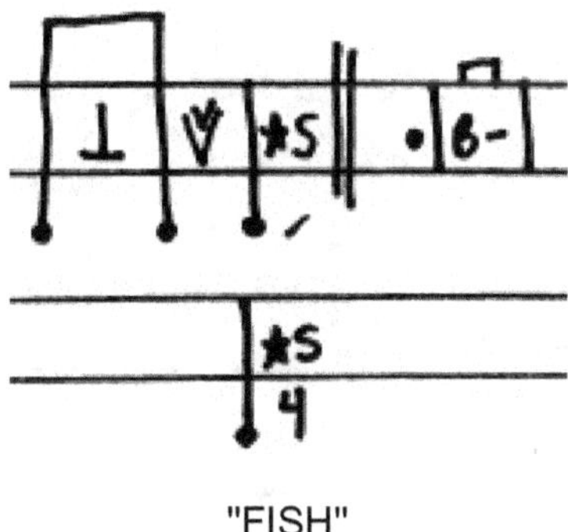

"FISH"

Here is the notation for one version of the sign glossed: "cereal":

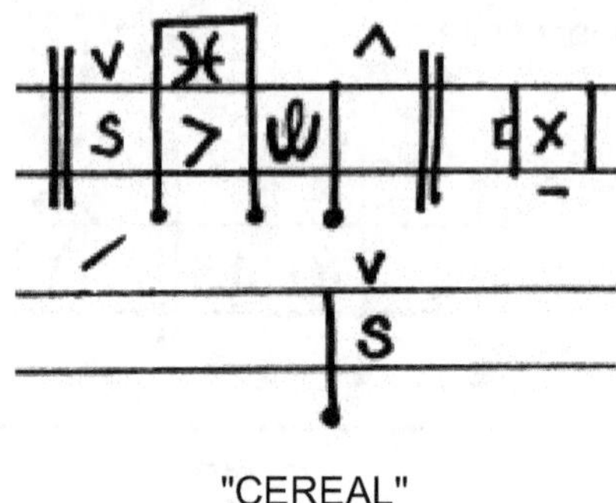

"CEREAL"

The following two signs have different contact notations both in terms of movement and detail. The second example includes the final HS, but is not necessary as the movement of "twisting" is usually a 90 shift in PO.

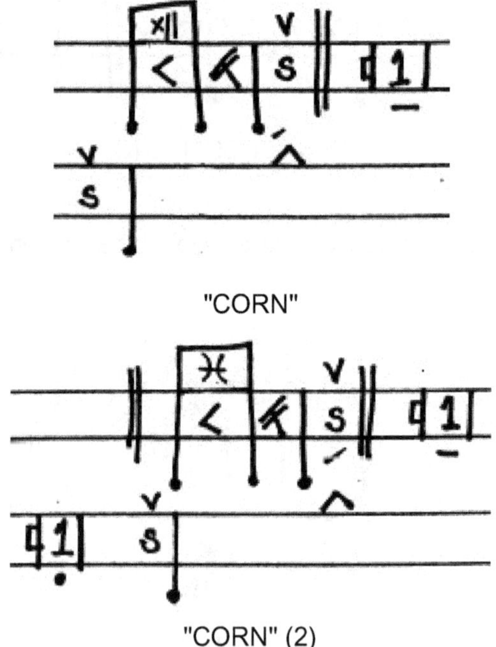

"CORN"

"CORN" (2)

This next sign an exciting sign to notate! You will notice that there is a directional notation in the MVT block. It might seem that this is additionally embedded movement, but for those MVTs that require direction, such as this bouncing movement, the direction is normally needed and is not an additional movement.

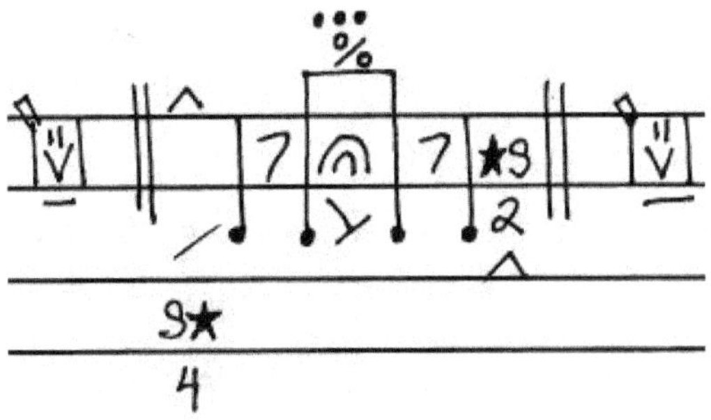

"ANIMAL GALLOPING AWAY TO THE LEFT"

And this is one version of an embedded movement sign glossed: "to happen over and over again".

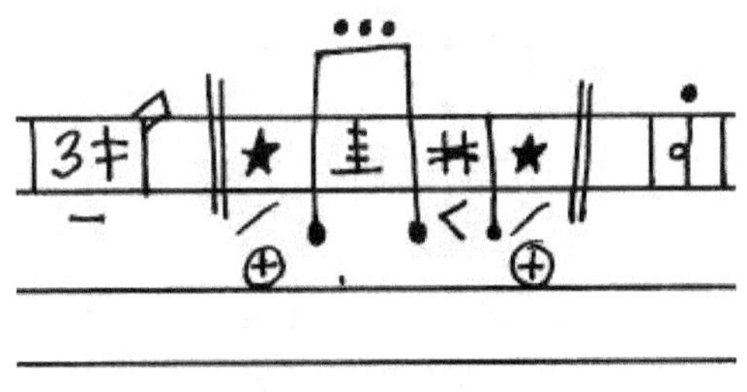

"RECURRENT EVENT"

When evaluating a sign for embedded movements, any sign that typically requires a direction notation along with the movement notation is not an embedded MVT sign. Look for movements which are done by the fingers or wrist and do not require a direction...these are often incorporated as internal or embedded movements within a larger external movement.

PARAMETER 4
FUN SURPRISES

Some movements are serendipitous. An example is the ASL sign for "government". The movement seems a bit complicated (using an index finger). However, it is actually identical to the sign for "?" that draws a question-mark in space, with the addition of being simultaneously rotated 90 degrees (I notated this as an embedded movement), and making contact at the temple:

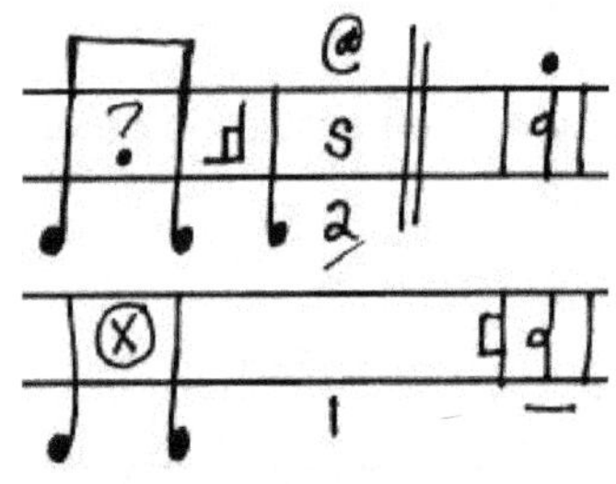

"GOVERNMENT"

You will also find sets of signs that have an unexpected connection. For example the movement for the sign glossed: "can't" is also the same movement, with the addition of direction, for the sign glossed: "absent":

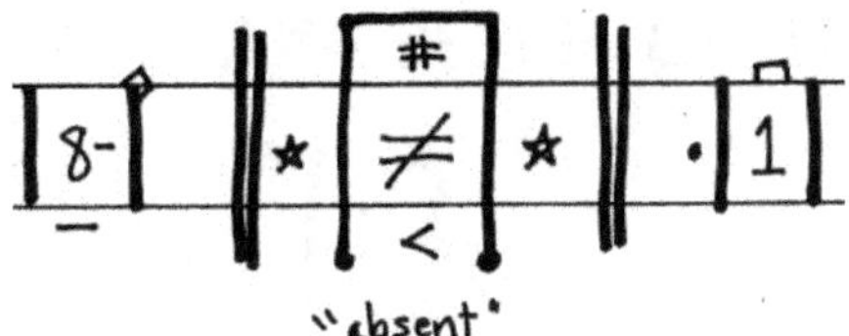

You will notice that the ending or second tier LOC and HS are omitted. This is due to a convention that would apply to the movement of "cutting", meaning signs using that movement have a generally agreed upon arching motion that is presumed.

It is possible to have more than one notation created for a sign, which is why it would be important to agree to the SN for any particular sign. Of course, you can work through each and still arrive at the particular articulation. But for educational purposes, it would be good to have standard notations. For example, here is an alternative, expanded version of the sign for "can't" with a different articulation:

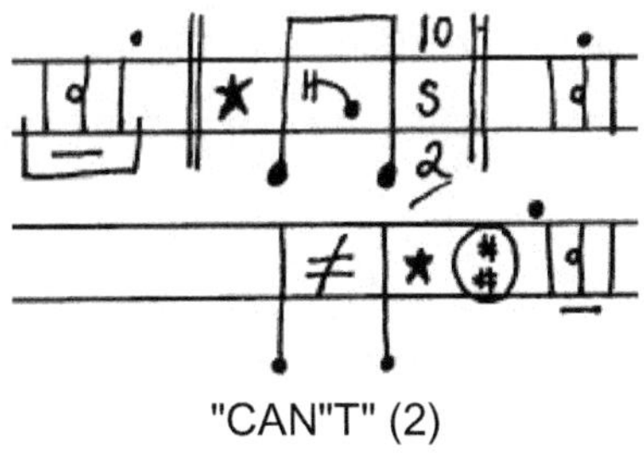

"CAN"T" (2)

Here is a suggested standard notation using BHSP:

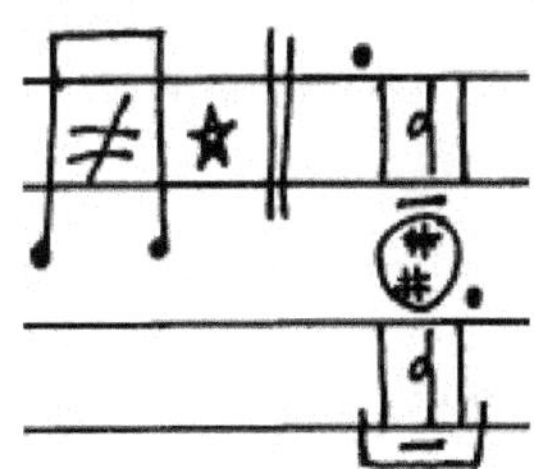

"CAN'T" (3)

DEPICTING VERBS AKA: CLASSIFIERS

Roll up your sleeves. There is a daunting category of signs which are now termed "depicting verbs" due to the fact that their use represents both the passive "to be" state and active verb use.

This is the most exciting part of SN! When you fill in the grammar block with the dV (depicting Verb) notation, a small 3D hologram of the item you are about to describe shimmers on the page! Solving our challenge of *how on earth to replicate the intricate descriptions that seem to defy recording*. Or perhaps we can just have a little video screen juxtaposed into our notations and simply watch the signer describe away...!

What we need to do is work through the task in the same manner that the signer mentally approaches the use of depicting verbs.

The basic "rules" are:

TYPE 1: TO BE

1. The signer identifies the item such as an animal.

2. The signer generates various dV HS that describe the creature in brief or elaborate detail, possibly veering off with tangential explanatory tidbits, and returning to give as colorful a description as imagination and time allow.

TYPE 2: TO DO

1. The signer identifies the item such as a "car".

2. The signer generates a depicting verb HS such as a "3" which is a pre-designated HS for this particular class of items in ASL.

3. The signer manipulates the dV in space to demonstrate the behavior or activity of the original item as represented by the dV HS, such as a car trip or path of travel.

TYPE 1+2: HYBRID SERIES

1. The signer identifies an item or group of items such as an engine with various parts.

2. The signer uses depicting verbs to explain relationships, connections, functions, malfunctions, processes AND descriptions etc...such as the flow of fuel, shape of a valve, break-down of a part, size of a fuse, etc...incorporating both static "to be" as well as functional "to do" aspects.

We need to:

1. Identify the grammar notation for a dV.

2. Notate whether this particular upcoming sign to be notated is intended to function as a TYPE 1 or TYPE 2.

DEPICTING VERB: TYPE 1 DEPICTING VERB: TYPE 2

3. Notate the HS, PO and starting LOC

4. Notate the relationship of the descriptor to the identified item for TYPE 1.

5. Notate the path or interactional features and MVT behavior for TYPE 2.

SKETCHING FRAMES

For #4 and #5 above, the PATH or INTERACTIONAL features need to be sketched and the RELATIONSHIP of the descriptor to the whole needs to be conveyed thru sketching.

Sketching will occur in a separate frame:

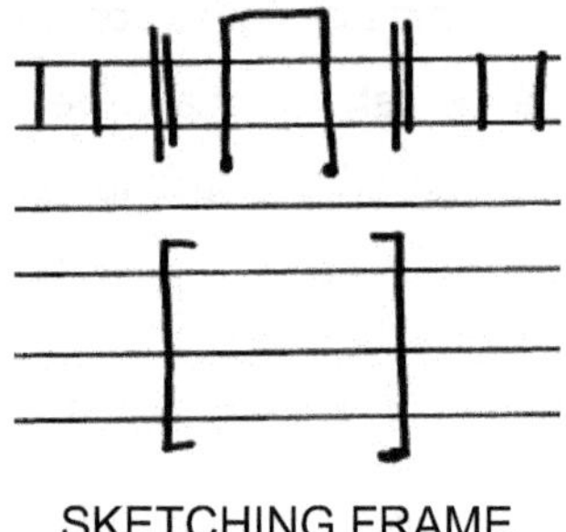

SKETCHING FRAME

The orientation of the frame of reference is needed. For sketching frames that are vertical such as would be needed to sketch the shape of a picture frame on a wall, add vertical frame marks:

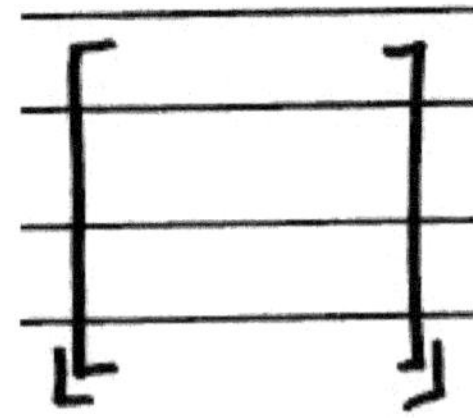

VERTICAL FRAME MARKS

For a horizontal frame such as would be needed to sketch the path of an airplane in flight use horizontal frame marks:

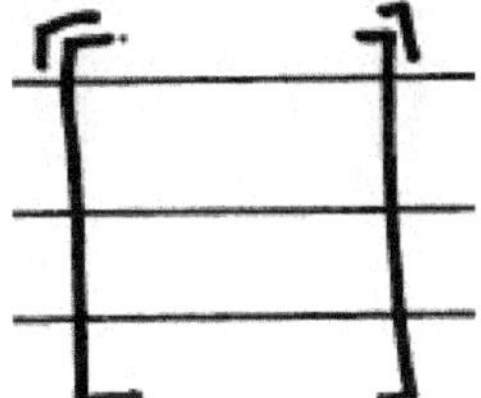

HORIZONTAL FRAME MARKS

DEPICTING VERB TYPE 1
TO BE/DESCRIPTIVE

Let's look at Type 1 dV first. There are a couple of novel adjustments we will need to make. First, it would be helpful for the reader to know if the item being described is an animate or inanimate object. This information helps the reader and signer contextualize the description. Of course, the signer should have introduced the type of item previously such as a house, dragon, or garden but for reading clarity we will use two notations to aid in comprehension:

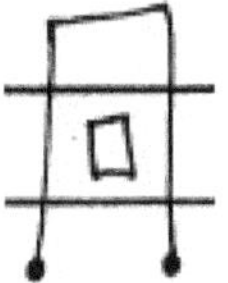

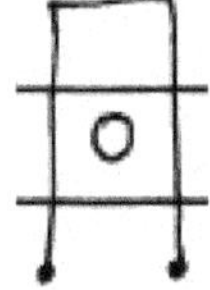

INANIMATE OBJECT ANIMATE OBJECT

The second thing we can do to make our notations more efficient is to indicate the starting and ending location side by side, following the order of operations outside to inside:

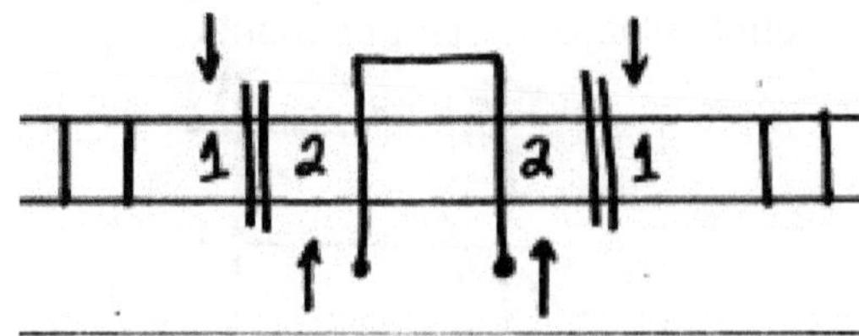

Here is an example of that strategy to notate a picture frame:

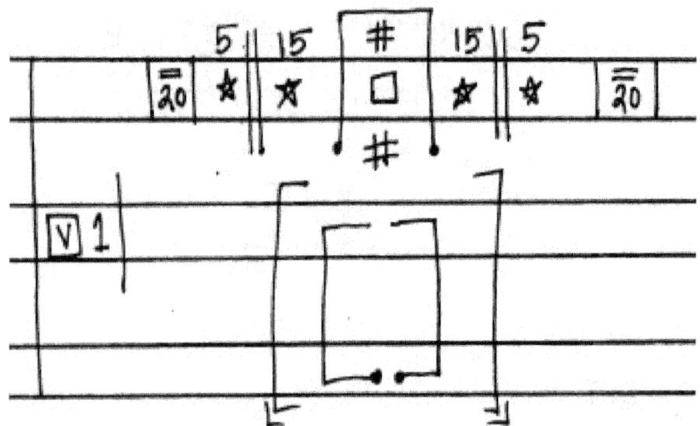

Of course, you could also notate the locations in the standard two tier format, and then perhaps need to move the sketching frame to the side of the notated sign, or reduce the frame size. It is nice to have options.

Here is another example showing a dV series of connected frames including the final frame with a place holding BHS index. Default is D HS if no other information is given except for HS:

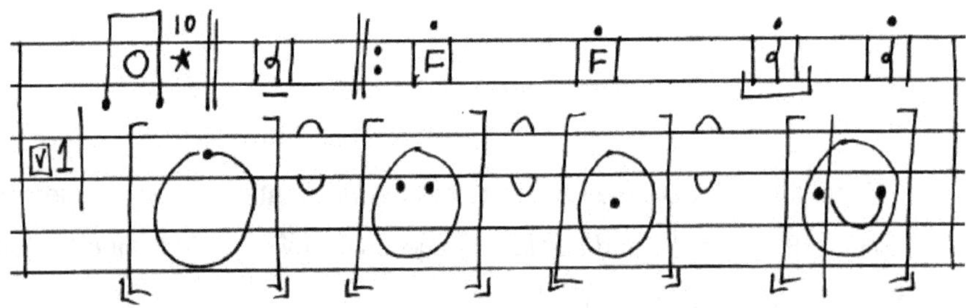

Here is the same basic information but notated by a signer using their own face as the point of reference for the depicting verbs. I also got lazy and only marked the vertical frame on one side of each frame:

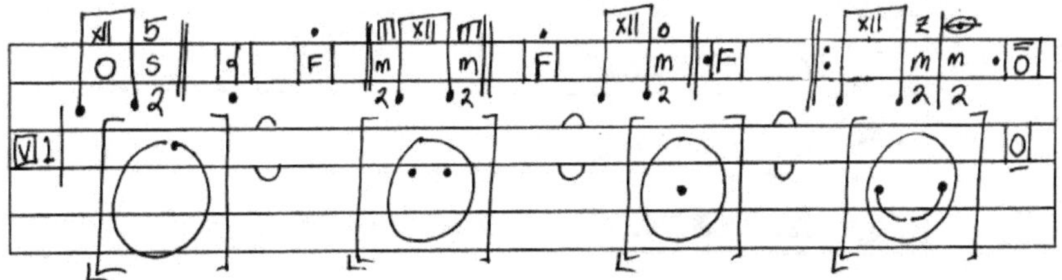

Visually, utilizing color to highlight the addition of each new dV detail and leaving the base shape a separate color would assist the reader in following more easily the development of the description.

DEPICTING VERBS TYPE 2
TO DO/ACTIVE

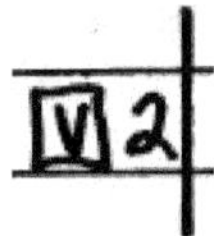

Type 2 dV require notation of several additional aspects including the path of movement and the type of movement. Regarding the type of movement, instead of indicating "animate" or "inanimate" as in Type 1 dV, we need a more extensive ability to identify the type of movement. Here is a very rudimentary sample chart of possible unique dV MVTS:

TYPE 2 DEPICTING VERBS "TO DO": ACTIVE

	A: WALKING/RUNNING/CRAWLING
	A: CLIMBING
	A: FLYING
	A: SWIMMING
	A: RESTING/STATIONARY
	IA: DRIVING/FLYING/STEERING
	IA: PARKED/STATIONARY
	IA: CONNECTING
	IA: DISCONNECTING
	IA: FLOWING/MOVING/PASSING BY

Notating these movements is needed because these inform the way a signer approaches using dV.

PATHWAYS

When sketching a movement path for a Type 2 depicting verb, we need to have some way of understanding the slope of the path. We can use the graph below to notate the type of slope:

= Uphill Slope

• • Downhill Slope

— Minimal or No Slope

X Arc Zone

M _X_ Bumpy Ride

NOTE: Color would be ideal to notate the shift in direction, ie: black for minimal slope, blue for an incline and red for a decline etc...

DEGREE OF SLOPE

In addition we will need to indicate the amount of slope or incline/decline. Let's agree to use the mathematical symbol for slope **"M"** in conjunction with a scale from 0-6:

0 = No slope...flat surface
1 = Minimal slope
2 = Small slope
3 = Medium slope (45 degrees)
4 = Significant slope
5 = Profound slope (85 degrees)
6 + = 90 degrees upward
6 - = 90 degrees downward

SLOPE NOTATION

Let's look at some examples. Here is the path of a standard vehicle or animal/person wandering back and forth with minimal to no slope. Notice the arrow indicating the pathway direction and endpoint dot. No slope is notated for this standard level pathway:

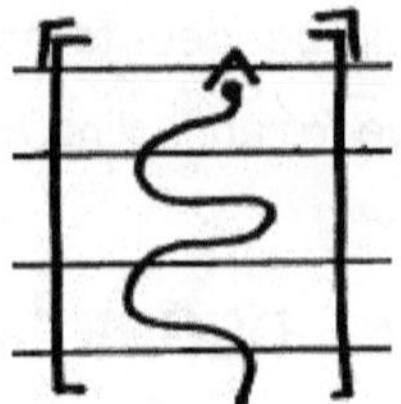

In this example, the route of a rocket is conveyed with a series of slopes along the pathway:

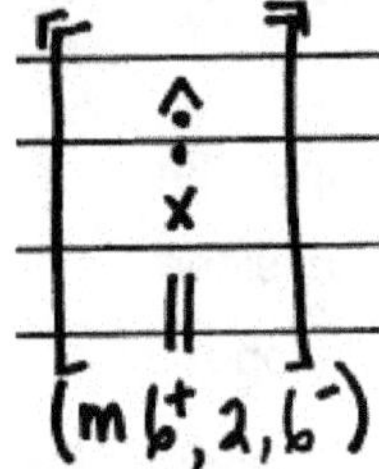

Here is an undulating pathway, and it is repeated three times, as notated with an exponent on the entire frame:

The pathway notated in the next frame shows a downhill, uphill, jog to the right, and then forward route, with moderate slope for the hill section:

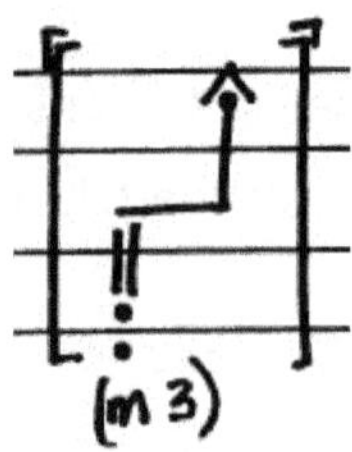

A bumpy ride to the left:

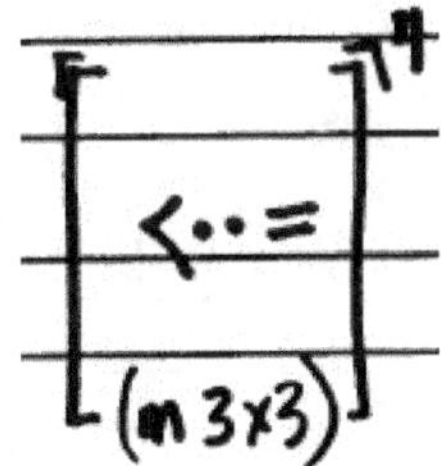

A race could be notated using an alternating movements notation:

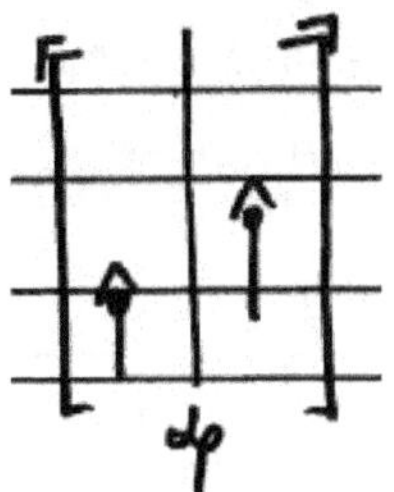

Individuals, vehicles, animals etc... meeting head on or one another can be sketched:

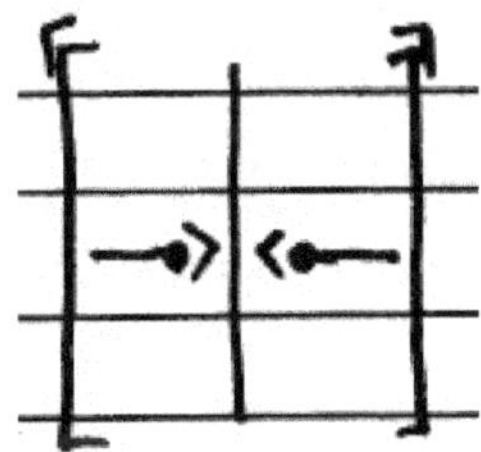

This next sketch notates an increasing slope of a set of hills encountered:

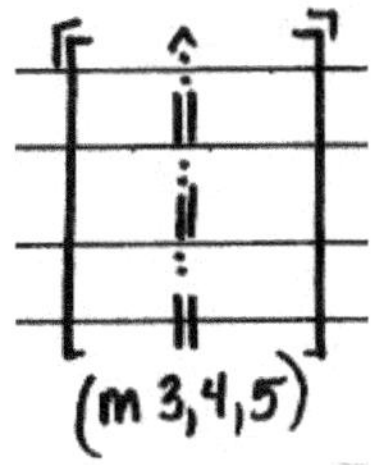

Sketches can also be created alongside the related sign notation details…

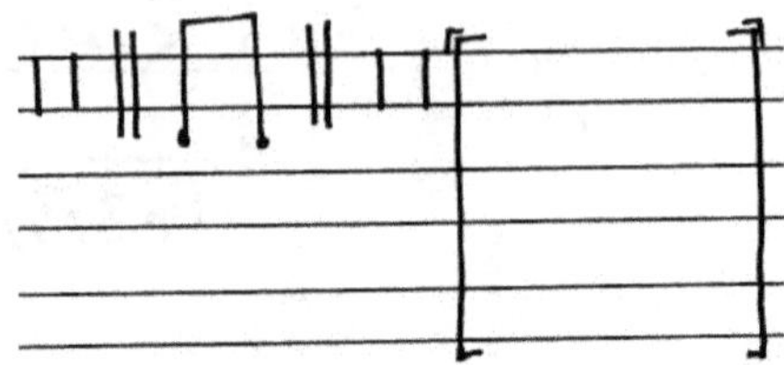

and be set into a series of events using the same initial handshapes, location, movement etc...such as this sample of a race that has a winner:

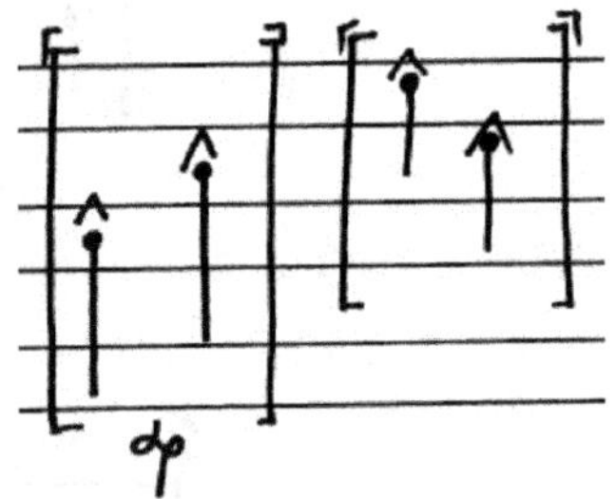

It reminds me of "**Car vs. Bike**" by 4jsabc! https://www.youtube.com/watch?v=2zeYdTjNrBg

How about this set...can you figure out what it is describing?!

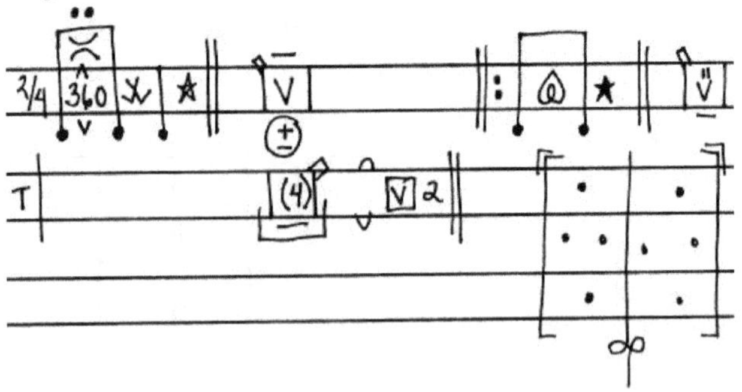

PUTTING IT ALL TOGETHER
V1 AND V2

Consider this example of a V1 and V2 series:

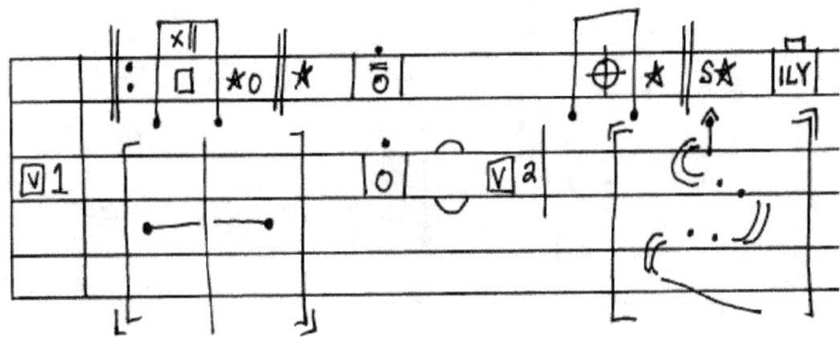

An airplane wing design is described and then the flight path of the aircraft depicted, swooping back and forth in banking turns and then leveling into a forward orientation. The only reason this would work is because....we would agree to these conventions as an approach to the complex three- dimensional aspects of depicting verbs recorded on a 2D surface.

Depicting verbs need an entire volume or volumes dedicated to exploring notations. The above is only a small sampling of how dV could be treated within SN. Further time can be devoted to this aspect of sign languages, if SN is seen as a viable and useful notation system.

"TV" MVTS

Some movements are unique and best conveyed through simple line drawings.

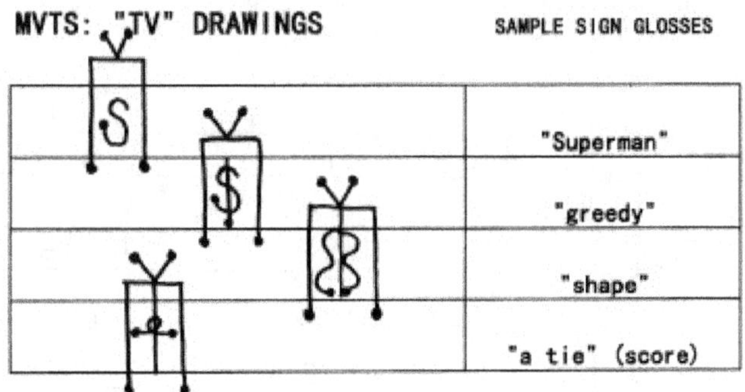

In order to convey the endpoint of the movement, use a period "." at the pathway endpoint. As with all SN, these "TV" drawings would become familiar for standard signs. Notice the midline on the sign glossed: "a tie" (related to a sports score). The actual pathway for the handshapes is a simple tying of a knot.

Here is an example for the sign "Superman" in longhand notation:

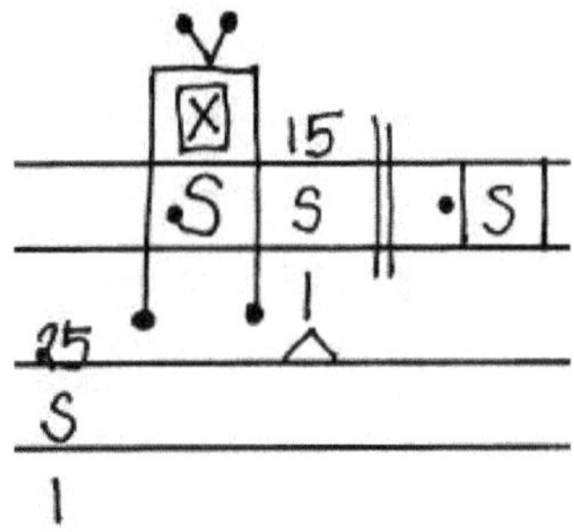

“SUPERMAN”

And another for "shape":

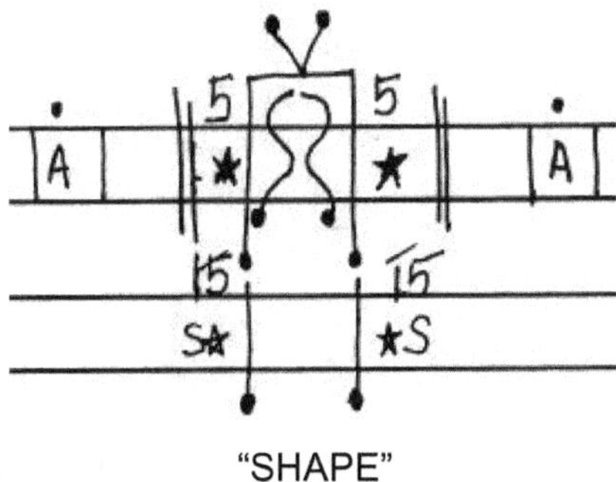

"SHAPE"

Or this option for "shape" (Mirror MVT):

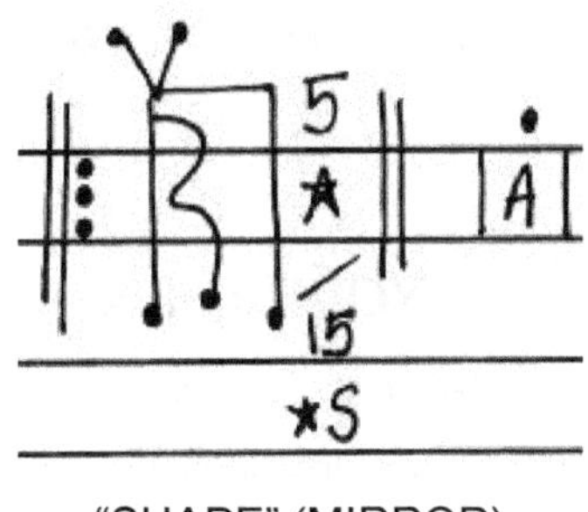

"SHAPE" (MIRROR)

Another sign that lends itself to using this notation is "house". Even though we can write the notation longhand, it works more efficiently to use a "TV" MVTS notation:

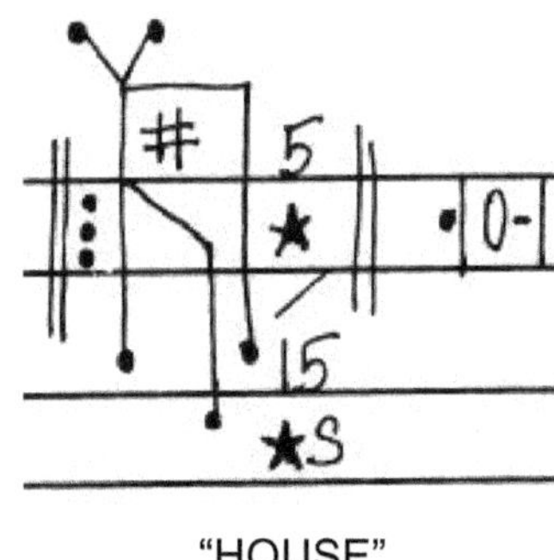

"HOUSE"

We could simplify even further:

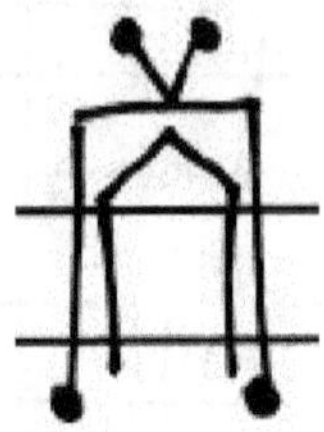

"HOUSE" (SHORTHAND NOTATION)

A grammar notation is usually required for shorthand notation. The "TV" symbol above the movement block provides this information.

YOUR TURN!

Create the depicting verb notation for a group of penguins sitting in a semi-circle facing the signer. Include the unique dV MVT. Check your answer in the back section under "YOUR TURN! ANSWERS" (#6)

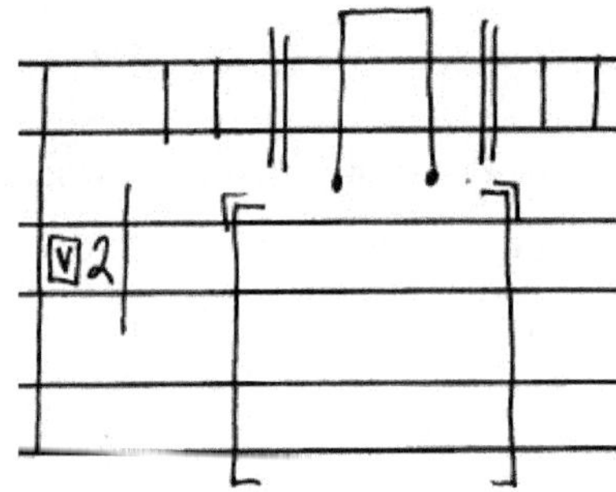

CONJUGATION OF VERBS

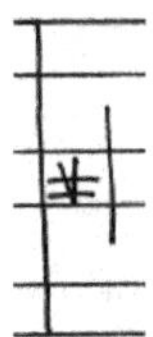

ASL has a set of verbs that are conjugated in the same manner that Romance languages conjugate verbs. Directional verbs take a root verb such as "teach" and conjugate or modify in consistent patterns to indicate first person, second person and third person. For example the verb "to teach" is modified directionally to express:

- I teach
- I teach you
- You teach me
- I teach her/him/all of you
- You teach each other
- She teaches him

Here is a very brief list of a few sample verbs that are similarly conjugated in ASL:

- Pay
- Give
- Sell
- Buy
- Come
- Go
- Help
- Drive
- Look
- Like

Not all directional verbs utilize all of the possible conjugated forms, but the basic pattern is consistent for these directionalized verbs.

When notating, we will use the root form of the verb and then add the applicable directional conjugate. Take the sign glossed: "to pay" as an example. Here is the fully notated form:

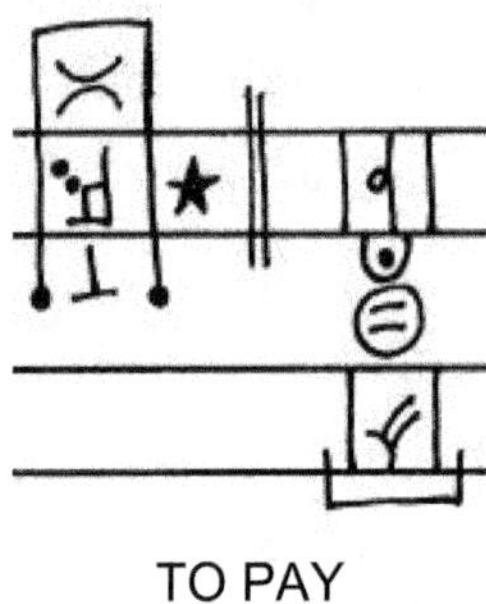

TO PAY

And another possible variation for the same sign using a different HS and MVT:

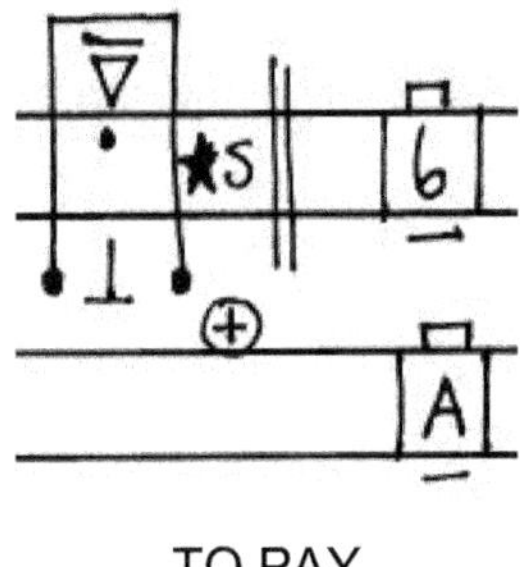

TO PAY

For the first example, we would notate the directional verb in the grammar block:

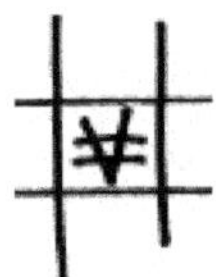

And then notate the root verb with the conjugate form next to the MVT block similar to an embedded movement:

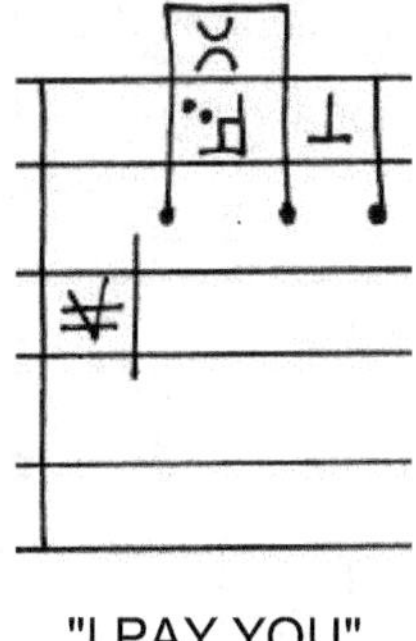

"I PAY YOU"

Or with a different conjugation:

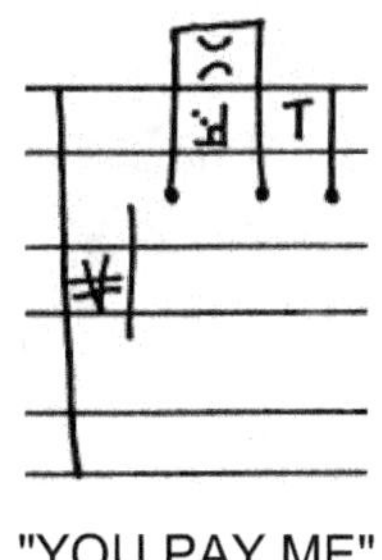

"YOU PAY ME"

When using conjugations, the root verb is maintained even though the directional movement has changed. It could be notated as a “stem changing” verb and the movements altered to match the clockwise/counterclockwise movements. Let's look at another directional verb, "to give":

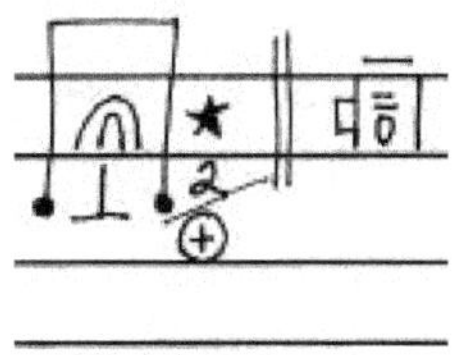

"I GIVE YOU"

In this case the notation includes the directionality, "I give you". If we notate that using the directional conjugated form it would look like this:

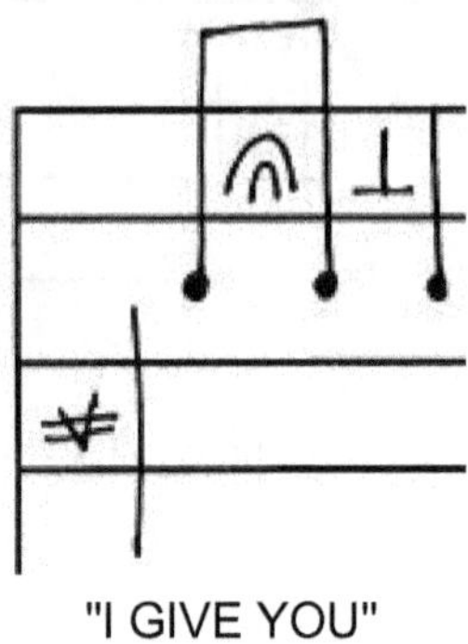

"I GIVE YOU"

If we need to further clarify, in the event there are more than one directional sign with a similar movement block, then we will add details as needed starting with HS:

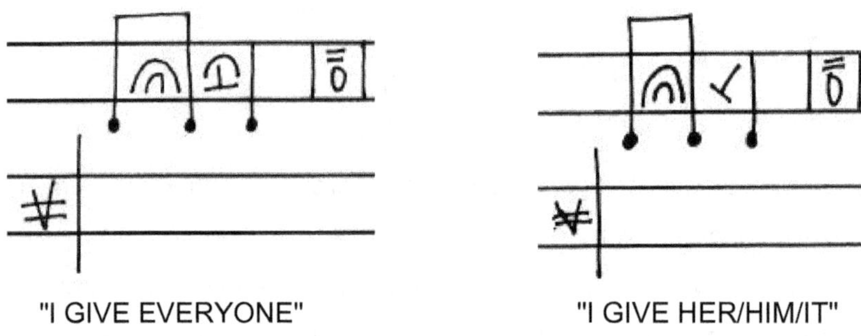

"I GIVE EVERYONE" "I GIVE HER/HIM/IT"

Notice in the examples above the PO is omitted. Only the required detail will be added until the notation is differentiated from other directional conjugates. Directional conjugates would need to be collected and recorded in a “Conjugated Verbs” notation chart/bank to ensure clear standardized notation.

FINGERSPELLING, NUMBERS AND DATES

Fingerspelling and numbers are vital to clear communication. Fingerspelling is not universal...each country has its own unique set of fingerspelling HS. Below is a sample of the American Sign Language alphabet:

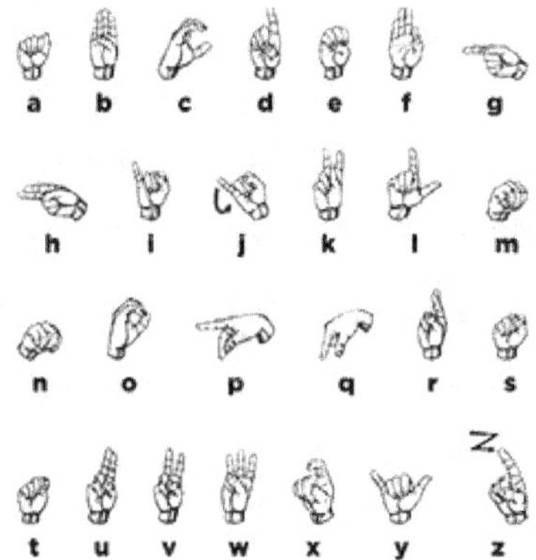

Source: http://jonkeane.com/images/Asl_alphabet_gallaudet.jpg
http://www.lifeprint.com/asl101/pages-layout/gallaudettruetypefont.htm
Retrieved 10/7/15

Likewise the numbering system is unique and well developed. On the SS, fingerspelling, numbers and dates are all recorded on the second tier, mid-staff.

FS Chloe Jones # 1956 6/2/83 FS Lincoln # 3/4

At times, there may be a dense data section which can be notated on all three tiers as needed, and read top to bottom, left to right:

Marie Mendoza	SSN 589-00-3671
VP 506-213-6895	DOB July 21, 1953
NS Dallas, TX	3362 Poplar St.

I chose to add some details above the actual info such as SSN, VP, FS, DOB, # etc… These are not required, but are helpful bits of info. If the signer actually signs "SSN" or "VP" these would be written along with the details on the mid-tier staff as part of the signed utterance. To notate a sequential series of data that requires multiple tiers use the notation for an extension:

Susan Smith Allentown, PA

DOB 6/ 17/ 59 • 18101

SSN 430-81-0563

A shift in the location of fingerspelling can be notated along with the

FS term. For example many times a signer will extend the arm and fingerspell a term or item closer to the recipient to connect with and maximize impact on the viewer:

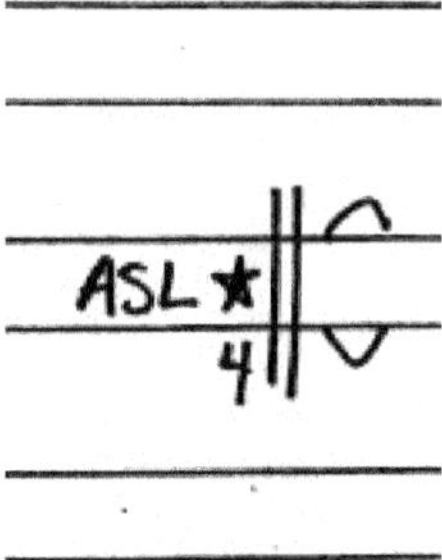

FINGERSPELLING WITH A BASE HS

At times, the signer may want to specifically direct the viewer's gaze to the fingerspelling as a means of emphasizing or highlighting a term, and is accomplished via an index BHS. This is often used in formal settings with deliberate register or as a pedagogical tool.

In the first example, Gallaudet can be bracketed below, to show the FS BHS is being used. In the second example, you can also notate using the standard BHS (index) on the third tier. The +/- contact details are unnecessary as this is an established BHSP format.

A signer may also just use an index BHS to highlight a specific letter or section of a sign. This can be notated:

ASL Nook

As well as if there is a unique motion associated such as a tap for emphasis. Samples of this usage can be seen in the notated sample from ASL Nook following the Grammar Notes section.

ASL Nook

When notating FS or number etc...it is not necessary to use the separation of signs notation on both sides of the term:

SEPARATION OF SIGNS NOTATION

A separation of signs is only needed when there is a subsequent sign, or change in the second tier such as a grammar notation. The separation notation belongs after the fingerspelled term, name sign, number, date etc...

NAD

LOAN SIGNS

Loan Signs are fingerspelled words which through repetitive use by the signing community, have taken on specific characteristics of bona fide signs that include movement and location, and have standard ways of being executed correctly. Examples include:

- #BACK
- #BANK
- #CHILD
- #EARLY
- #EMAIL
- #FIX
- #IF
- #KILL
- #OWN
- #STYLE
- #WILD

The standard linguistic notation for loan signs would also be written on the second tier:

#early

NAME SIGNS

Name signs are unique signs, letters or combinations of HS that identify a particular person. Since they are so prevalent, it would be good to have a shorthand way of denoting them as parts of discourse.

On the SS, name signs are recorded on the second tier, mid-staff. Notice the location of the NS for MJ is over the heart in location "X".

NS Julie — NS MJ (heart) || X — NS L (lion) — NS A (long wavy hair)

Another approach would be to list the name, indicate the NS above, and then provide the full notation for the desired name sign:

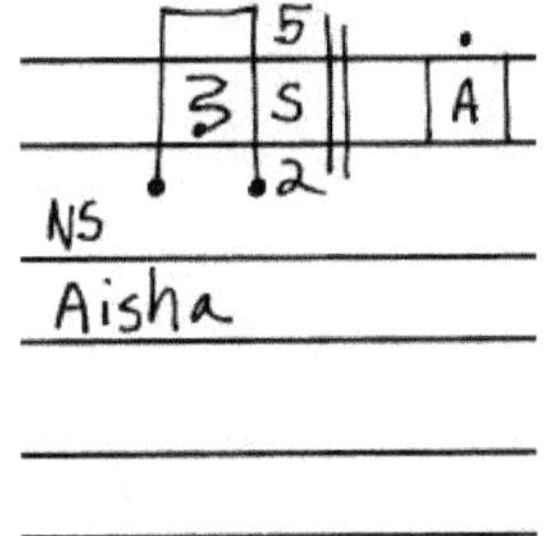

SAMPLE NAME SIGN: "AISHA"

TIME

On the SS, the time is also recorded on the second tier, mid-staff.

1:30 pm 1 sec 3 min 2.25 hrs

YOUR TURN!

Watch this video on Youtube: ASLized, **Signily: New Additions!** https://www.youtube.com/watch?v=lfoJgmxS_Eg

At around :08 the signer mentions a term that combines a sign with fingerspelling. Notate the fingerspelling and then check your answer in the back section under "YOUR TURN! ANSWERS" (#7)

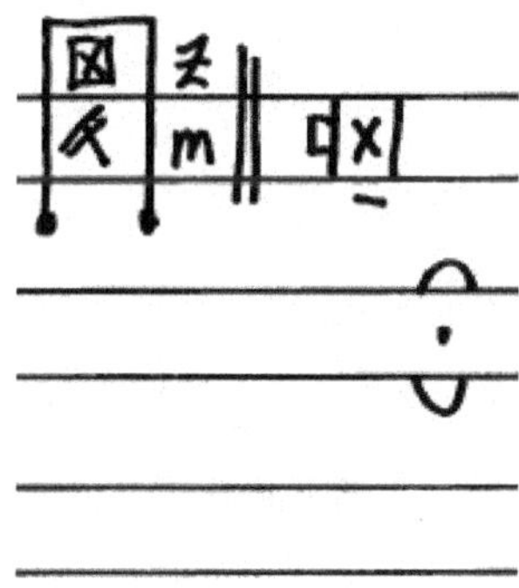

PARAMETER #5

FACIAL GRAMMAR (FG:NMGS)

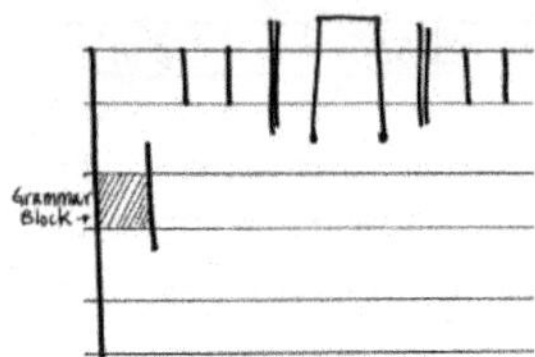

In order to match the correct facial grammar (FG), with the utterance, the signer needs to know which grammatical type is being utilized for any particular sign or signed utterance. SN assumes the user is familiar with the common sentence types in his/her signed language and can then apply the correct NMGS in a standardized manner. For example, in ASL specific facial grammar is used for any "WH" questions and a separate specific facial grammar is used for Topic, Comment sentence structure. Once identified, the grammatical type remains consistent until a new grammatical type is introduced on the SS staff.

Below is a list of the most commonly occurring grammatical types in ASL and the notation for each. Novel grammatical forms can be added...this is an experimental starter list:

GRAMMAR BLOCK

S	STATEMENT
T	TOPIC
C	COMMENT
|•|	GREETING (HI, HELLO, WHAT'S UP?)
•|•	PARTING (BYE, SEE YA LATER, HAND WAVE)
!	EXCITED UTTERANCE
	CONDITIONAL STATEMENT (2 PARTS:
if	IF
¬	THEN
⇑	ORDER, COMMAND, IMPERATIVE
?	QUESTION
WH?	WH QUESTION
RH?	RH QUESTION
Y/N?	YES/NO QUESTION
⇐	REPLY TO QUESTION (RH? OR OTHER)
[V]	DEPICTING VERB
[V]1	DEPICTING VERB 1
[V]2	DEPICTING VERB 2
"	QUOTATION
	TENSE MARKERS:
↵	PAST
↓	PRESENT
↳	FUTURE
–	NEGATION

ꟼ	INDEX REFERENCING
ꟼ	BHS (FLAT B) REFERENCING
⩷	DIRECTIONAL VERBS
Ꝑ	MANUAL LISTING (SEE LIST OF TYPES)
[	LATERAL LISTING (+2, 3 ETC...)

Notice that these function similarly to punctuation as far as their impact on the SS reader.

YOUR TURN!
GRAMMAR BLOCK

Record your own observations!

GRAMMAR BLOCK

Three sections of the Grammar Block are available to record relevant grammatical information:

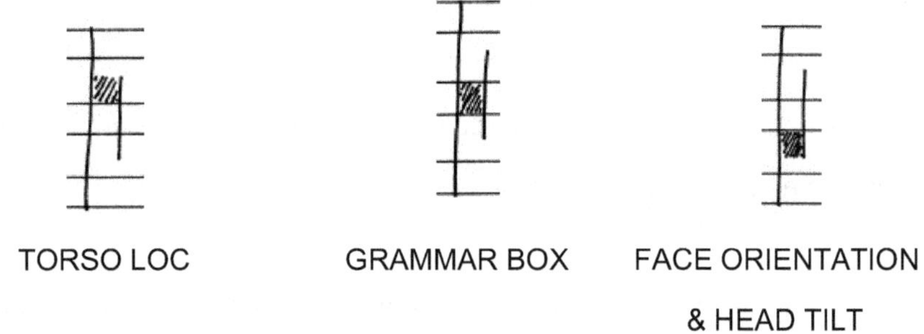

TORSO LOCATION: BODY SHIFTING

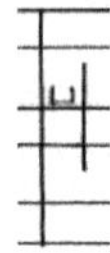

In ASL this is commonly referred to as "body shifting" and frequently occurs to express a change in speaker in a dialogue. It can serve other purposes, but our goal is to notate those grammatical torso shifts. **Default is facial orientation matches the torso position**, such as a person body-shifting right and facing right. We will use a simple set of positions:

3
|1 0 2|
4

*/0 = Neutral "narrator"

1 = Lateral shift Left

2 = Lateral shift Right

3 = Lean Forward

4 = Lean Back

The notation below would indicate the signer moved into the right hand lateral signing space, and is still facing forward:

⌊2⌋

This notation would be a marked movement back in the signing space (imagine an expression of surprise!):

⌊4⌋

And a return to the neutral Center position would need to be notated once, as it is the presumed default position:

⌊0⌋ or 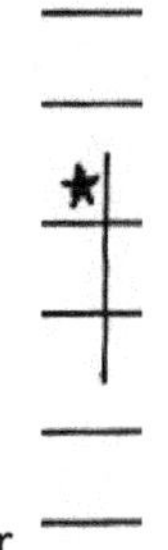

Because the space Is so small, we can dispense with the "basket" drawn around the numbers, and notate using the numbers 0-4,and L,R and the numbers in combination with L or R positions.

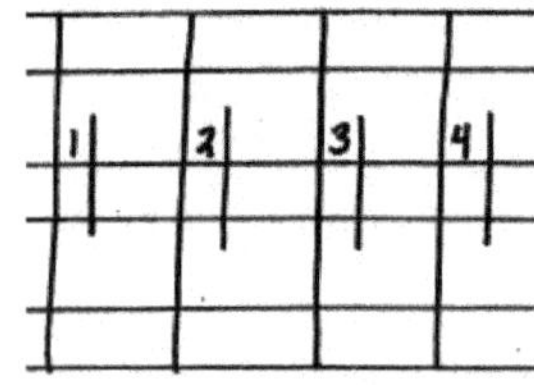

We will need to have the identical torso range of motion for a LEFT facing shift and a RIGHT facing shift. Of course, some positions will be very rarely used, but the framework needs to be available.

LEFT RIGHT

So a fairly common position would be to turn the torso to the Left in the "0" position, notated simply:

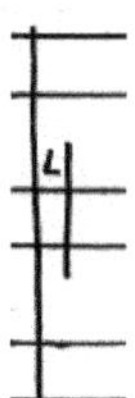

And then to body shift the torso to the Right, again in the "0" position in a dialogue exchange:

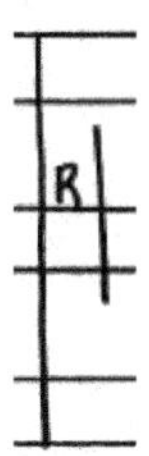

More detailed torso shifts can be labeled "R#" and "L#" as needed:

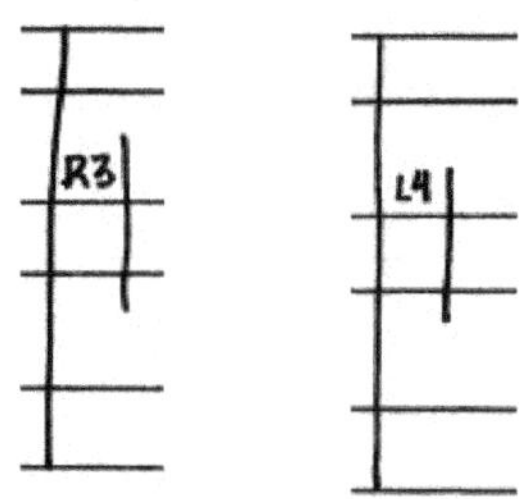

And a return to the neutral Center position can be notated to return the position to center-forward.

0 or “*”

Note: **Default is that each notation only affects the one specific sign being notated and does not carry to the next sign**...however in a dialogue situation, a torso shift may be held for a phrase or longer monologue. The repeats can be notated in the grammar block and the return to center or new torso position notated when needed.

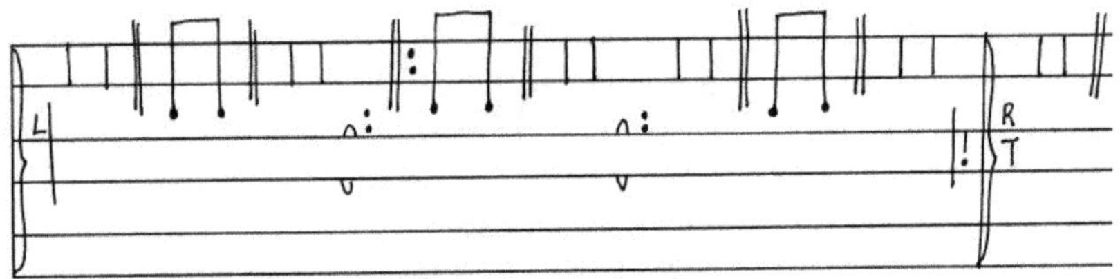

GRAMMAR BOX

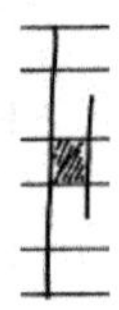

The grammar box is essential to record the relevant grammatical type as described above in the GRAMMAR BLOCK charts at the beginning of this section, (ie: Topic/Comment, Statement, WH?...)

T	C	S	Wh?

We will see many more of these grammatical types notated in the grammar box throughout this text. Here is a sample of a notated RH?:

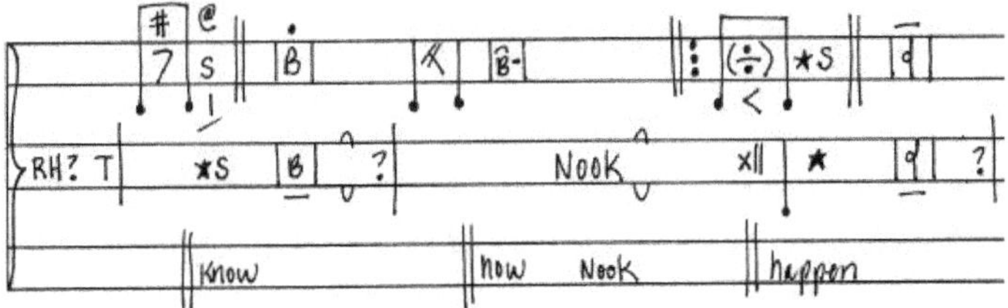

FACE ORIENTATION & HEAD TILT

To notate the face orientation of the signer, which is separate from a torso shift, we can use a "joystick" approach for each of the 8 standard positions:

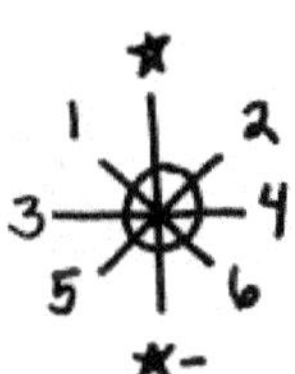

The most common will be 1 (facing left at an angle), 2 (facing right at an angle), 3 (facing direct left), 4 (facing direct right) and neutral *. Of course the **default position is "*" or forward facing** and will not need to be notated for the majority of signs. Positions to the rear are: 5 (left rear),

6 (right rear) and directly behind: 

A head tilt upward at any of these positions will be notated with an upward tilt arrow:

^

Or a downward tilt arrow:

v

Here the signer is facing leftward:

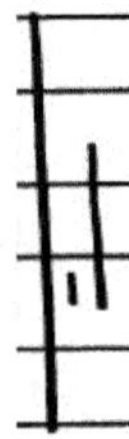

And directly to the right:

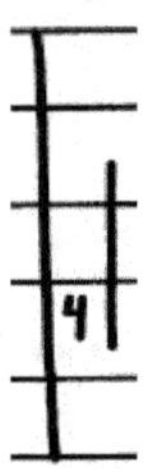

A person looking straight down at a person or item would be notated:

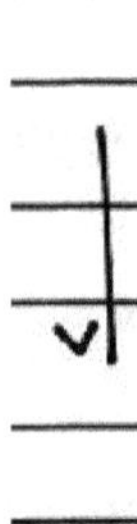

Perhaps a person is looking up and to the right to check the scoreboard at a game:

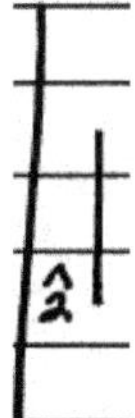

And someone looking upward, watching a bird flying by from right to left would be notated using a collapsed "21" for the area including and between zones 2 and 1:

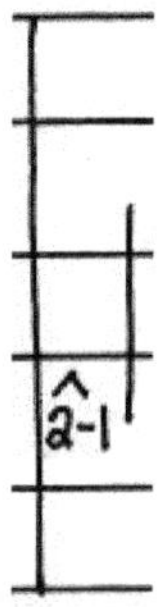

A fan watching a volleyball game could be notated using a repeat (meaning the signer's face orientation shifted back and forth a total of 4 times, or generalized, multiple times):

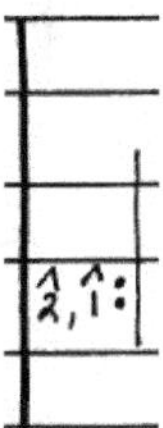

The last two are the left and right side head tilt:

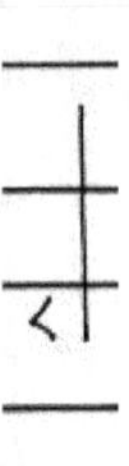

LEFT SIDE HEAD TILT

RIGHT SIDE HEAD TILT

An example of this notation is the sign below which includes one crossed arm, a left head tilt and the D HS grasping the chin. Facial grammar has also been notated on the third tier:

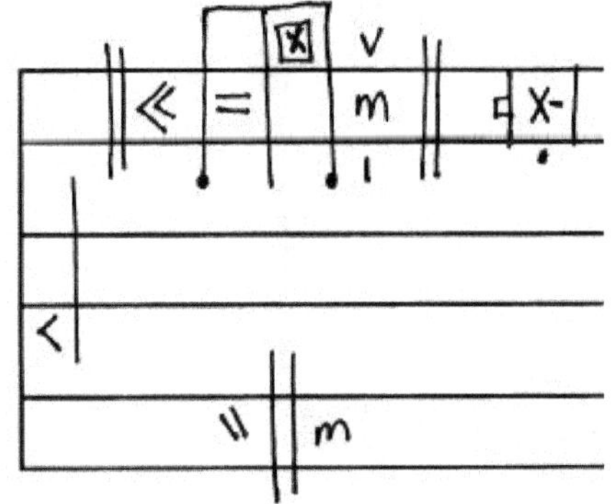

"TO PONDER OR CONSIDER...HMM…"

RETURN TO NEUTRAL CENTER

To return the signer's face orientation or head tilt back to central neutral, notate using the "*" position:

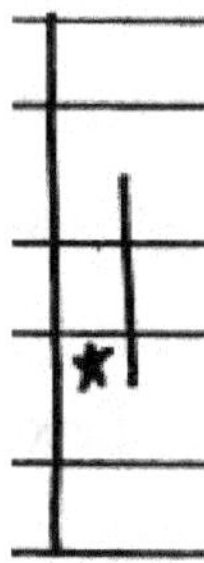

Default is a grammar block notation only affects the specific sign being notated and not the subsequent signs...however there may be times when this position is held for multiple signs and therefore a repeat sign would be needed in the grammar block section for these few signs, and then a return to neutral can be notated for the first forward-facing standard position.

NOTE: **Default is the eye gaze and head tilt are coupled.** If the head tilt is marked (or the eye gaze is marked in the facial grammar block), the eye gaze is presumed to match that orientation (up or down). In the following section, we will discuss notating eye gaze in the facial grammar block. The reason for two separate sections to notate this is that at times the head tilt and eye gaze need to be de-coupled. For example, perhaps the eye gaze is upwards but the face remains forward in the neutral zone. This de-coupling needs to be clearly notated.

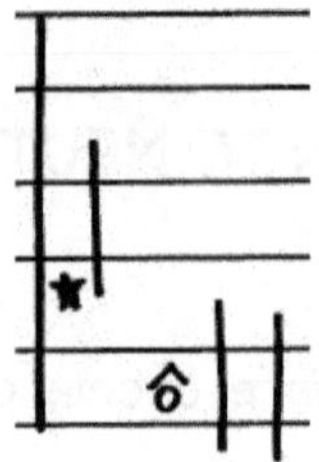

DECOUPLED EYEGAZE AND HEAD TILT

A signer might look up to see the time on the wall without moving her/his head position, or s/he might look over the shoulder and downwards simultaneously to check for a child following behind. These changes in eye gaze will be notated in the third tier Facial Grammar block.

GRAMMAR BLOCK SHIFT

When a signer ends a sign with a different grammatical form than the beginning of a sign, the entire grammar block can be shifted to the applicable tier using a simple arrow, to differentiate it from a facial grammar block shifted to the side section:

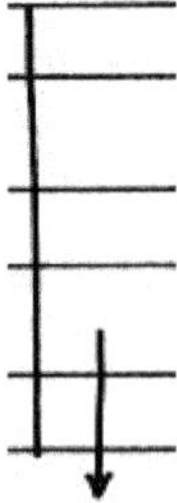

An common example of this would be when a signer has a torso shift forward in the later phase of the sign articulation:

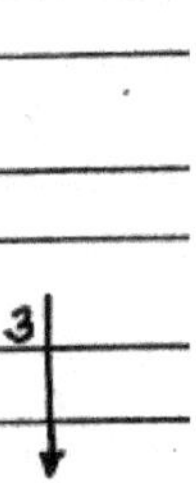

FORWARD TORSO SHIFT

PARAMETER #5A

FACIAL GRAMMAR

(EYES, NOSE, MOUTH)

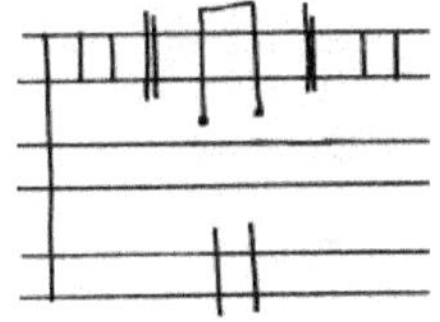

In addition to the basic set of grammatical types with inherent facial grammar listed above, there is an addition component of actual facial expressions that can be made that are required grammatical components for many specific signs. In actuality there are a gazillion different facial expressions that are made throughout a signed story or dialogue, but we are going to focus on and tackle some of the *grammatically* vital ones which indicate adjectival details etc...such as the size or shape of an item. This is offered only as a sample...The Deaf community would need to revise and update these as appropriate.

As an aside, many spoken languages rely on word order for grammatical management. ASL also uses some standard English grammatical constructs such as Subject-Verb-Object. In the Grammar

Box, very often a “statement” grammatical type “S” is a sentence that closely follows a standard English sentence pattern. ASL however has a wide range of acceptable grammatical constructs and these are clarified and managed by facial expression in the same way word order precisely dictates "correct" or "incorrect" grammatical usage in English. In fact, a native or near native signer is often identified by community members by facility with and incorporation of these facial grammatical markers.

Below are charts for each of the three sections:

FACIAL EXPRESSIONS: EYES

		SAMPLE SIGN GLOSSES
—	SQUINTY EYES	"tiny amount"
⑊	FURROWED BROWS	"OIC···" (concerned)
Λ	RAISED EYEBROWS	"OIC···" (surprised)
III	BLINKING EYES	"unaware of···"
⩚	ANGRY EYEBROWS	"mad"
O	OPEN EYES	"or"
⊙	WIDE EYES···SHOCKED!	"tricked me!"
⚲	EYES TRACK SIGN, EYES ON HS	"look at page"
⌂	EYE GAZE UP	"trying to remember"
∨	EYE GAZE DOWN	"looking for item"
⌓	ROLL EYES	"Oh brother!"
⊠	COVER EYES	"purposefully oblivious"

FACIAL EXPRESSIONS: NOSE

		SAMPLE SIGN GLOSSES
÷	NOSE WRINKLE UP AND DOWN	"Yes"
⊥	NOSE WRINKLE HELD	"perplexed, bizarre"

FACIAL EXPRESSIONS: MOUTH

		SAMPLE SIGN GLOSSES
o	Oooo..MOUTH IN TINY "o" SHAPE	"small incision"
cha	CHA! LARGE ITEM	"large amt of cash"
pah	PAH!	"finally got my license!"
bing	BING!	"tend to"
m	"m" MEDIUM SIZE	"average distance"
M	"M" HMMM..HARD M	"very bad"
o-o	PUFFED CHEEKS	"chubby, fat"
-o	SINGLE CHEEK PUFFED	"cyst"
⊔	JAW DROP	"what?!" (shocked)
	"FSH"	"finished!"
	"OIC" LIP (LOWER LIP UP-AND-DOWN)	"thinking about it..."
∞	BOTH LIPS POUCHED OUT	"make a decision"
♡	KISS	"kiss-fist"
	OPEN MOUTH	"obsess over"
⊃C	BLOWING AIR	"windy day", "heavy"
	"EEE" LOWER TEETH EXPOSED	"accidentally ruined"
▭	"EEE" ALL TEETH EXPOSED	"brush teeth"
	"SCHJAH, SCHJAH"	"speech practice"
	BITE TONGUE BETWEEN TEETH	"fascinated to learn"
	MOUTH OPEN, TONGUE OUT	"exert effort"
=	TONGUE BACK-AND-FORTH	"crazy awesome!"
(=	TONGUE SWIPES CHEEK	"I'm a natural!"
	MOTOR BOAT/RASPBERRY	"bored"
	"POW"	"went out of business"

	SMILEY FACE	"was beaming!"
	FROWNY FACE	"went from happy to sad"
	COVER YOUR MOUTH	"feel nauseaus"

YOUR TURN!

	FACIAL EXPRESSIONS	SAMPLE SIGN GLOSSES

Record your own observations!

These are recorded left to right: EYE, NOSE, MOUTH:

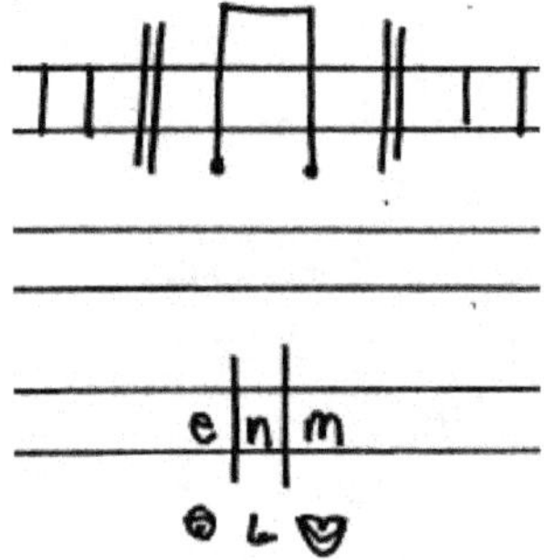

In a pinch, there may be times all three tiers are being utilized to notate a more involved sign, and the side section can also be used to notate facial grammar:

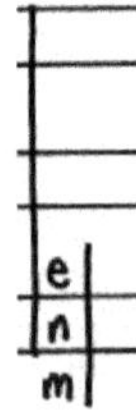

For example:

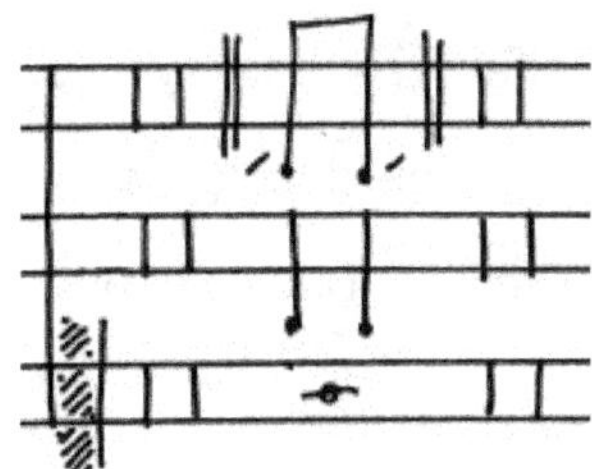

Below is the notation for the sign glossed: "tend to" with facial grammar notated:

"TEND-TO"

Check it out these vlogs to see “bing” in action!

The Daily Moth

https://www.youtube.com/channel/UCaayieDFpDIZ1b_mspO_Rzg

Deaf Bing Ep. 1 (ASL)

https://www.youtube.com/watch?v=eVsvH5TjS6g

Deaf Bing by Indiana School for the Deaf Students at Butler University's Hands on Fire | ASL

https://www.youtube.com/watch?v=c_AFeNUMgcQ

EYE GAZE

A signer can very effectively use eye gaze to highlight an item by focusing on the sign itself. This directs the viewer to jointly recognize the item being signed as if the item had been placed in a spotlight. This is notated:

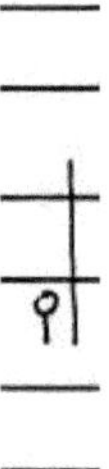

SPOTLIGHT EYE GAZE

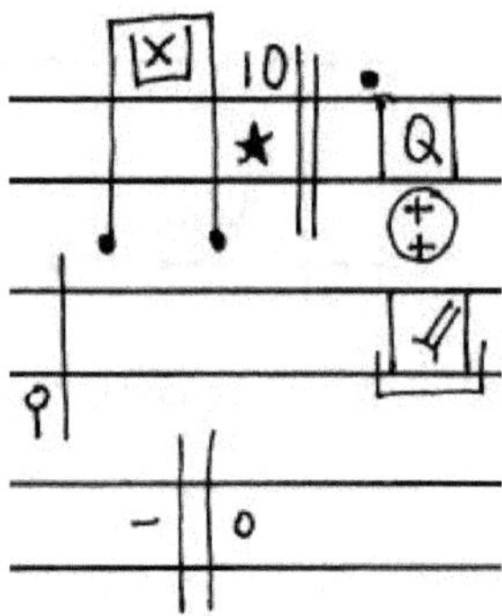

"A VERY SMALL AMOUNT OF SOMETHING"

The spotlight icon is also useable in the eye grammar section. It is just so handy I wanted it to be available in both locations:

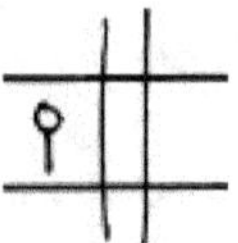

SPOTLIGHT EYE GAZE OPTION #2

YOUR TURN!

What is the facial grammar notation for this commonly occurring ASL sign?! Check your answer in the back section under "YOUR TURN! ANSWERS" (#8)

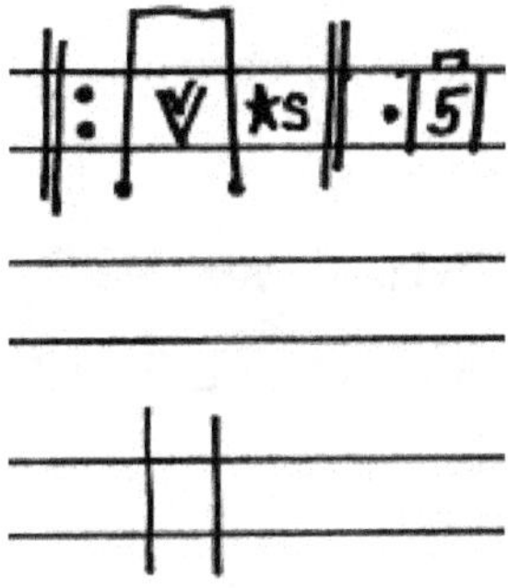

LISTING STRATEGIES
"LET ME COUNT THE WAYS..."

ASL has an extensive repertoire of listing strategies. SN will need to create a notation for each type of listing method.

LISTING METHOD #1
MANUAL LISTING

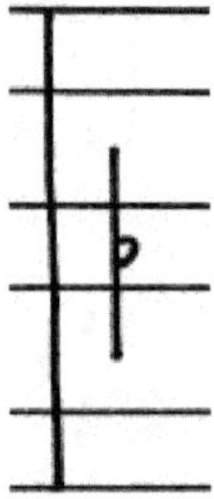

There are two primary types of manual listing. The first is when a signer wants to propose the concept of "listing items" as a generic proposition, or prior to commencing an actual list. These types of listing will be notated in the MVT block:

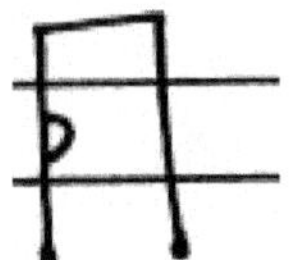

GENERIC LISTING

Typically the ND HS of an open "5" facing the signer is used as the listing template, and the D HS interacts to express the specific type of list intended:

ND "5" HS

For the notation below, the list format would be a sweeping motion by the D HS "index" arcing the perimeter of the ND “5” HS, without any contact:

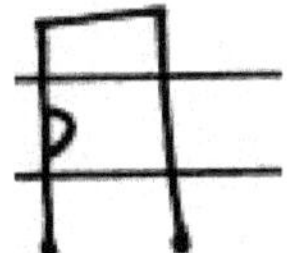

Here is a sample set of possible additional listing notations:

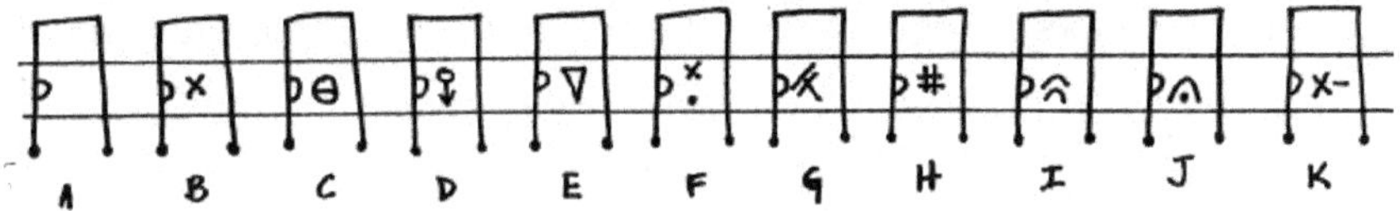

A. D HS "index" air-lists without contact
B. D HS "index" lists with contact, touching each ND fingertip
C. D HS "open 5, palm facing outward" sweeps across in an arc with contact
D. D HS "index" rotates or spirals while air-listing
E. D HS "index" clicks off options while air-listing
F. D HS "index" drags across in a sweeping arc with contact
G. D HS "index" twists while making contact with each finger (1st, 2nd, 3rd)
H. D HS air-counts: "1st", "2nd", "3rd"...with corresponding digits
I. D HS "bent B, thumb extended" bounces down air-listing on ND BHS

J. D HS "bent B, thumb extended" air-lists in a smooth, sweeping "moving down the page" movement

K. ND HS starts with only the thumb extended, and works through list, extending each finger one at a time as if ticking items off a list (1,2,3,4,5...)

SPECIFIC LISTING

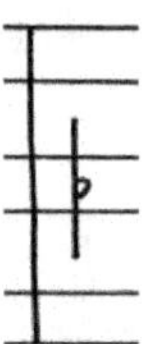

To create an actual list of items, the notation needs to shift to the grammar block, with identification of the type of list being initiated. Then the first specific item listed is notated (for example the color “red” in a series of colors), with subsequent items numbered in the listed series:

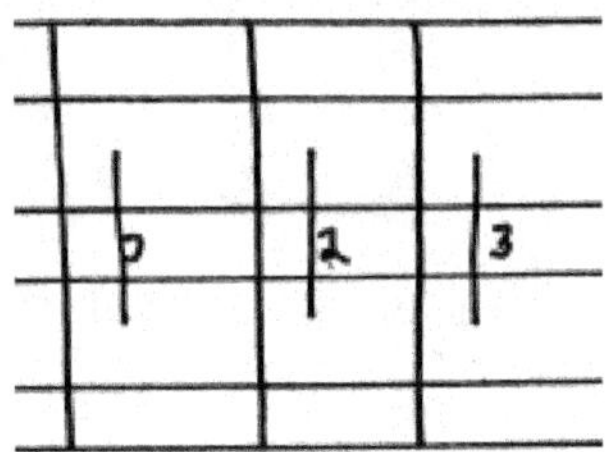

SPECIFIC LISTING

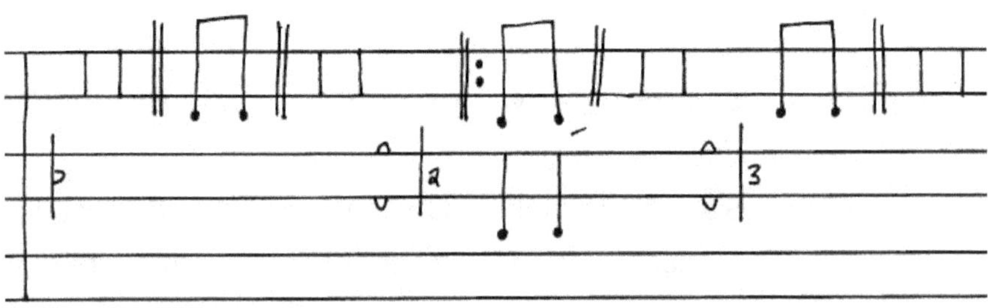

Let's look at an actual example. The signer mentions an upcoming list, and then proceeds to create the list of specific named items:

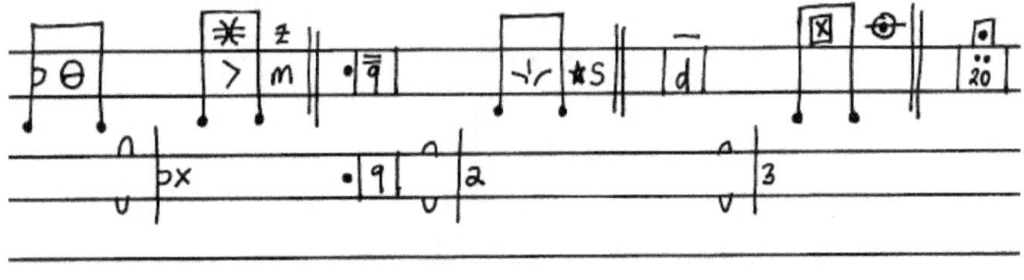

Can you figure out what the listed items are? The signer first uses a sweeping listing strategy to introduce the topic and then proceeds to list each item using a fingertip-contact list. The items are…cat, dog and bird. Of course the signer could elaborate on each item, inserting additional signs between the listed items, but the listing would resume until completed.

Here is the companion notation for the specific listing notations when creating an actual list of items. The first notation is count "1" and the numbering begins 2,3,4,5,etc...

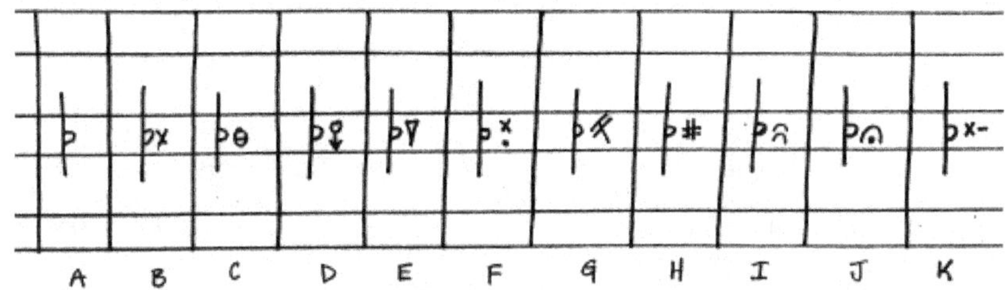

Can you think of other listing types?!

LISTING METHOD #2
LATERAL BODY SHIFTING

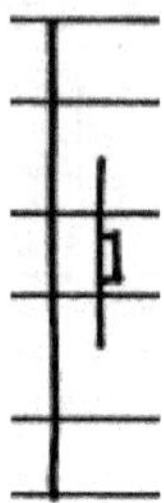

This type of listing involves overt and sometimes very subtle shifts in the torso to create a list of items. For example, a person might be explaining the items required to apply for a position opening. The listing may involve a "back and forth" method in which the signer shifts his/her weight side to side laterally, listing through each item, or it may be one continuous "left to right" series of smaller shifts. An example can be seen in this video by Jr. NAD:

SHARE: Looking for YLC Staff for Summer 2015!
https://www.youtube.com/watch?v=FrxDzpLQj0M

We will use an approach similar to specific listing in the previous section. The lateral body shift listing will be notated on the grammar block, and then numbered either in a series: 2, 3, 4, 5 or back and forth 2.1.2.1 etc... with "1" representing the first lateral shift, and 2 being the second lateral shift position:

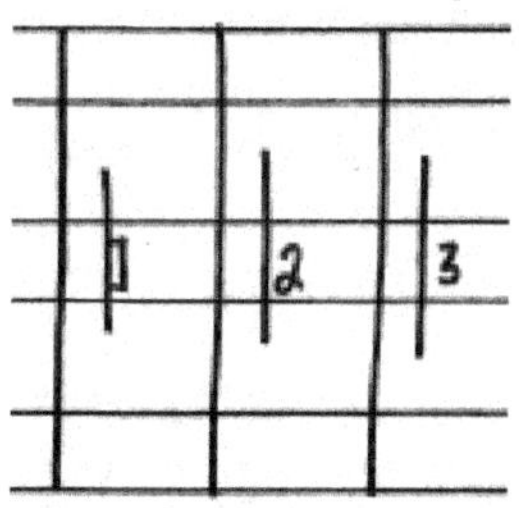

CONTINUOUS LATERAL LISTING

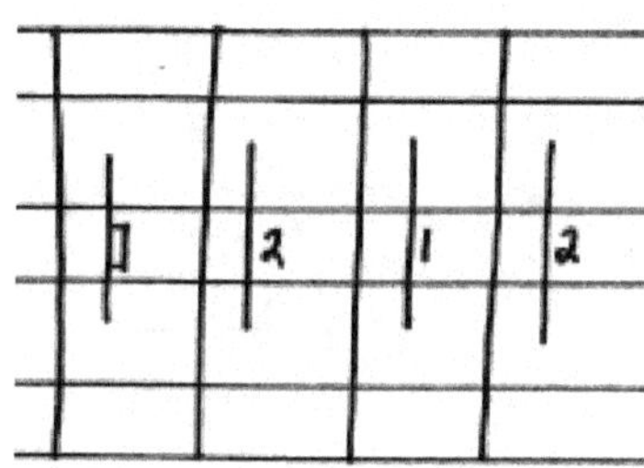

BACK AND FORTH LATERAL LISTING

LISTING METHOD #3
INDEX REFERENCING: SPATIAL

Another common approach is to provide examples of items and set them up in locations in space, available to be re-referenced. This type of content mapping allows the user to identify referents and then efficiently re-reference those items using an index finger "1" HS. No lateral shifting of the torso is required.

For example, a signer might want to ask a question about three items: a car, a boat and a bus. First those three items will be identified, and placed in a spatial sequence in the SSS*. Then the signer can use the index to review the list of items by re-referencing their locations in space, and pose a question, such as "Which one is the fastest?"

This method of listing will be noted first in the grammar block on the second tier:

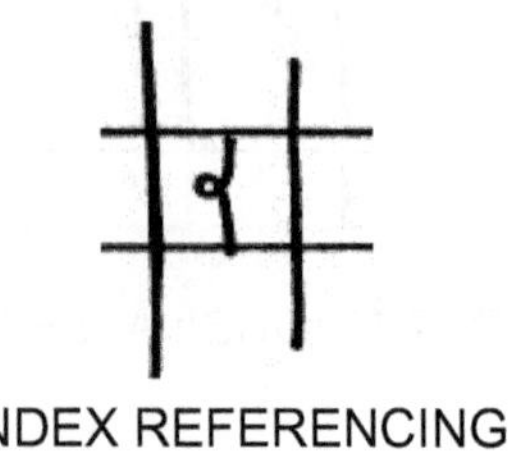

INDEX REFERENCING

When the first item in the series is notated (such as the car) we will notate on the top of the first tier:

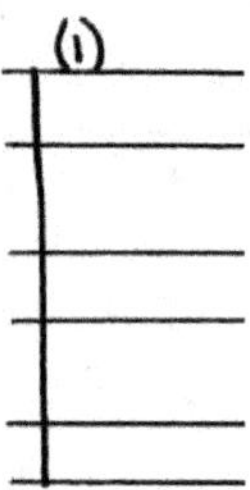

Each subsequent item in the listing set will be numbered similarly (2), (3) etc...Once the items have been numbered, later during the signed utterance when it is time for re-referencing using the D HS index, we will borrow from the mathematical notation for "remainder" in long division:

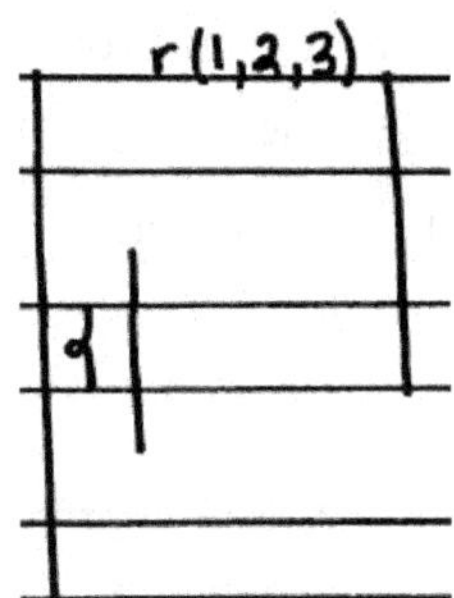

REMAINDER NOTATION: INDEX REFERENCING

Once items have been set up in space and numbered, they can be re-referenced as needed for the duration of the conversation.

Here is an example using the car, boat and bus:

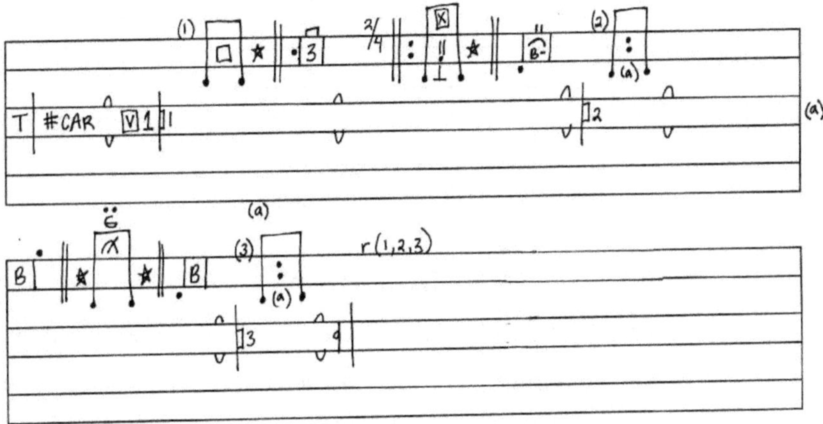

You will notice that the depicting verb is notated once ("3" HS vehicle depicting verb facing forward in a neutral location) and then is "copied" for the subsequent vehicles in the list.

This set can also be produced without the repeated depicting verb if the signer chooses to only use a depicting verb for the first item, and then places the other two items in the listing spaces:

YOUR TURN!

Let's practice!...Watch the first 15 seconds of this video by NADvlogs: **SHARE: FCC Update re: TTY Compatibility & Prison Communications** https://www.youtube.com/watch?v=MavGD6kArHU Then notate which type of listing strategy is being utilized by the signer. Check your answer in the back section under "YOUR TURN! ANSWERS" (#9)

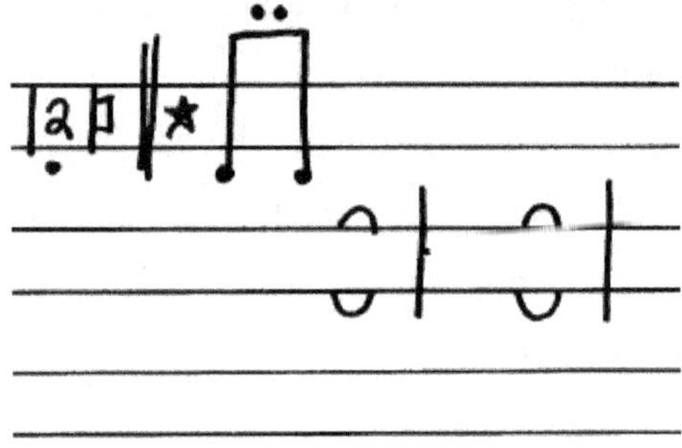

PUTTING IT ALL TOGETHER

Now that we have all 5 parameters addressed, (yay!!!) it is time to put it all together on the SS. You will want to read through the GRAMMAR NOTES in the next section for more important details. Here is a sample of the basic structure for recording on the SS:

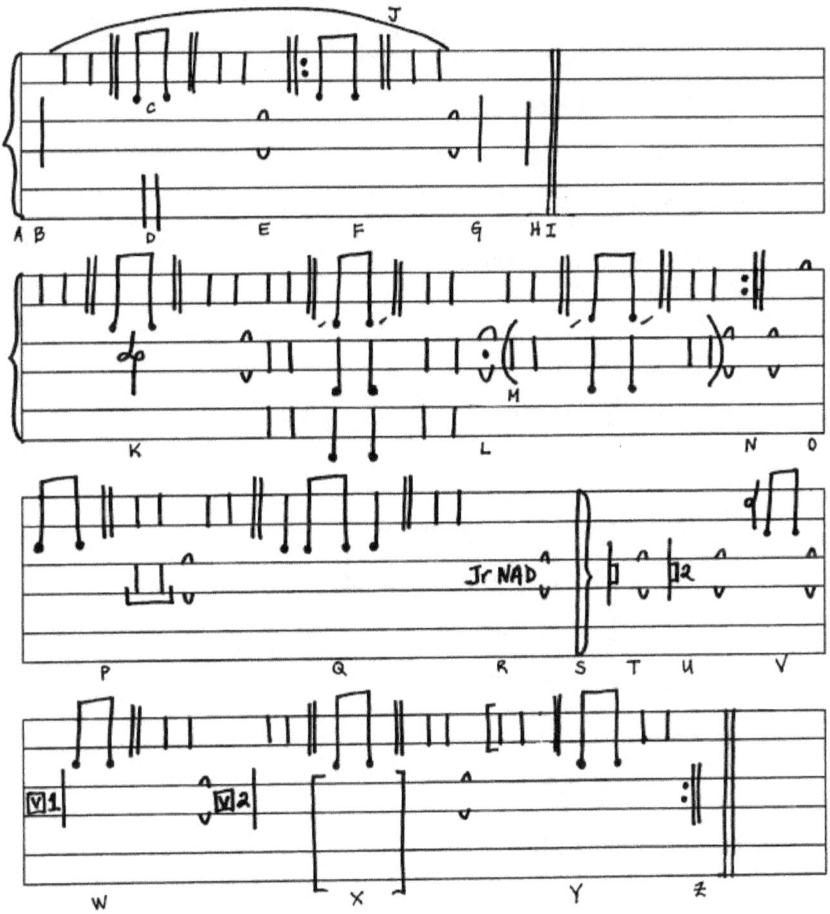

J
C
A B D E F G H I
M
K L N O
Jr NAD
P Q R S T U V
W X Y Z

(A) Beginning of a paragraph or set of connected utterances.

(B) Grammar Block

(C) Sign notated

(D) Facial Grammar Block

(E) End of a sign/sign boundary within signed utterance

(F) Mirrored sign

(G) New Grammar Block within signed utterance

(H) Punctuation Block

(I) End of signed utterance or paragraph

(J) Phrase mark

(K) Alternating sign

(L) Extension

(M) Stress

(N) Repeat of previous sign

(O) Rest

(P) Base Handshape sign

(Q) Embedded movement

(R) Fingerspelling

(S)* End of signed utterance and beginning of next signed utterance within set of connected utterances

(T) Listing of first item

(U) Listing of second item

(V) Pronoun

(W) Depicting Verb 1

(X) Depicting Verb 2

(Y) Lateral Base Handshape Pair

(Z) Repeat prior phrase

* Other options for sentence boundaries within a paragraph:

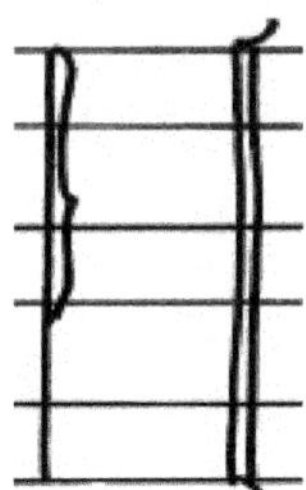

GRAMMAR NOTES

The following grammatical notes provide further guidance for accurately notating sign languages.

ATTENTION GETTING

ASL uses some signs to elicit the attention of the viewer. The notation for these types of signs is:

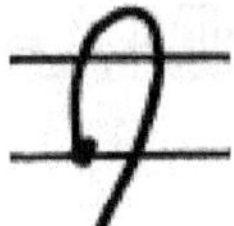

ATTENTION GETTING

This is similar to a bass clef in musical notation. Here is the notation for a common attention-getting sign in ASL:

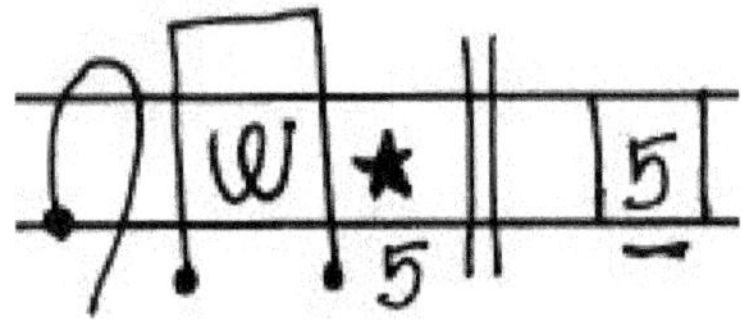

"FINGER-WIGGLE"

And here is another version of the same sign, but instead of the fingertips wiggling, they bounce up and down, and have been notated in a different location:

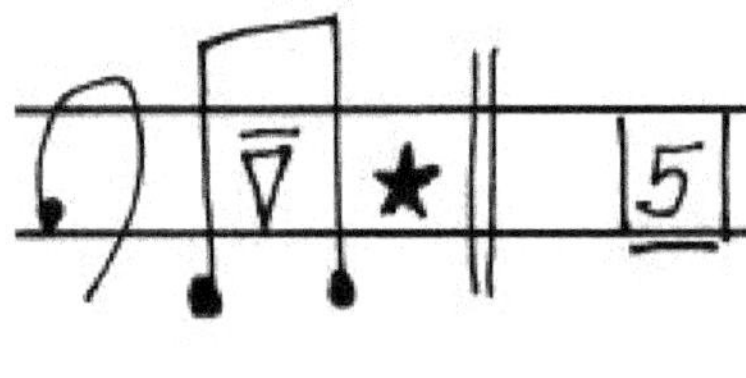

"HAND-BOB"

Shorthand notation for these two common attention-getting signs is:

FINGER-WIGGLE HAND-BOB

A third common articulation involves a hand-bob and simultaneous vibration:

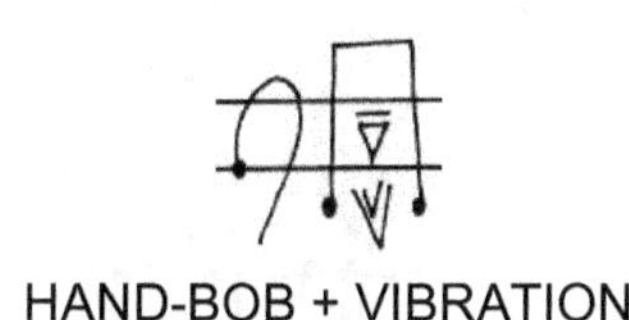

HAND-BOB + VIBRATION

There are more attention-getting signs that can be notated similarly. One attention-getting sign in ASL is an inverted "penguin" with the signer gesturing to tap another person:

TAP-TAP (YOU)

TAP-TAP (YOUR NEIGHBORS ON EITHER SIDE)

BODY-ONLY MVTS

ASL uses some signs that are purely body-only movements. The notation for these types of signs is:

This is borrowed from the treble clef in musical notation. Here is the notation for a common body-only movement in ASL:

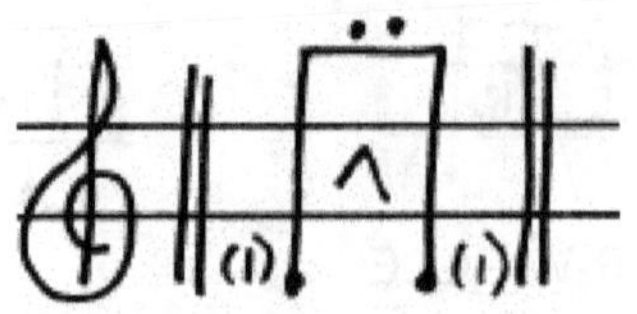

SHOULDER SHRUG

The shorthand SN for a shoulder shrug is:

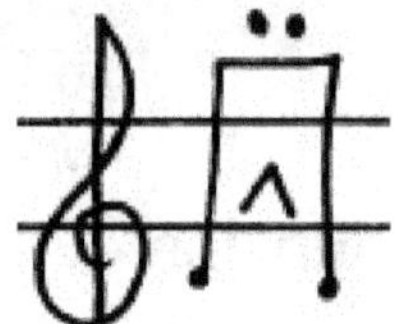

And after notating the International Signs at the end of the Grammar Section, we can add:

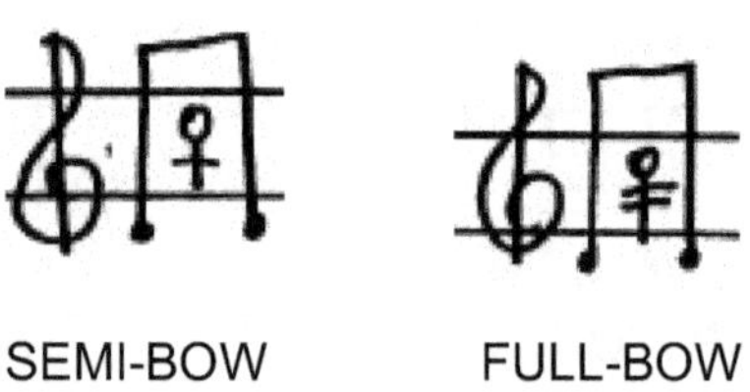

SEMI-BOW FULL-BOW

CIRCULAR MOVEMENTS 360

There are three dimensional planes: vertical, horizontal and lateral. Consider these three ASL signs. All involve a 360 degree movement. I have not included the time signature for these which would be 2/4. Also these would normally be written as mirror movements, but seeing them longhand is helpful for this discussion:

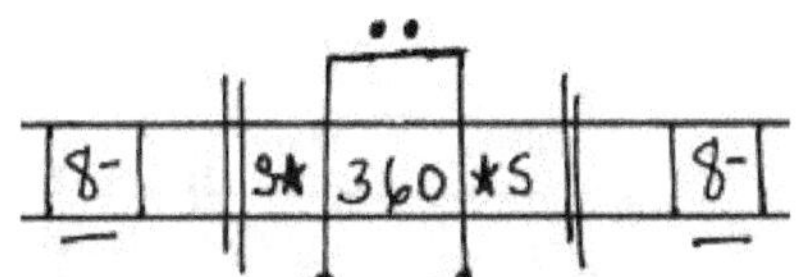

TAPE RECORDER (HORIZONTAL)

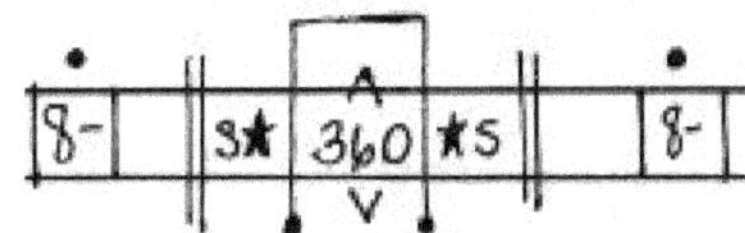

SYMPATHIZE WITH (VERTICAL)

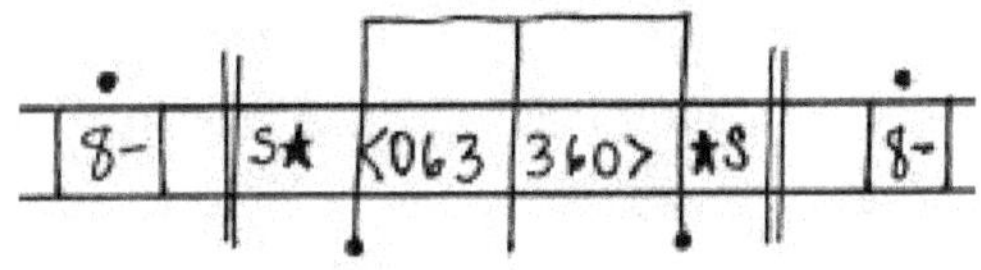

COMPUTER (LATERAL)

The default is horizontal, and directional marks must be added for vertical and lateral movements. Another option is to incorporate these planes into the 360 notation:

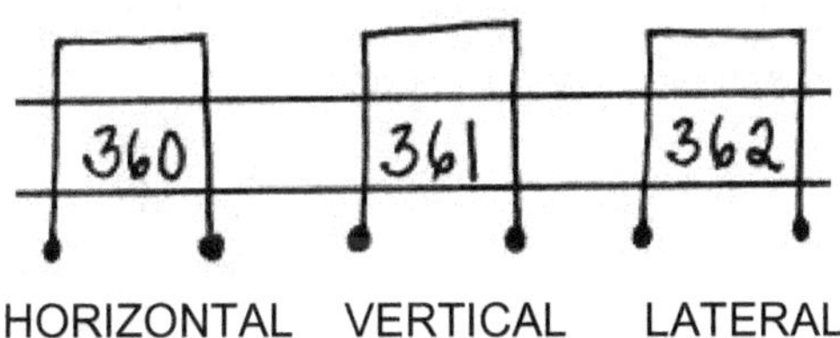

HORIZONTAL VERTICAL LATERAL

Here are those three signs, using mirror notation and this alternative notation:

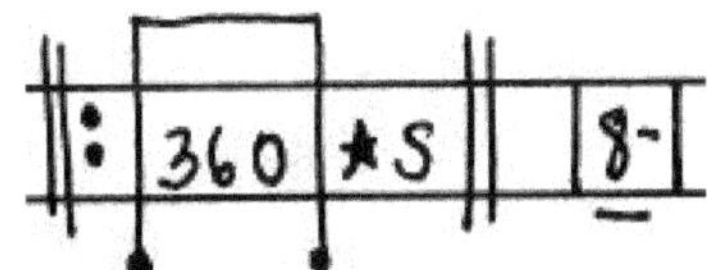

TAPE RECORDER (HORIZONTAL

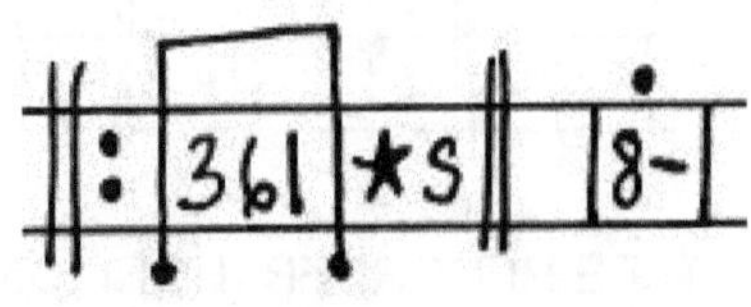

SYMPATHIZE WITH (VERTICAL)

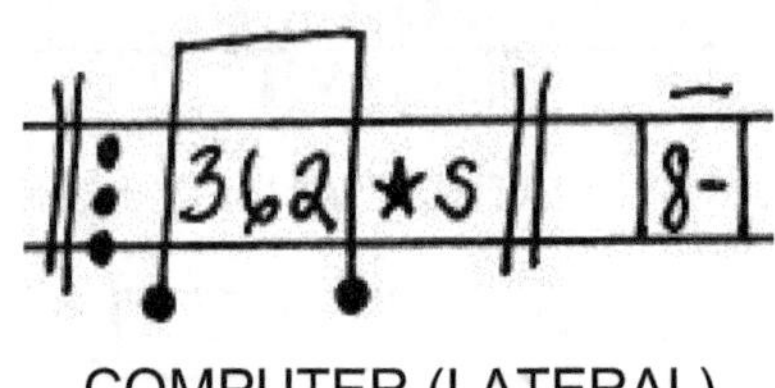

COMPUTER (LATERAL)

Which approach do you like best? Counterclockwise movements would be notated 063, 163, 263 respectively.

COLLAPSED MVT BLOCK: PASSIVE HS

Occasionally you will want to clarify that only one HS (usually the D HS) is doing a particular MVT. Notate using a collapsed MVT block:

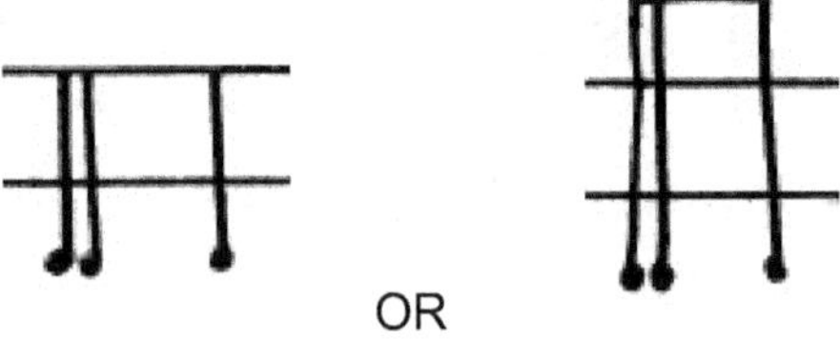

In this example, the set on the left does not have any contact, so the upper section is deleted...you can always notate with all three sections including the contact section of the MVT block (set on right). The HS that is not involved with the MVT (passive HS) will have this collapsed adjacent section. If the N HS is active and the D HS is passive, the collapsed section will be on the right.

CONJUNCTIONS WORD BANK

It could be useful to designate some words/signs as being part of a word bank within a specific language community that have agreed upon use and standard articulation, to be written in the mid-tier along with other fingerspelled words. For example, many people don't consider some "English signs" as being a natural part of natively derived ASL, and instead these signs represent contact language with the English speaking community. Conjunctions, articles, prepositions etc...may fit into this category. Of course, as has been stated elsewhere, these would be agreed to conventions amongst the signing community using SN. Here are some examples of terms that have very standard signs and would fit into this type of word bank. The purpose would be to expedite notation, and any of these could be notated longhand if desired.

- and
- a
- an
- the
- so
- for
- but
- with
- because
- after
- off
- on

Here is the SN for Word Bank items:

And a few snazy examples!:

because so and

You can also notate if a signer uses both hands simultaneously by using two tiers:

and

and

NOTE: You might wonder why it wouldn't be easier to generate a giant word bank of signs and skip notation all together. If our goal is to represent a signed language in an authentic way, including important variations in articulation, the integrity of the base sign notation must be preserved independent of the written form of the adjacent spoken language. Conventions support but do not replace longhand SN.

CRADLING: ARMS CROSSED

The notation for a cradled position is arms crossed:

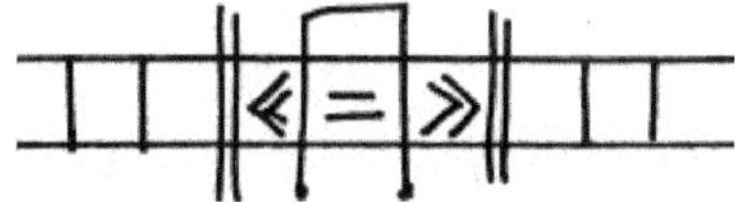

with a movement notation added. Here the notation for daughter, incorporates the arm as a BHS :

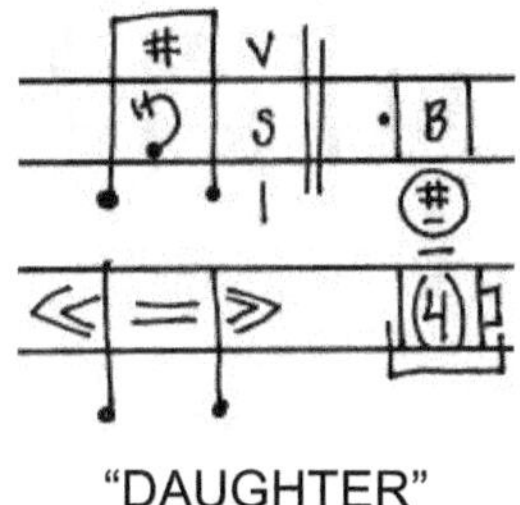

“DAUGHTER”

The notation for son:

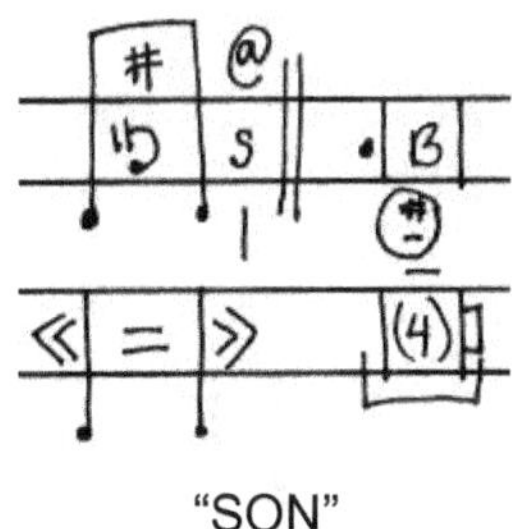

“SON”

The notation for baby:

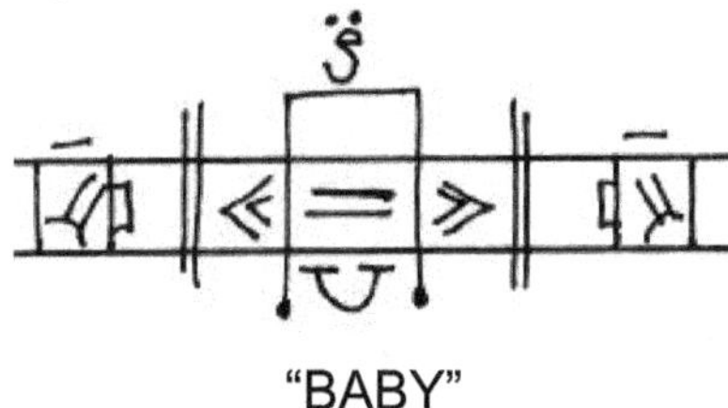

“BABY”

CROSS-OVER LOCATIONS

Some signs involve a shift in location from one side of the signing space to the other. For example the sign glossed: "bear" puts the D HS on the ND side, and the ND HS on the D side. When the D HS is on the other side of the signing space, it is notated:

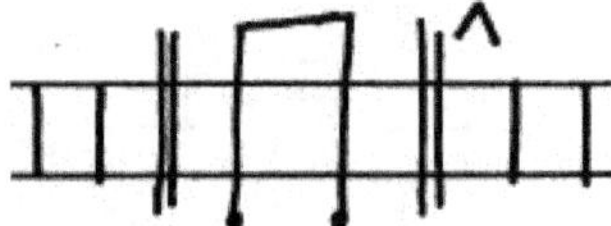

When the ND HS is on the other side of the signing space, it is notated:

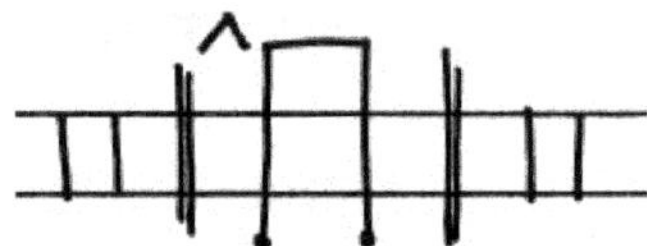

When both hands are on the opposite side of their standard signing side, you can notate it either using:

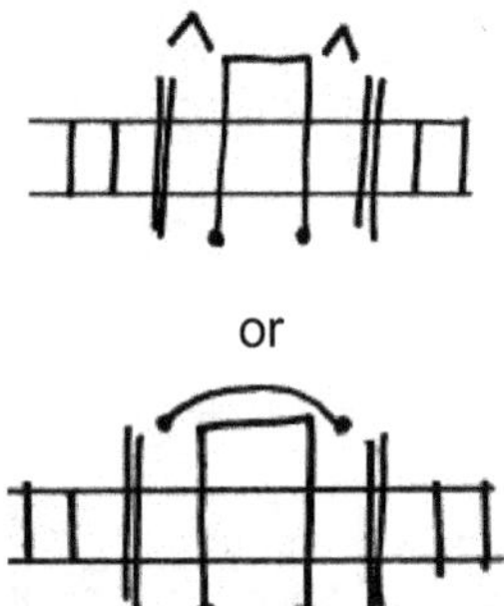

Here are two examples using cross-over notation:

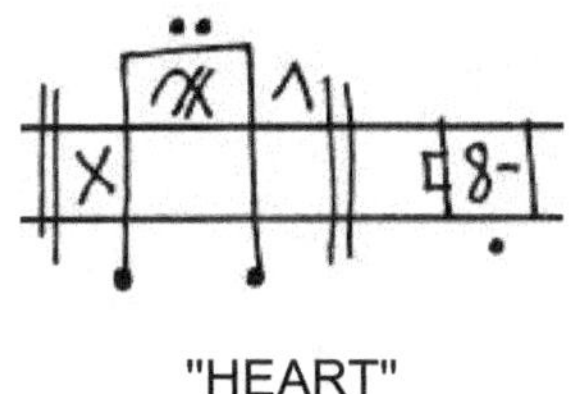

"HEART"

"BEAR"

D AND ND JOINT MVTS

To notate that both D and ND handshapes are using the same MVT simultaneously you can use an upper bar segment on the MVT block:

D/ND JOINT MOVEMENT

Default for a two-handed sign is that both D and ND are using the same movement. But it can be useful at times to add this for clarity, especially for shorthand notation.

ENTRY MVTS

Some signs include an additional flourish or entry movement, usually for emphasis. These can be notated above or within the MVT (including contact) section as space permits:

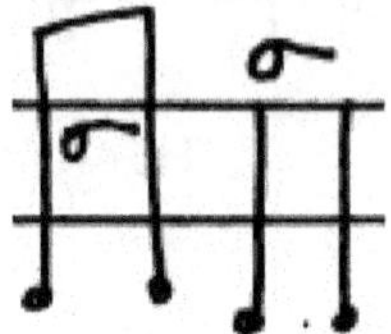

ENTRY MOVEMENT

EXTENSIONS

Anytime you need an extension to the adjacent set of tiers, you can use an extension notation on the second tier:

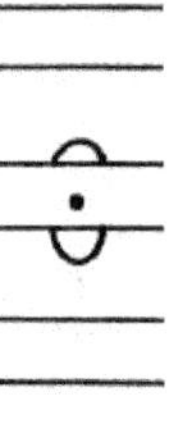

EXTENSION

Here is an example of a compound sign construction that would necessitate an extension notation:

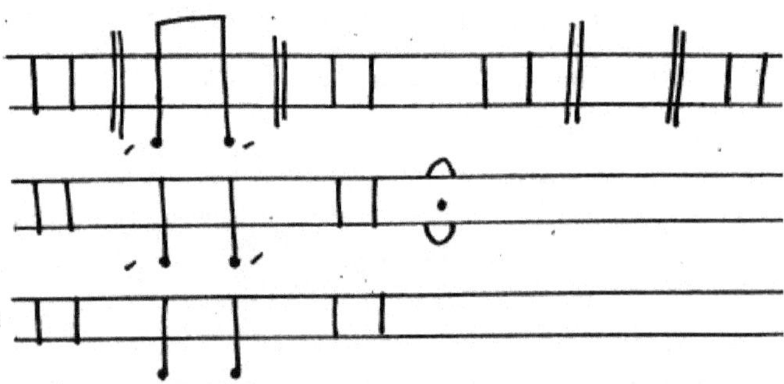

FINAL HOLD

Sometimes, a signer will hold a sign...for emphasis, import, etc... The SN for a final hold is:

And it occurs in the third tier:

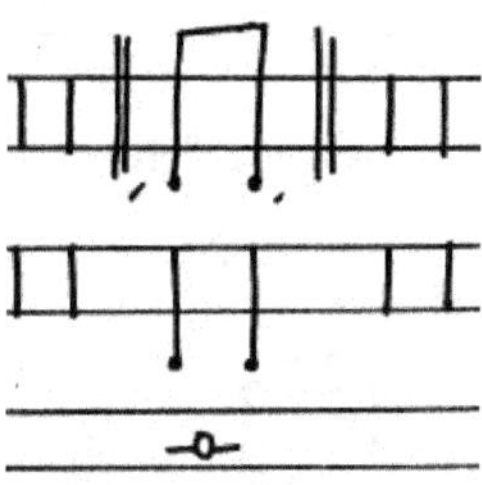

FINAL HOLD

GREETINGS, PARTINGS AND SOCIAL COURTESIES

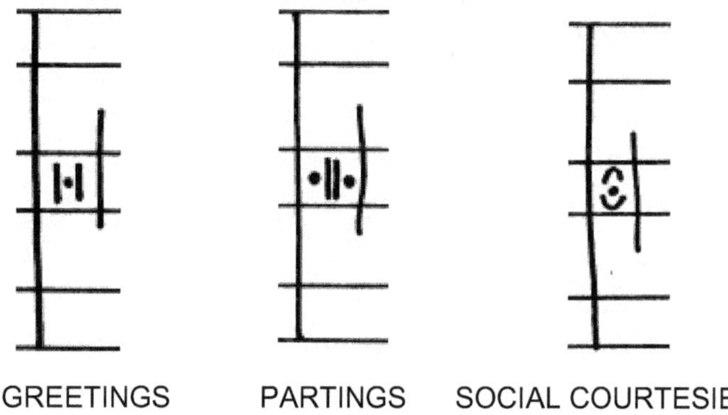

GREETINGS PARTINGS SOCIAL COURTESIES

Greetings and partings are such a common component in communication encounters that it would be helpful to generate shorthand notations. We start with the exploration of some common greetings and partings, fully notated:

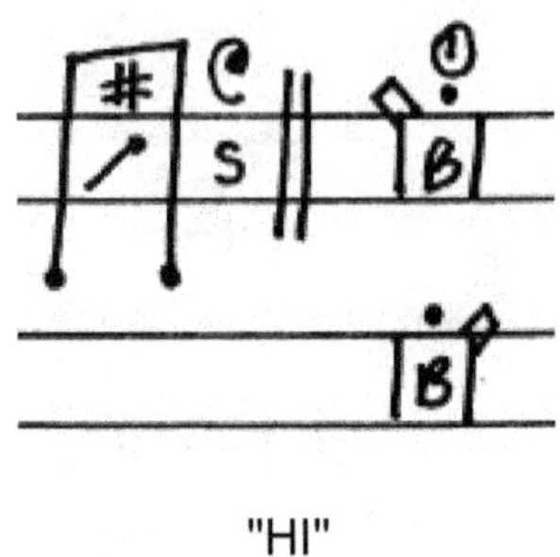

"HI"

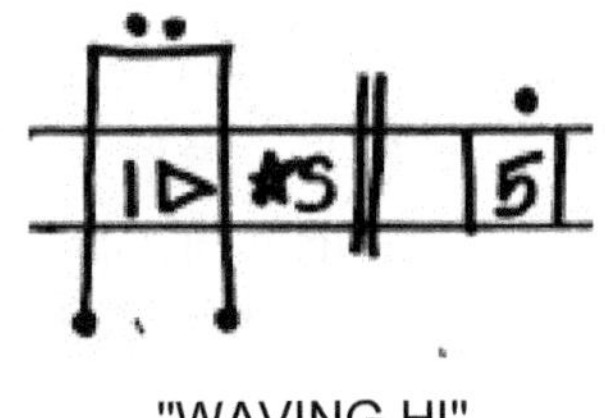

"WAVING HI"

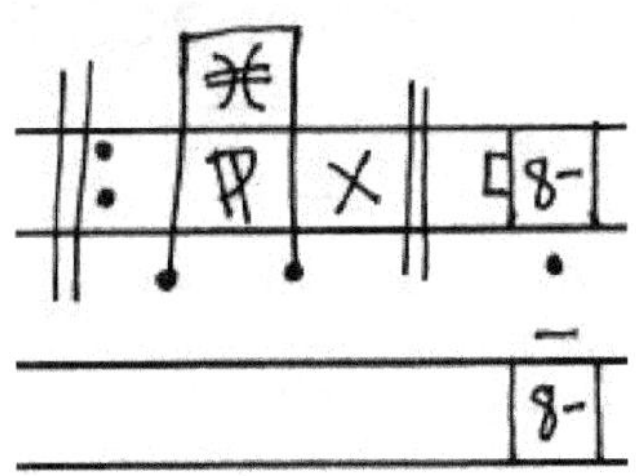

"WHAT'S UP?!"

NOTE: This is another sign where the movement of “scooping” as a specific articulation for this sign glossed, “what’s up?”, would have an agreed range of motion so the final location would not be notated.

Using shorthand notation, indicate the grammar type and movement:

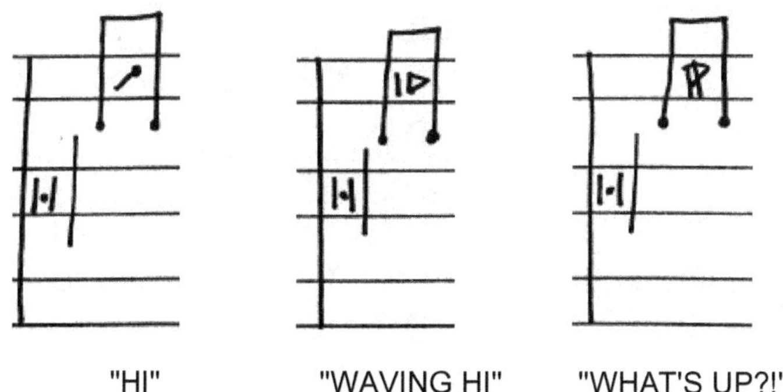

"HI" "WAVING HI" "WHAT'S UP?!"

A direct saluting "Hi!" is notated:

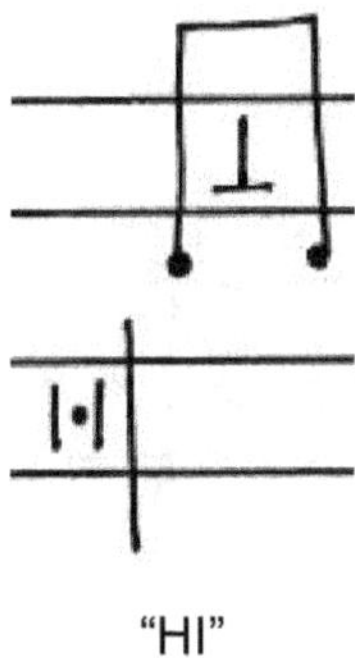

“HI”

"Welcome!" as an introductory greeting uses the MVT notation for "to enter":

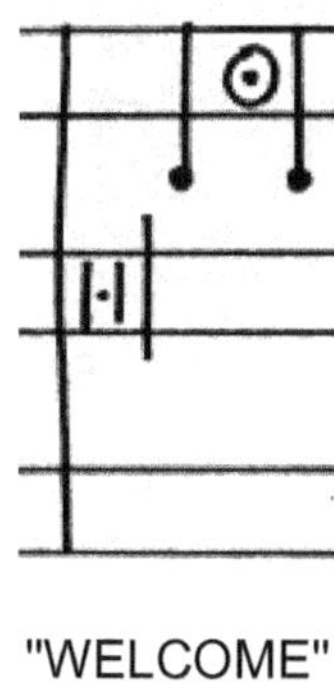

"WELCOME"

Partings can also be fully notated with variations in articulation:

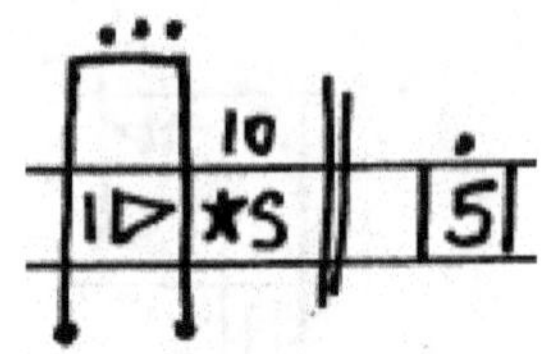

"BYE"

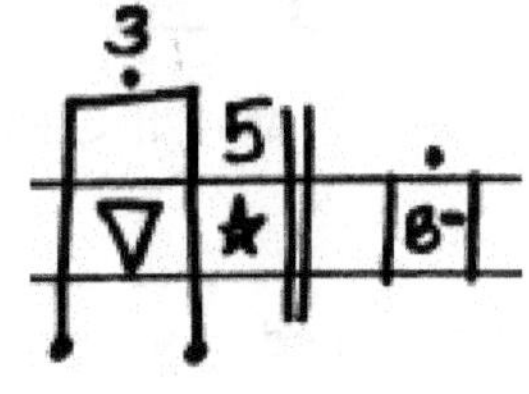

"BYE BYE"

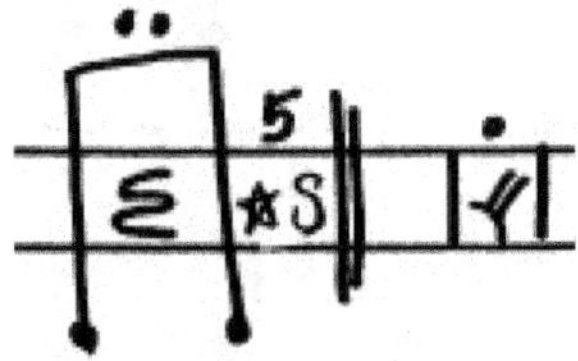

"WAVING BYE"

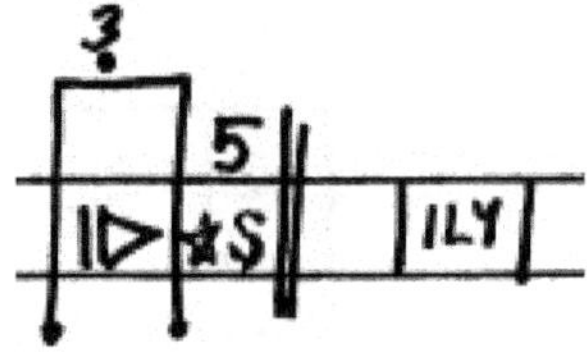

"ILY-BYE"

Using the MVT block and a grammar notation, you can notate these shorthand:

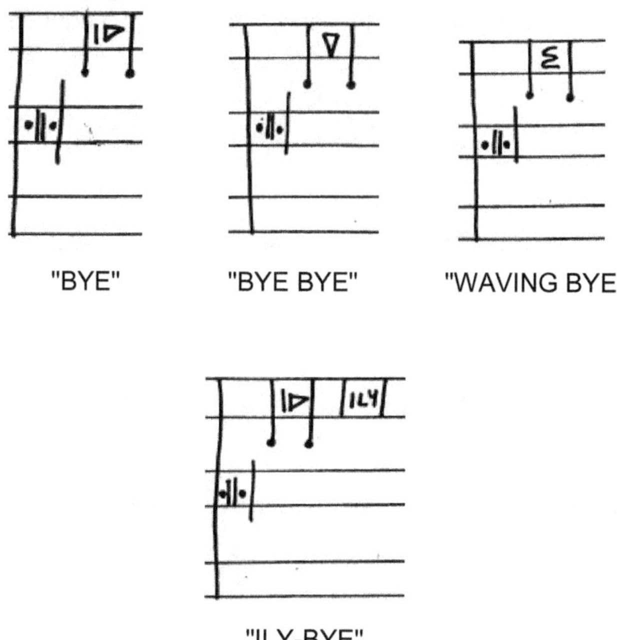

"BYE" "BYE BYE" "WAVING BYE"

"ILY-BYE"

There are many more greetings and partings, and the shorthand notation would be created using the same approach with the addition of the HS for clarity as needed.

For example in ASL a commonly used parting is: "See you later!" (I used "SL"...the actual HS is "KL")

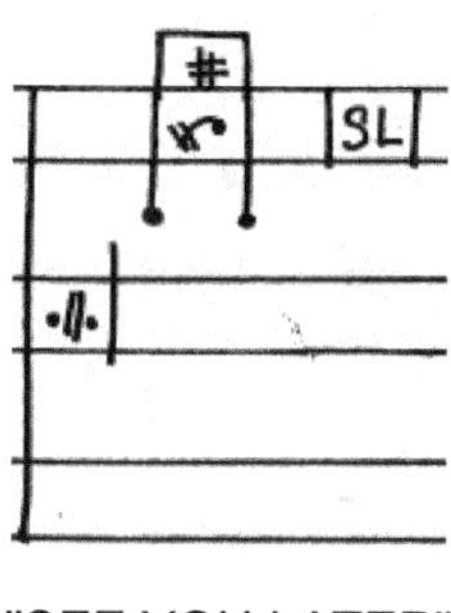

"SEE YOU LATER"

And either of these could be used to notate a two-handed wave:

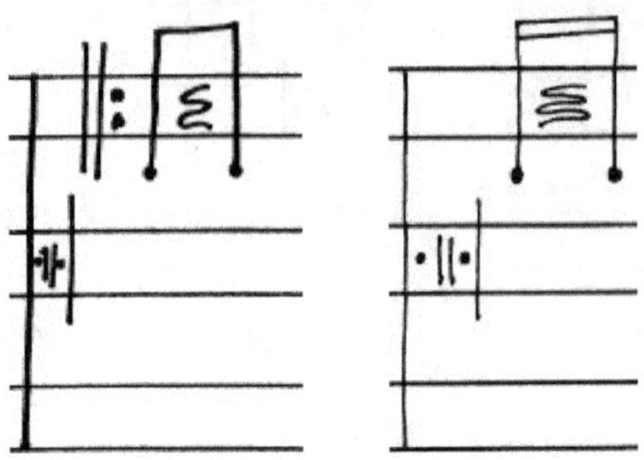

"WAVING GOOD-BYE" (BOTH HANDS)

Social courtesies are usually phrases such as: "Good morning!", "Excuse me" or "Thank you". Many phrases could be seen as social courtesies...and as independent statements by others. Determining which category a statement falls into is somewhat subjective. The signing community could create shorthand notations for high frequency social courtesies...or choose only to alert the reader to the upcoming social courtesy grammar type, and then use long hand notation for the statement. In the examples below, "Thank you" is notated as a social courtesy. It can also serve as a farewell, as in the ASL Nook video transcribed using SN at the end of the Grammar Notes section.

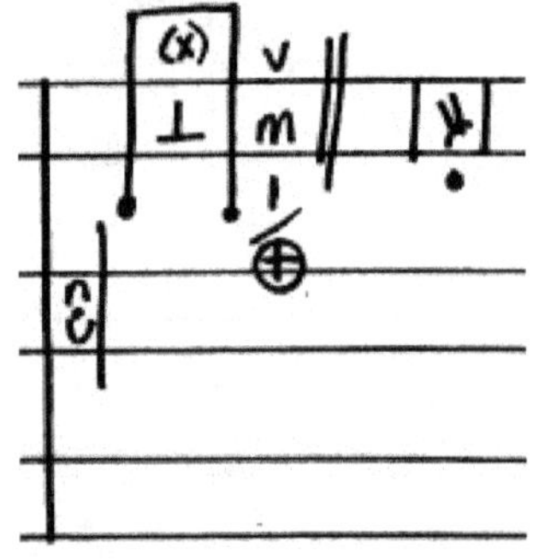

"THANK YOU" (LONGHAND NOTATION)

The shorthand version of "thank you":

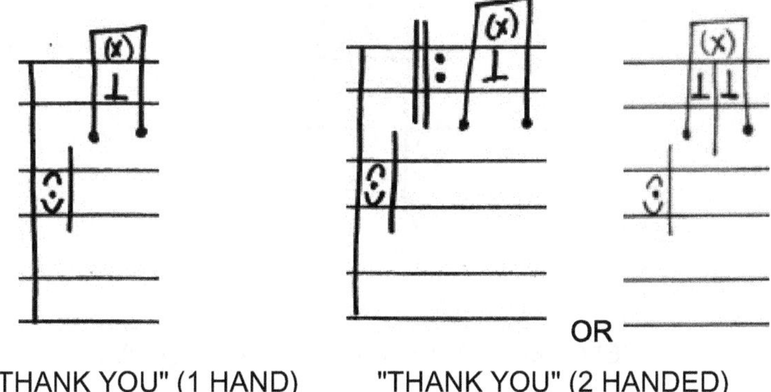

"THANK YOU" (1 HAND) "THANK YOU" (2 HANDED)

The social phrase: “Welcome!” (to our home, this event, etc…), would be similarly notated but using the Social Courtesies grammar notation and a directional component as needed for pluralization:

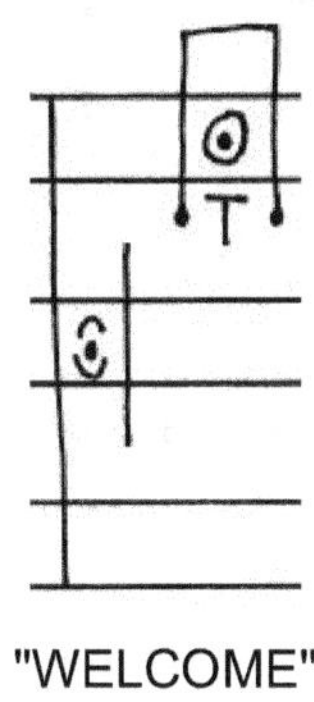

"WELCOME"

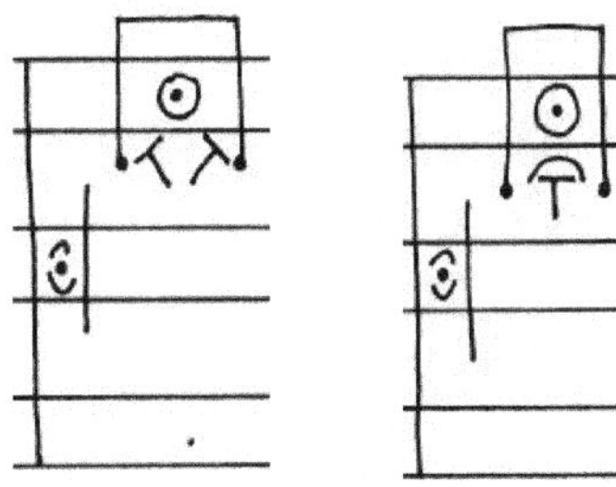

"YOU ARE BOTH WELCOME" "WECOME EVERYONE"

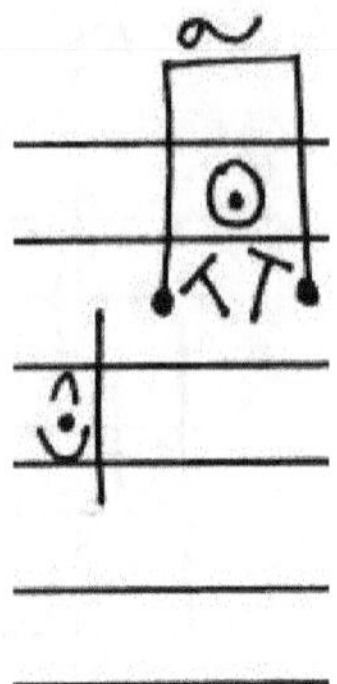

WELCOME" (WITH INTRO FLOURISH MVT)

The social courtesy of "You're welcome" as a response to someone saying, "Thank you!" would have a different directional element:

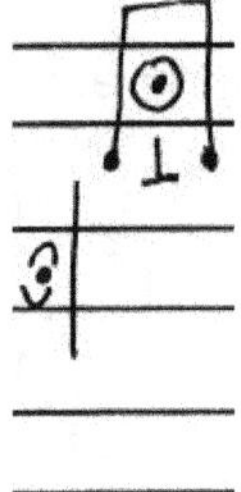

"YOU'RE WELCOME"

HEAD NOD AND SHAKE

Shorthand notation for a head nod or shake can be notated on the MVT block, which incorporates these important grammatical components with the sign movement articulation:

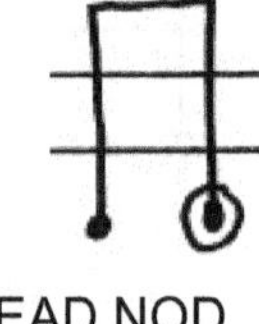

HEAD NOD

HEAD SHAKE

INDEX HANDSHAPE VS. REFERENCING

We need to differentiate between use of an index to reference a location and that does not constitute a formal sign, and those signs which do incorporate an index HS.

For signs that use an index HS, we can use either of the following handshapes in the HS block (PO is flexible):

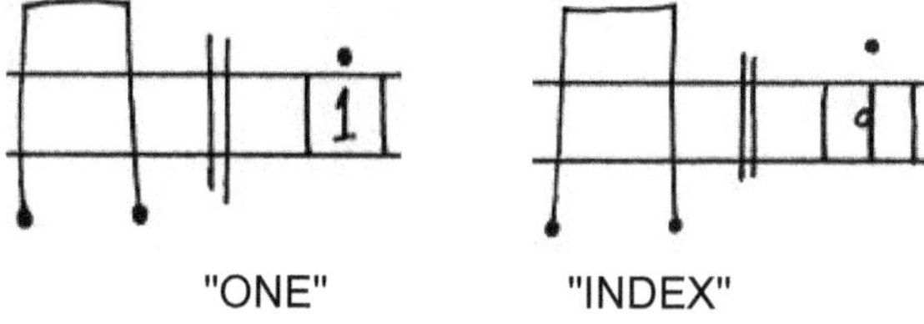

"ONE" "INDEX"

For example here is the sign glossed: "to cry" or "a tear":

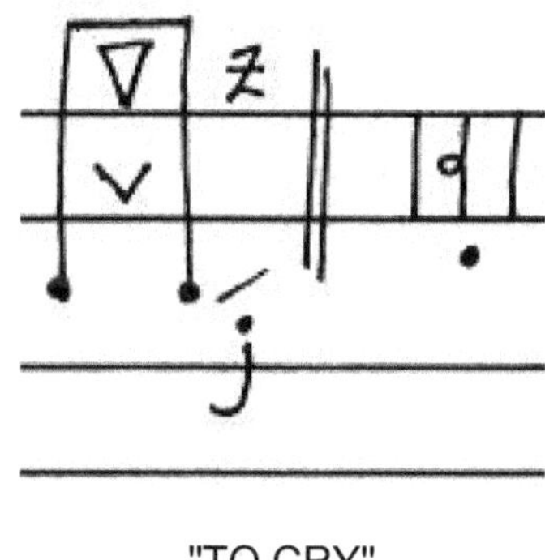

"TO CRY"

When an index is being used to reference a location, it will be notated in the grammar block and the location will be identified along with contact/movement:

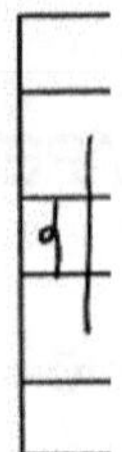

INDEX NOTATED IN GRAMMAR BLOCK

Here the location of the cheek itself is being referenced:

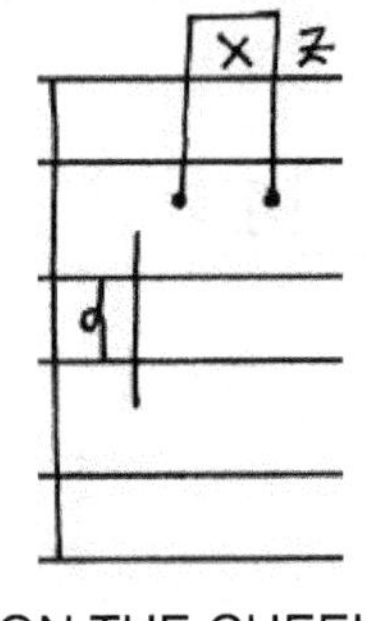

"ON THE CHEEK"

"FLAT B" HANDSHAPE REFERENCING

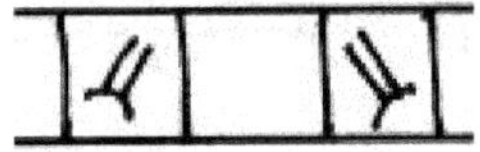

The BHS can be used to reference something is "there" or "here". The grammar notation is:

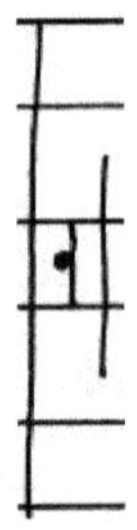

“FLAT B” BHS NOTATED IN GRAMMAR BLOCK

An example is the concept of "here" or "there you have it":

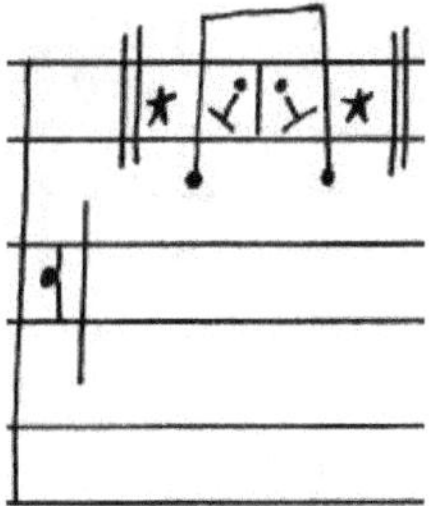

MOUTHING

Comprehension of some signs is enhanced by mouthing of an English gloss (or the spoken language of the contact culture). For educational purposes as well as the grammatical value of mouthing, the term to be mouthed can be notated in the Facial Grammar section on the lower tier. Here is an example:

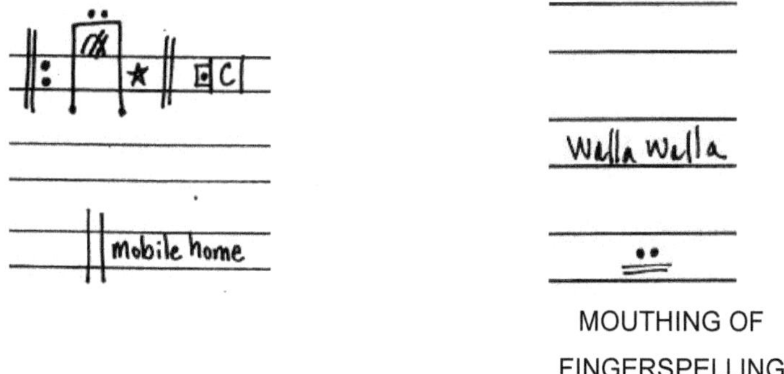

MOUTHING OF FINGERSPELLING

MULTIPLE CONTACTS

It may be necessary to notate more than one contact in the contact block of a movement. For example, a sign might maintain a parallel position as well as incorporate a contact. These are notated with a comma between:

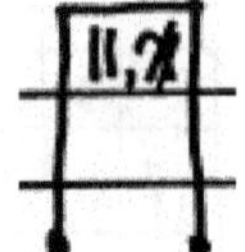

Here is a sample:

"UP TIL NOW"

NEGATION

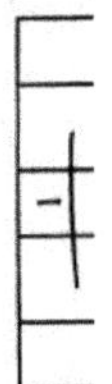

Each of the commonly used signs for negation can be notated longhand. Here is the notation for the ASL sign "not":

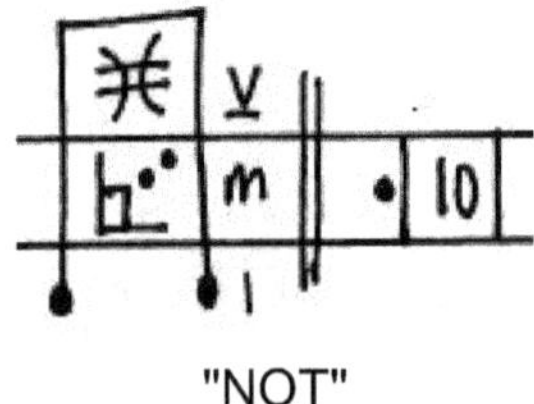

"NOT"

A short list of negation signs includes: "not", "never", "can't", "won't", "not-yet", "No", and a negating "head shake". We can use the principle of conservation and mark negation "-" in the grammar block and then utilize MVT makers to notate in shorthand form:

Here is a visual comparison of the same set with the larger movement block:

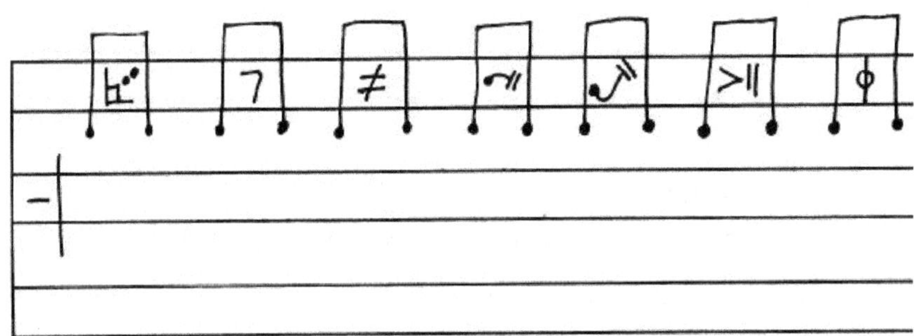

"NOT" "NEVER" "CAN'T" "WON'T" "NOT YET" "NO" "NEG HEAD SHAKE"

Let's add "DON'T":

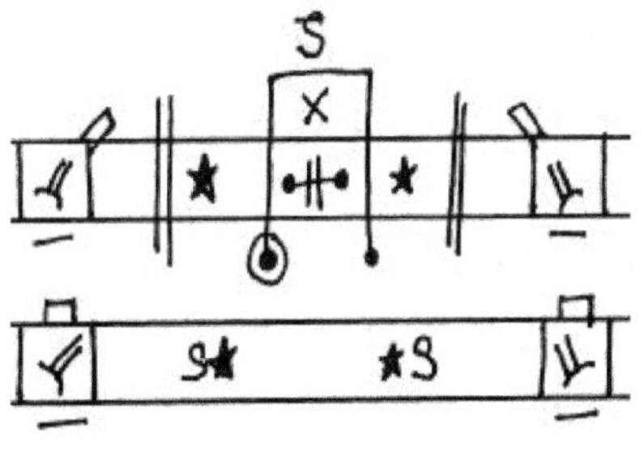

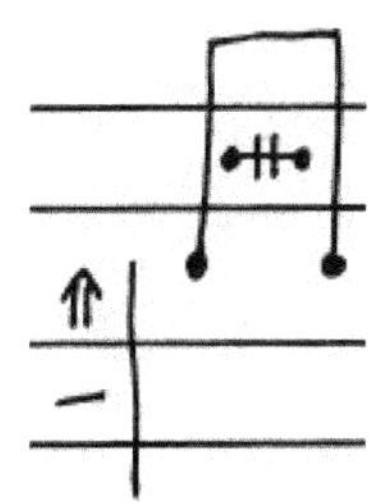

"DON'T" (LONGHAND NOTATION) "DON'T (SHORTHAND, COMMAND)

"NOTHING/NONE"

Similarly, high frequency signs conveying concepts related to negation of: nothing, none, nada, zero, zilch, absolutely none left, not one bit, etc...can also be given shorthand SN. The grammar notation "negation" is also used for this set. Each of these can also be notated longhand:

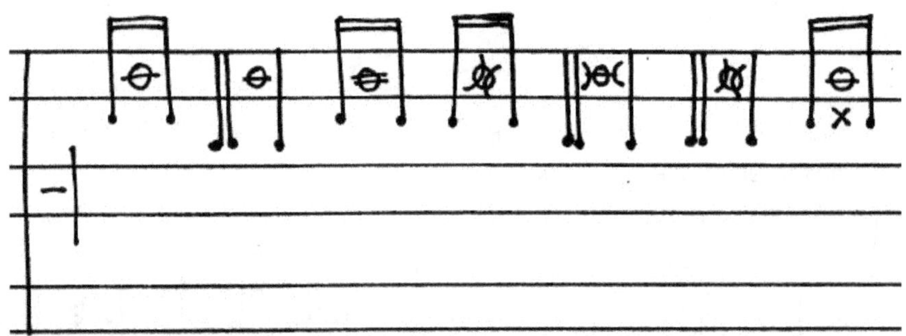

From left to right:

1. Two handed sign with "O" HS moving straight forward simultaneously once. ("zero")
2. Same as #1, but using only D HS. ("zero")
3. Two handed sign with "O" HS shaken back and forth. ("nothing")
4. Two handed sign with "B" HS cross and separate in front of the mouth while blowing. ("not a speck, completely gone")
5. One handed sign using "O" HS held by mouth while blowing through the empty space ("absolutely none")
6. Same as #4, but using only D HS.
7. Two handed sign with "0" HS that cross and separate emphatically in front of signer's torso. ("zero")

ORDER OF OPERATIONS

As in mathematics, establishing an order of operations provides a consistent application of the notation pattern for each sign.

The tiers of the Sign Staff are to be read top to bottom: 1st tier, 2nd tier and then 3rd tier.

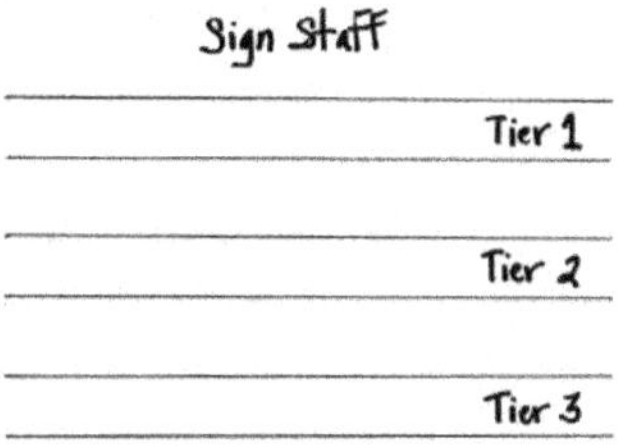

Sign Staff

Tier 1

Tier 2

Tier 3

The order along each tier is outside>inwards. Each hand is to be read separately. The order of operations is:

HS

LOC

MVT

****

HS

LOC

MVT

****

HS

LOC

MVT

Or

HS>LOC>MVT:MVT<LOC,HS

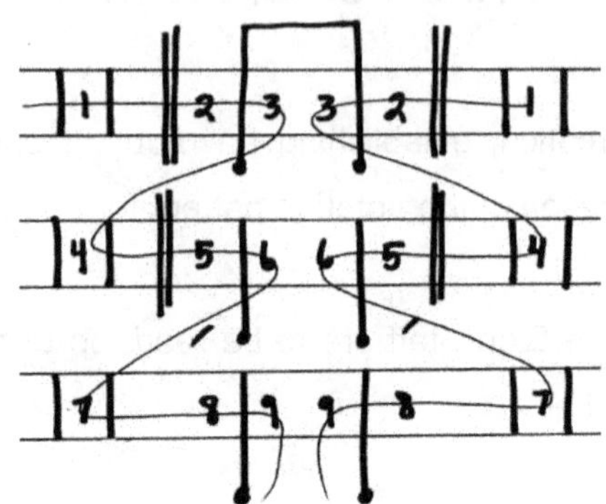

Additionally, within the MVT block the upper portion is reserved for Contact MVTS.

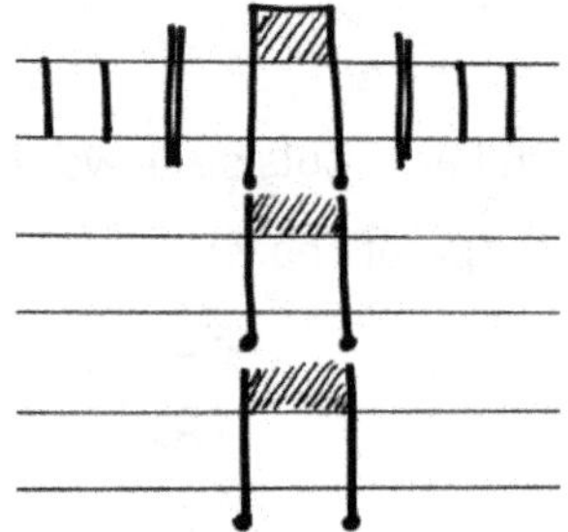

The mid and lower sections of the MVT block are for non-contact MVTS. Occasionally it may be useful to notate a contact in the mid and lower sections. For example:

ORDINALS

Ordinals can be notated longhand. For example this is one articulation of the ordinal "1st" with the location shifting upward:

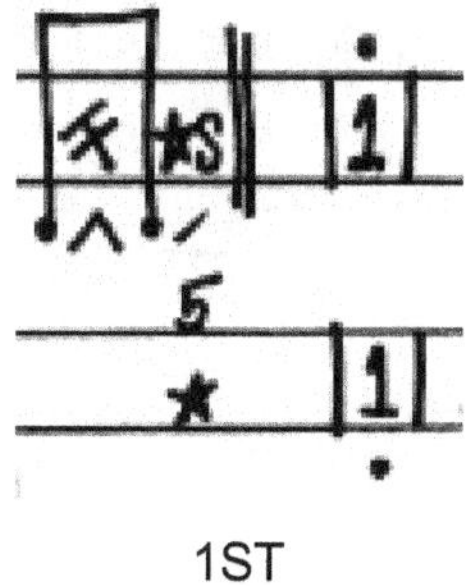

1ST

Ordinals can also be notated on the second or mid- tier:

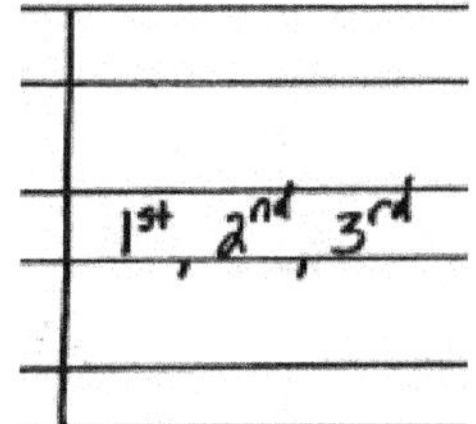

And if a specific articulation is desired, that can be notated and then the remaining ordinals written mid-tier to clarify the type of numbering being used. In the notation below, no upward shift during articulation is included:

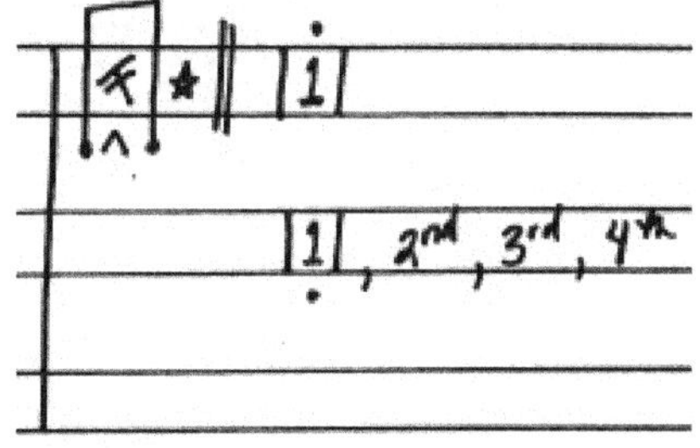

PAUSES AND RESTS

Signers will at times pause during an utterance. Below is the notation for a pause between signs:

You can also have a pause mid-sign articulation which would be notated:

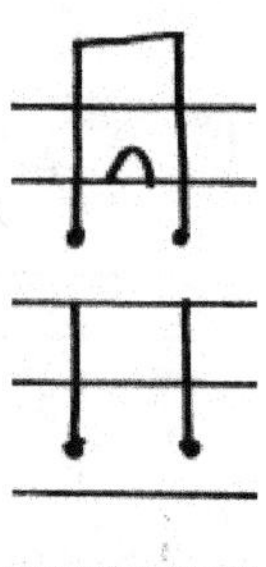

As well as a pause that incorporates a resting posture such as hands clasped, hands open or arms crossed:

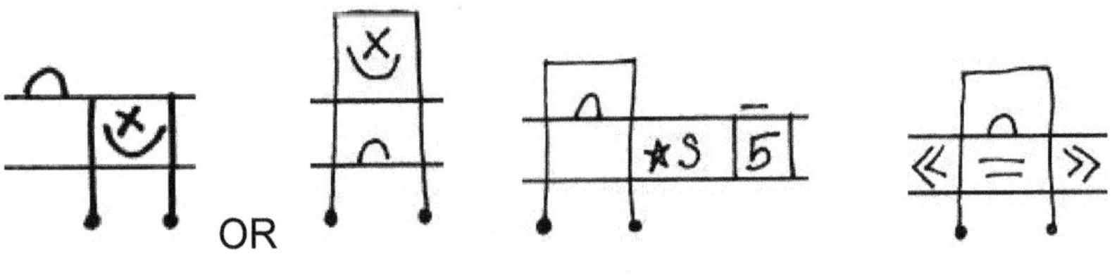

PERSON-MARKER

ASL uses a specific construction known as a person-marker to denote the difference between the verb form and the noun (person) form. For example: dance vs. dancer, teach vs. teacher, to cook vs. the cook. To notate the person-marked form of a sign use the notation shown below, on the third tier directly below the MVT block:

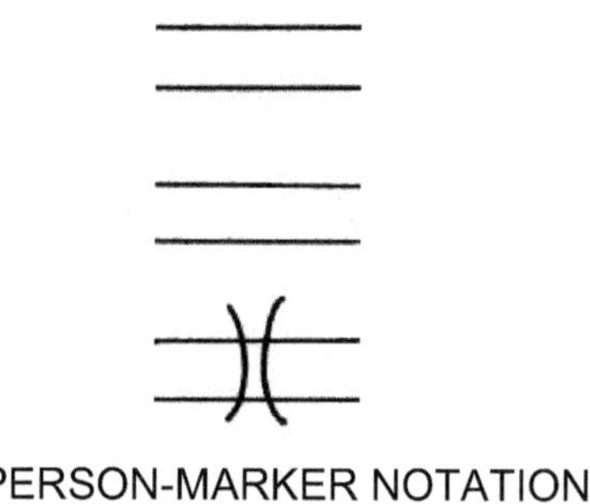

PERSON-MARKER NOTATION

Here is a sample notation of the ASL verb "teach":

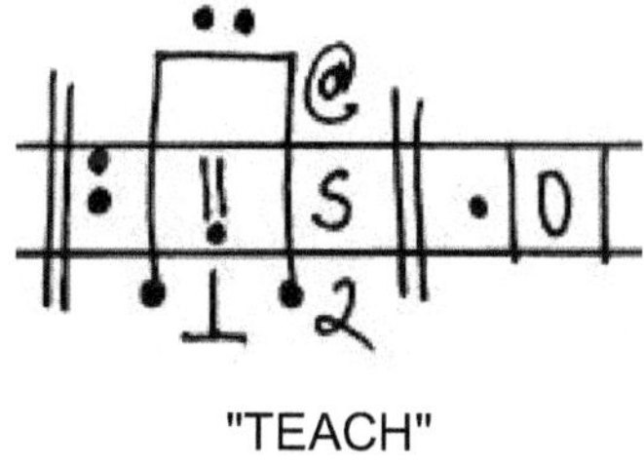

"TEACH"

And here is the same sign, with only one repetition and the person-marker "teacher". Fluent signers are familiar with the standard articulation for person-marked signs that creates a compound sign from two unrelated signs. In this case, "teach" + "person":

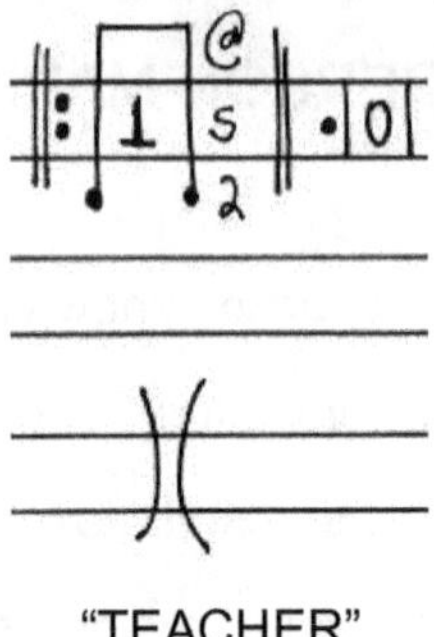

"TEACHER"

PHRASE MARKS

When a set of signs should be considered as a block or phrase and signed smoothly as a unit within an utterance, use the musical notation for a phrase:

PRONOUNS

We need a shorthand notation for pronouns. Below is the pronoun marker notation:

PRONOUN NOTATION

Here are examples of this notation for each pronoun incorporating the principles of shorthand notation:

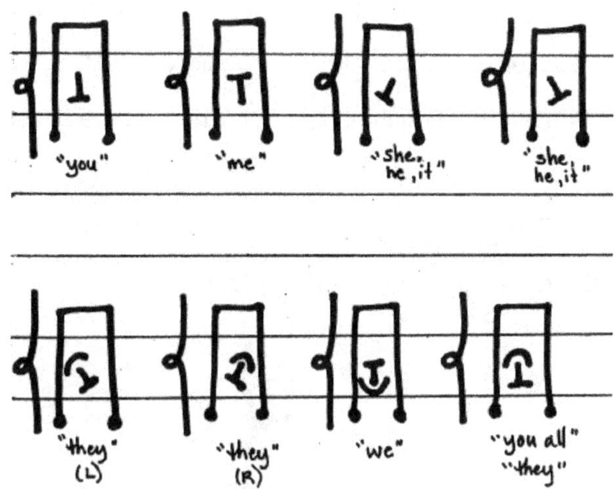

For a non-index pronoun, add the HS. A great example of this is the sign glossed "everyone" or " the masses of you":

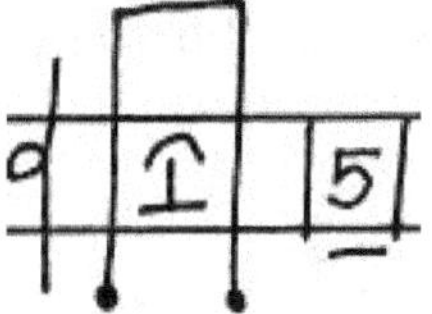

"EVERYONE OUT THERE"

You can watch Tar2006 (Youtube vlogger) use this beautiful, inclusive sign regularly.

FORMAL PRONOUNS

ASL also has a formal version of pronoun identification, using a flat

"B-" BHS with the palm facing up. It can be used alone or to "draw" a line up and down, directly beside the ND index similar to the way an English speaker would say "One would..." or "This item..." in a deferential, neutral or formal manner. Another common function is to reference oneself when formally introducing yourself, or to show respect as in a Dr./patient relationship. The Dr. may ask the patient, "if s/he has any further questions?..." and incorporate a formal pronoun to address the patient. Formal pronouns function similarly to "Usted/es" in Spanish. Below is the formal pronoun marker notation:

FORMAL PRONOUN NOTATION

Formal pronoun notation is used in the same way as pronoun notation above. For example, here is the formal notation for oneself when introducing yourself:

There is an additional use for formal notation and that is to specifically highlight an example. We will use an added notation with double lines for this function:

FORMAL PRONOUN NOTATION: "IT/THIS/ONE"

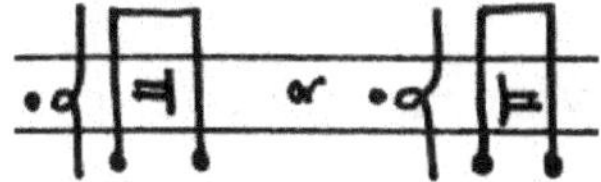

POSSESSIVE PRONOUNS

Similarly, we need a shorthand notation for possessive pronouns, which use a flat "B-" handshape oriented towards the party being indicated. Below is the possessive pronoun marker notation:

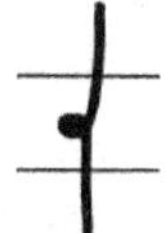

POSSESSIVE PRONOUN

Here are examples of this notation for each possessive pronoun:

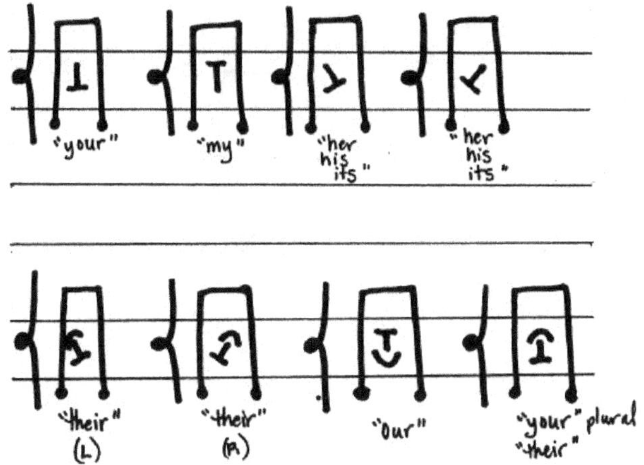

NOTE: The default location for all pronouns and possessive pronouns is in the SSS * unless otherwise noted.

FORMAL POSSESSIVE PRONOUN NOTATION

The formal possessive pronoun involves placement of the possessive pronoun handshape of a flat "B" against the ND index to emphasize formally the concept of "their". This can be used both for animate and inanimate objects. Check out this video to see a great example in use mathematically:

PLACE VALUE IN ASL

https://www.youtube.com/watch?v=r9GrtuDKzSA

Here is the notation format:

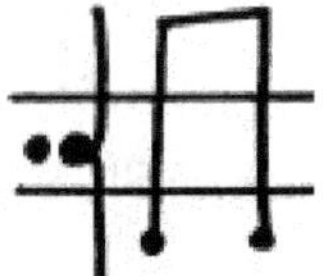

FORMAL POSSESSIVE PRONOUN NOTATION

An example is "its":

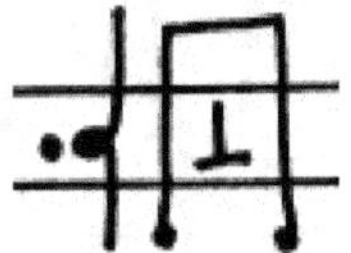

And in the place value example given in Mr. Behm's Math Video above, a possible notation could be:

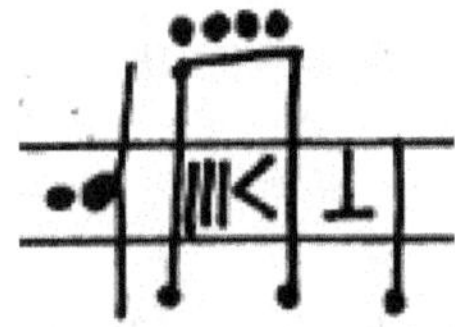

SERIES OF REPEATED "THEIR" OR "ITS", MOVING LEFT

"SELF" PRONOUN NOTATION

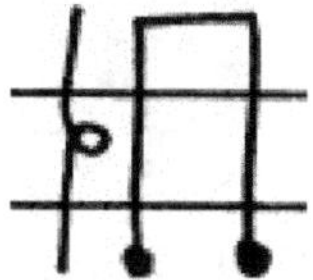

Here is the notation for "self" as in "myself, yourself, him/herself, yourselves and ourselves". Below is an example of this notation, and it functions the same for all other reflexive pronouns:

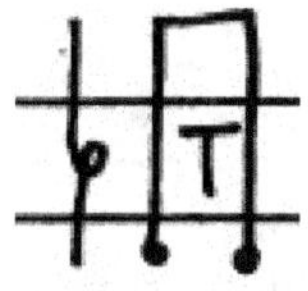

"MYSELF"

FORMAL "SELF" PRONOUN NOTATION

The formal expression of reflexive pronouns includes a an index "1" BHS: "yourself" formal. Below is an example of this notation longhand:

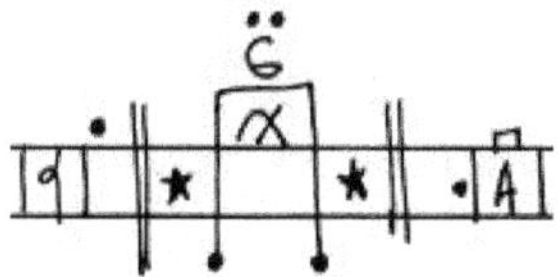

"SELF" PRONOUN FORMAL

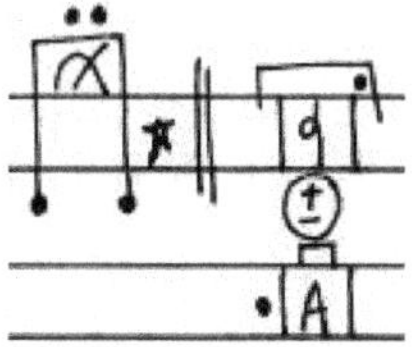

"SELF" PROUNOUN FORMAL (BHS NOTATION)

And in standard shorthand notation:

"SELF PRONOUN" (FORMAL)

Here is an example of "herself" using formal reflexive pronoun notation, based on the context of a previously identified female:

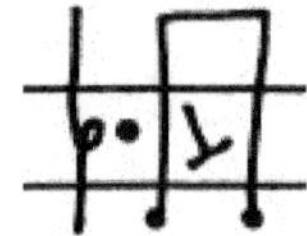

"HERSELF" (FORMAL)

QUESTION NOTATION

There are several high frequency question signs that would be good to notate shorthand. Below are four common question notation samples. All of these are listed without location or palm orientation. The default is palm facing forward, and the location is SSS*, in an "I ask you" grammatical structure. From left to right:

1. Simple drawing by index finger of a question mark. "Question" This sign often functions as a topical marker indicating that a question will be subsequently asked.
2. "X" HS with index wiggling: "qq?" Emphasizing curiosity or needed response from viewer.

3. Question mark is thrust slightly forward in throwing or flicking motion. "Ask-you" is a more directed question to a particular viewer(s).
4. Question mark is thrust further forward in a throwing or flicking motion. "Ask you!" Puts the question out into discussion, or is more emphatically directed to viewer. Directional verb.

Both #3 and #4 examples can be directionally marked by shifting the second movement notation:

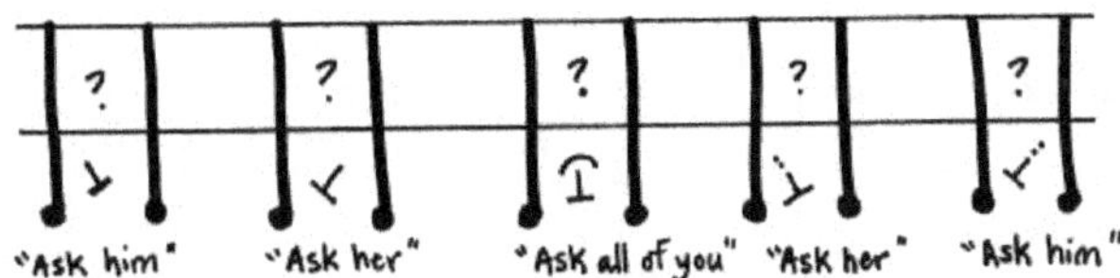

REPEATS WITHIN A PARAGRAPH

Within a limited block such as a paragraph, it can be useful to incorporate the concept of a repeat. Musical notation has a range of repeat strategies:

Figure 1.84. Repeated Measures

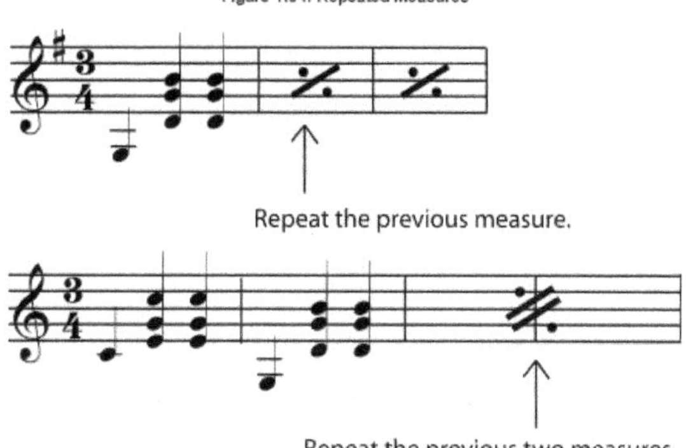

Figure 1.85. Repeat Dots

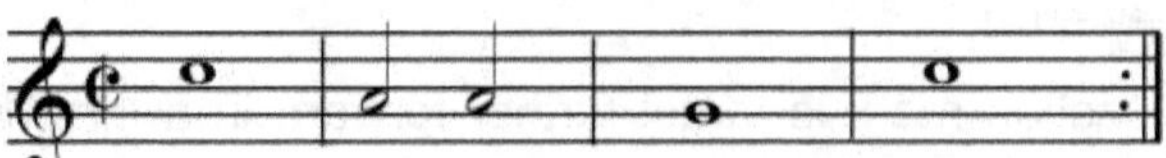

Go all the way back to the beginning and repeat once.

Repeat (once) only the measures in between the repeat dots.

Figure 1.88.

Example 1:
Play to the D.C., then go back to the beginning and play until you reach "*fine*", then stop.

Example 2: Play to the D.S., then go back to the sign and play until you find the "to coda". Go directly to the coda and play to the end.

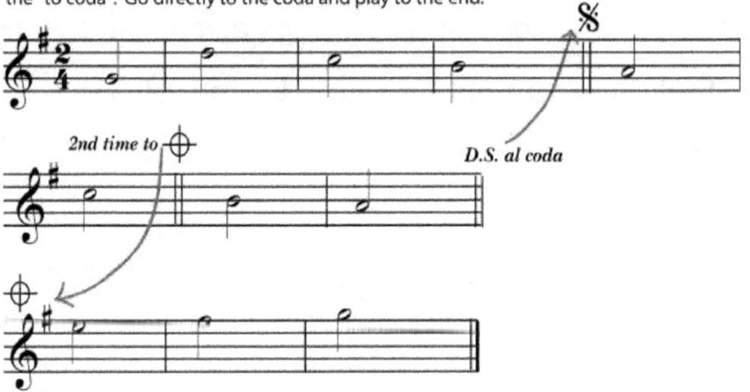

Source:

EarMaster Music Theory Online

http://www.earmaster.com/music-theoryonline/ch01/chapter-1-2.html

Retrieved 2/28/16 Creative Commons

For our purposes, a sign with longhand notation may be replaced with a repeat within a paragraph or set brief passage. A record of the repeat notations used is kept at the beginning of the passage, and identified below the sign and at the end of the Sign Staff block. For an example of this see the "ASL Nook's Introduction" notation sample at the end of the Grammar Notes section. Signs that have an established shorthand notation should not be replaced by a repeat. Here is an example of a longhand notation eligible for a repeat notation:

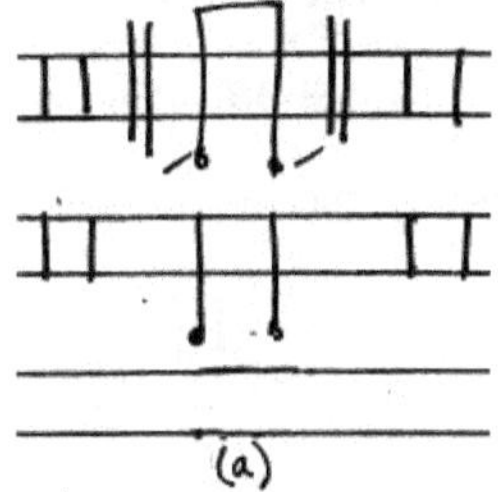

NOTATION TO REPEAT SIGN (a)

The actual repeat occurs within a subsequent utterance and is notated:

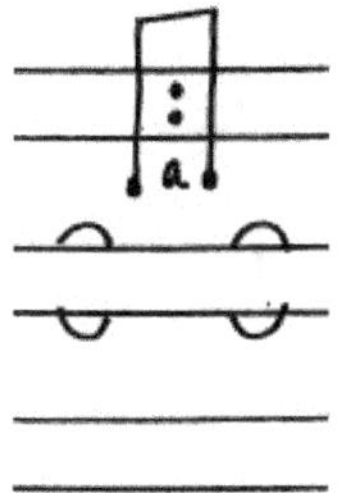

A running record of repeat references within a paragraph block, using lowercase alphabetical characters, is kept at the beginning of each paragraph block and end of the staff:

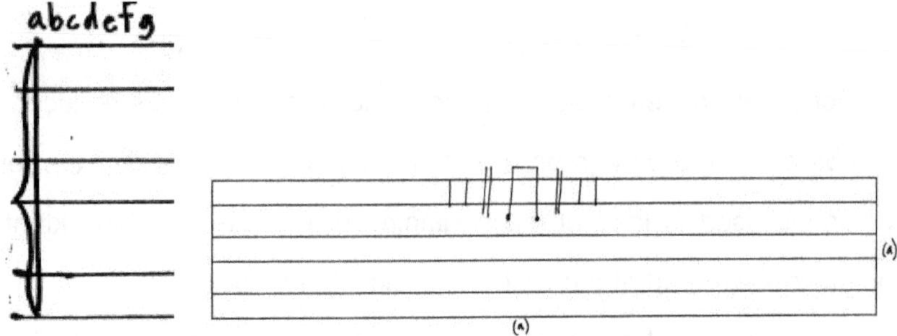

If notating with color is an option, repeats would be a great place to assist the reader by notating in color.

To notate a repeat in the location block, keep the parentheses to aid the reader in identifying a repeat notation. This often occurs when referencing an established depicting verb as a location:

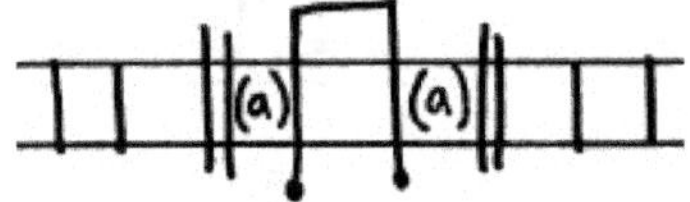

REPETITION IN MVT OR CONTACT

REPEATED MVTS

Use dots above the MVT block to notate the number of reps:

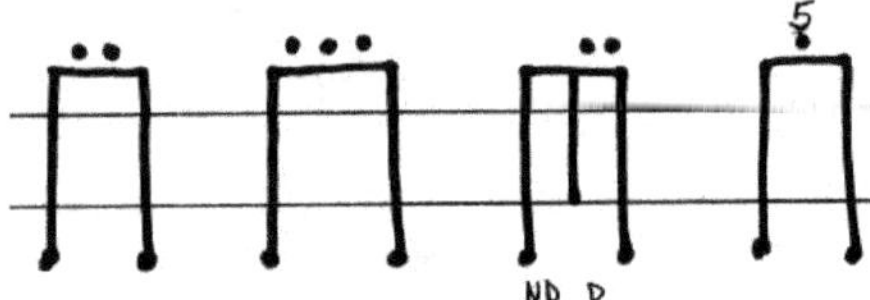

In ASL, nouns commonly have two smaller reps and verbs have one stronger rep. Many signs have only one MVT or Contact and do not need any rep dots. You can separate the ND and D HS rep sections, and also add a number for multiple-rep MVTS. The general rule is to use rep dots for 1-3 MVT reps and a single dot with the total number of reps written as a number for 4 or more reps.

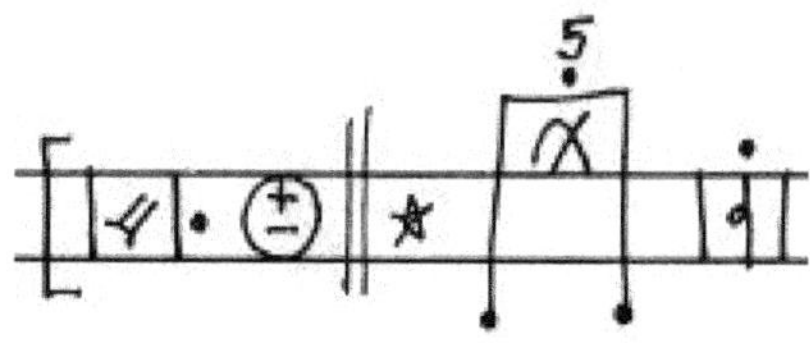

"ALARM GOING OFF" (X 5)

CONTINUOUS MVTS

Occasionally you may want to emphasize that a movement is continuous throughout the signed movement, such as with an embedded movement. Default for embedded movements is continuous movement, but a (:) can be used to clarify if desired:

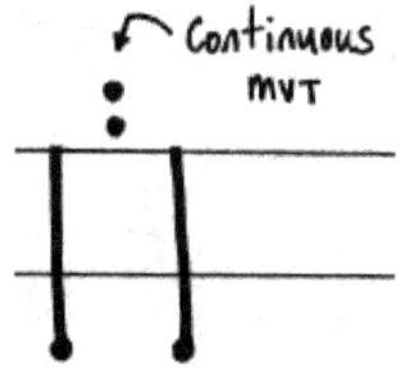

NUMBER HS REPETITIONS

When using numbers that have a movement as a HS you will need to identify the number of reps *within the HS block.*

REPETITION OF PREVIOUS SIGN

At times, you may need to notate a repeated sign unit. A repeat of the identical sign is notated:

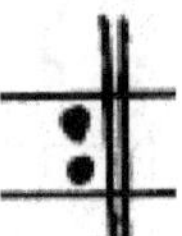

A repeat of the mirror image of that sign by the opposite hand is notated:

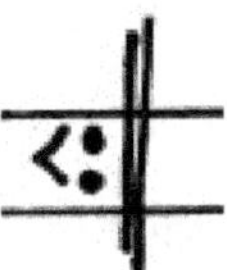

Here is an example of a repeated identical sign notation, often used with lateral listing:

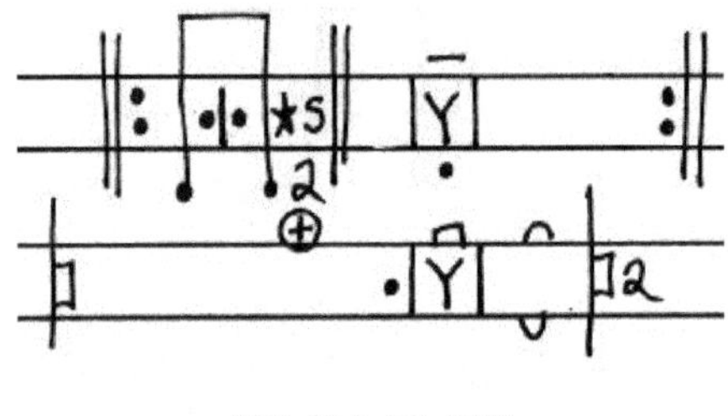

"PI AY, PLAY"

PHRASE UNIT REPETITION

At times, you may need to notate a repeated phrase unit. A repeat of the identical sign phrase is notated on the second tier, either back to the last grammar block or between repeat notations:

SIGNOTATION

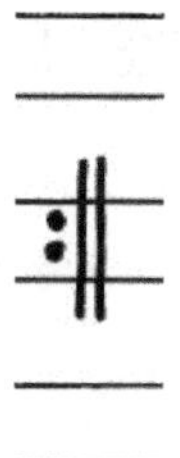

PHRASE UNIT REPETITION

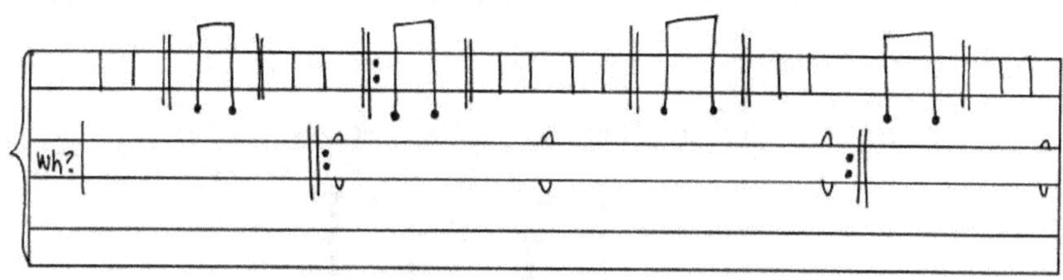

RETURNING TO "NEUTRAL" POSITION

In the Grammar Block, a return to the neutral "narrator" position and forward eye gaze and level head tilt is notated with an asterisk:

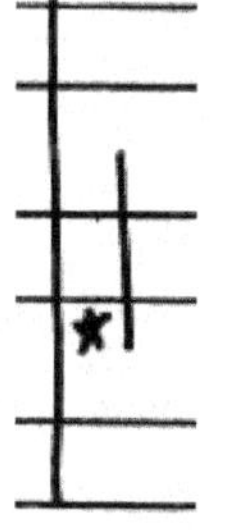

NEUTRAL EYE GAZE/HEAD TILT

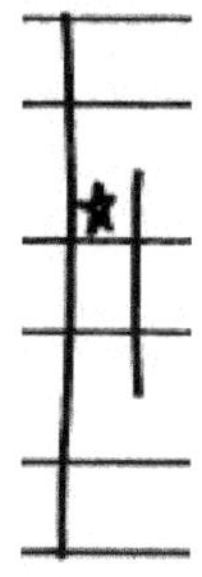

NEUTRAL TORSO LOCATION

REVERSAL OF MVTS

Some sign movements represent the reversal of the initial sign movement, or are comprised of both an original and reversed movement. We will be using a degree symbol along with the original movement to represent these reversals of any established movement. For example below are the signs for “throw” and "put something onto" on the first tier, and the reversal (“catch”, “take off”) listed below on the second tier:

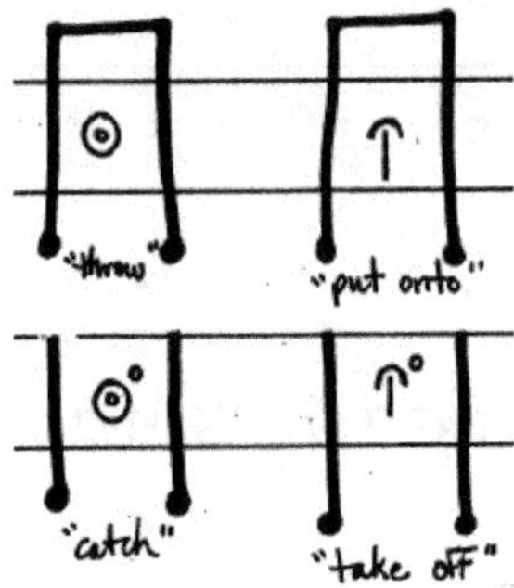

The sign for "microwave" is a good example of a reversal MVT sequence. You will notice that the second tier HS is un-noted...this is because the movement "throwing" has a standard open, collapsed "5" HS endpoint that does not need to be notated.

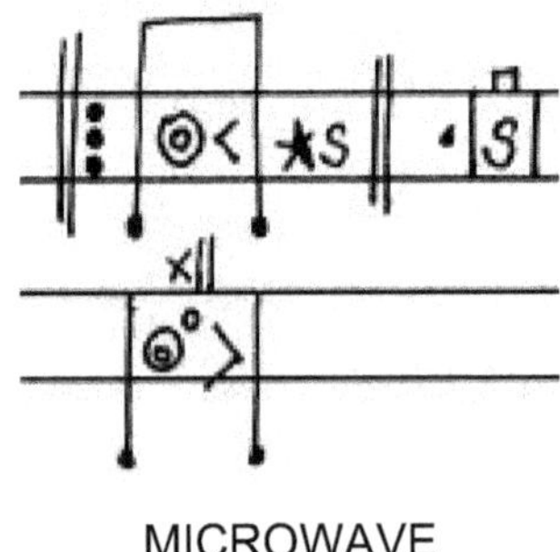

MICROWAVE

The sign for "baptize" is a good example of a sign that reverses "back to the starting point" which is another function of a reversal MVT notation:

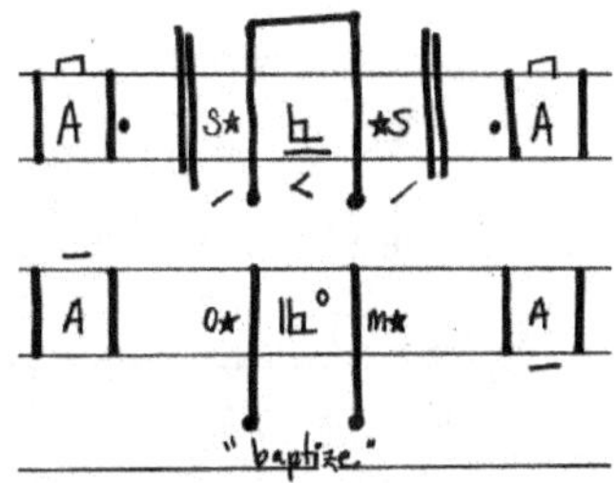

SEPARATION OF LOCATIONS

To mark the separation between locations on the SS tiers, use a forward slash (/):

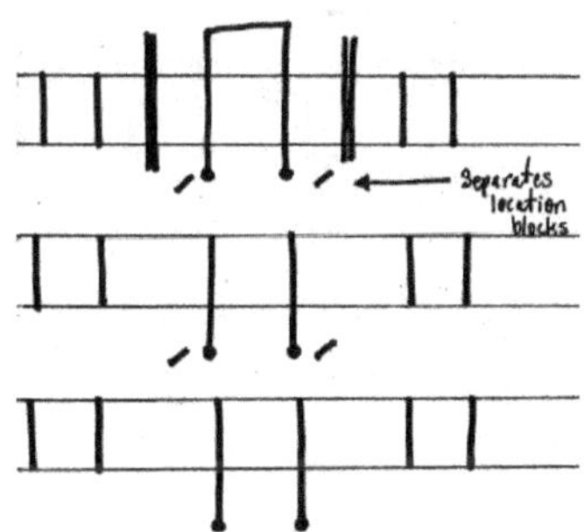

SEPARATION OF SIGNS IN A PHRASE

Separation between signs that are within a phrase is notated:

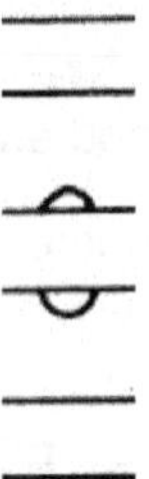

Here is a sample statement using this notation:

SHORTHAND SIGNOTATION

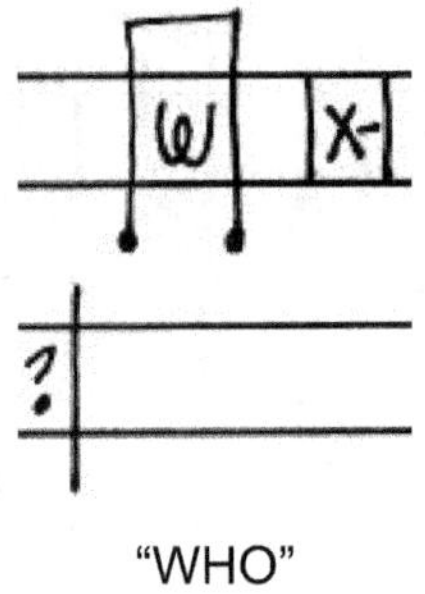

"WHO"

We will adopt a strategy used in mathematics and many other disciplines. Once a longhand notation has been established, it may be useful to develop a shorthand version for the sake of efficiency. We will adhere to four basic principles:

1. Create a **grammar notation** that identifies this particular shorthand SN set.

2. Use the **MVT block** to differentiate unique morphemes (units of meaning).

3. To further differentiate, **add HS, PO, LOC as needed**.

4. Shorthand notations require standardization and publication in order to be clearly understood by all SN users.

STACKED NOTATION

We need a way to indicate when a sign involves a set of stacked handshapes. For example, there are many signs that have the D HS directly above the ND HS. If the sign is a BHSP, then we do not need to indicate "stacked", but for those sign HS that have a set position in relation to one another, it will be helpful to have a clear notation of the eight basic positions.

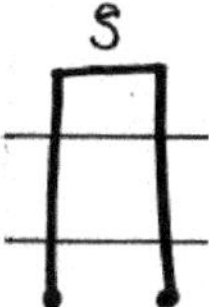

D/ND VERTICAL STACK

An example of this is the sign "make":

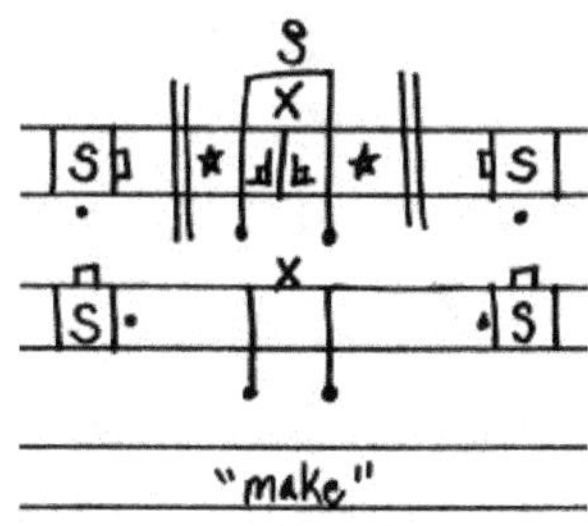

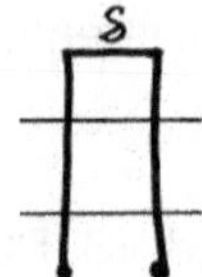

ND/D VERTICAL STACK

An example of a ND/D Vertical Stack is the sign "support":

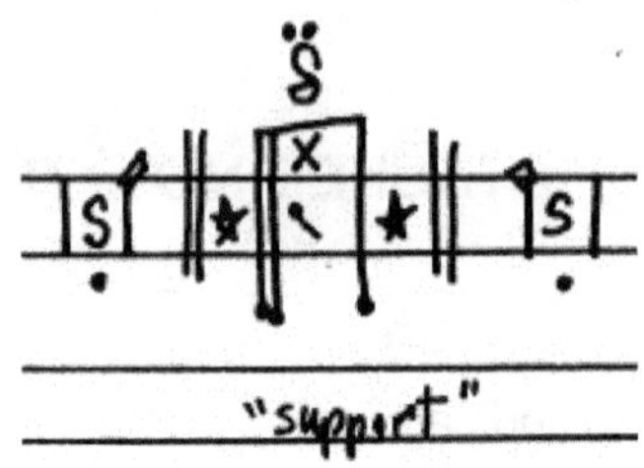

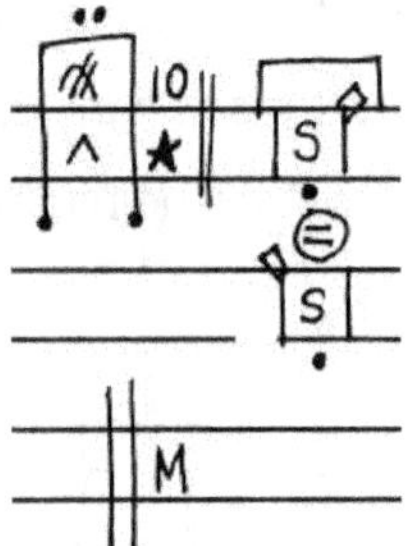

"SUPPORT" AS BHSP AND "TAP-TAP" ARTICULATION

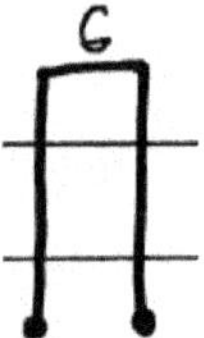

D/ND HORIZONTAL STACK

The D HS is closest to the signer. An example of this is the sign "protect":

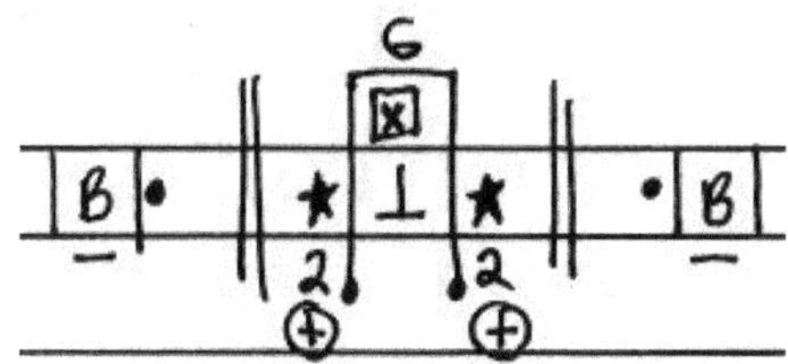

"BLOCK", "PROTECT"

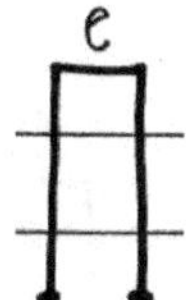

ND/D HORIZONTAL STACK

An example of this is the directional or conjugated sign "oppress me":

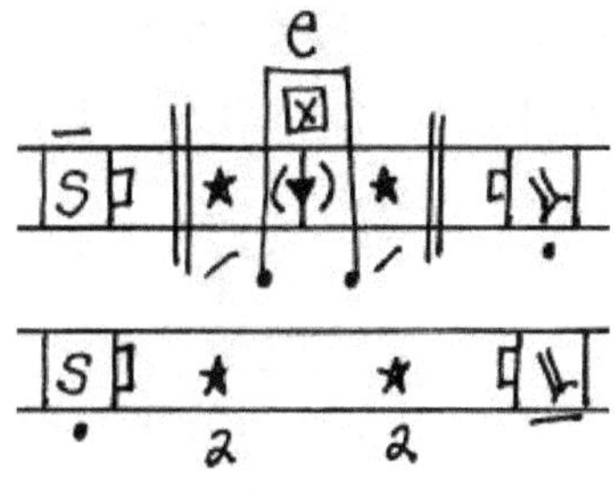

"OPPRESS ME"

%

OFFSET STACK

Offset stacks are notated above the MVT block:

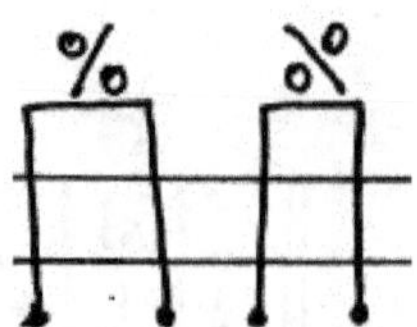

HORIZONTAL OFFSET STACKS

In the example above, the sign notated on the left has the ND HS forward in the signing space and the D HS to the rear. An example is the sign glossed, "feedback".

"FEEDBACK"

And the sign notated on the right above shifts those positions with the D HS forward and the ND HS to the rear. The sample below notates a conversation between two people:

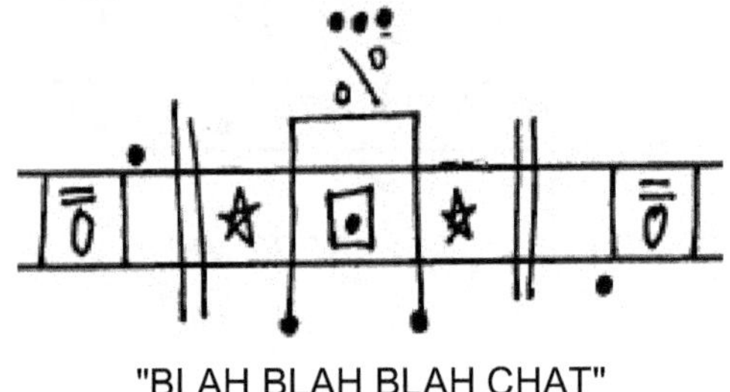

"BLAH BLAH BLAH CHAT"

The examples above are in the horizontal plane. Similar positions that occur in the vertical plane are notated with filled in dots:

VERTICAL OFFSET STACKS

STRESS

At times, a portion of a sign will have more stress than another. To notate the stressed tier or tiers, use large parentheses:

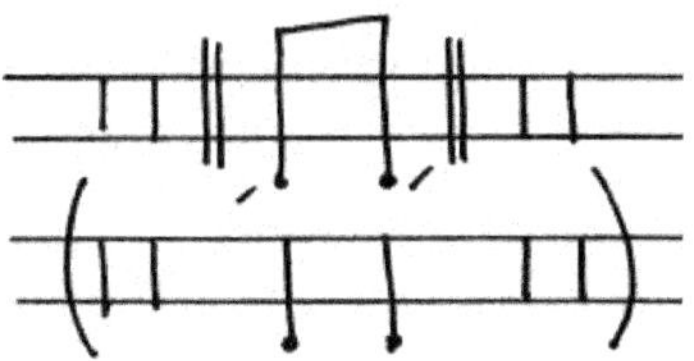

Here is an example of a sign with stress notated. This is the sign glossed: "to obsess" and is a complex BHS sign combination. Facial expression has also been notated.

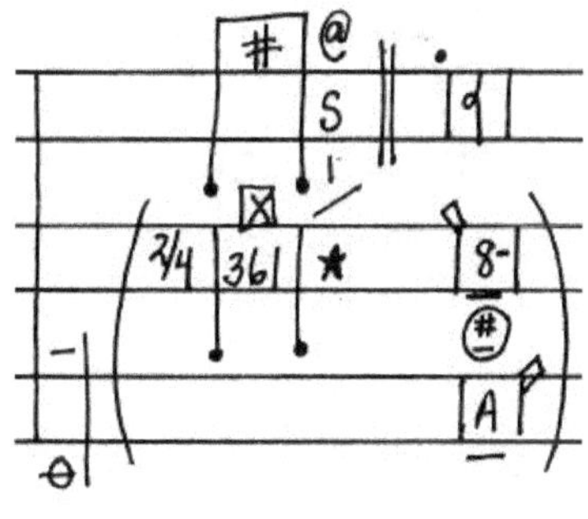

"OBSESS"

THIS AND THAT

The signs glossed: "this" and "that" occur commonly during conversation. The longhand notation for these signs is:

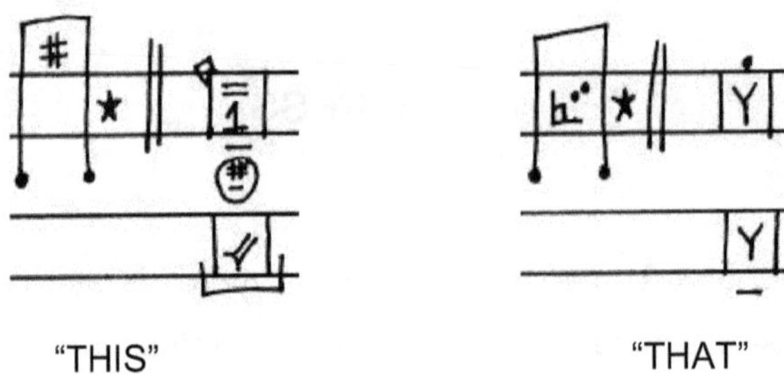

"THIS" "THAT"

Let's create a set of shorthand notations. There are three primary handshapes used: an index, a BHS or flat "B" and a "Y". What differentiates meaning is whether the item is referenced as a point in space (singular) or as a line in space (plural) and whether it is near the speaker ("this" "these" "that nearby") or far away ("that over there" "those"). The referencing grammatical notations are:

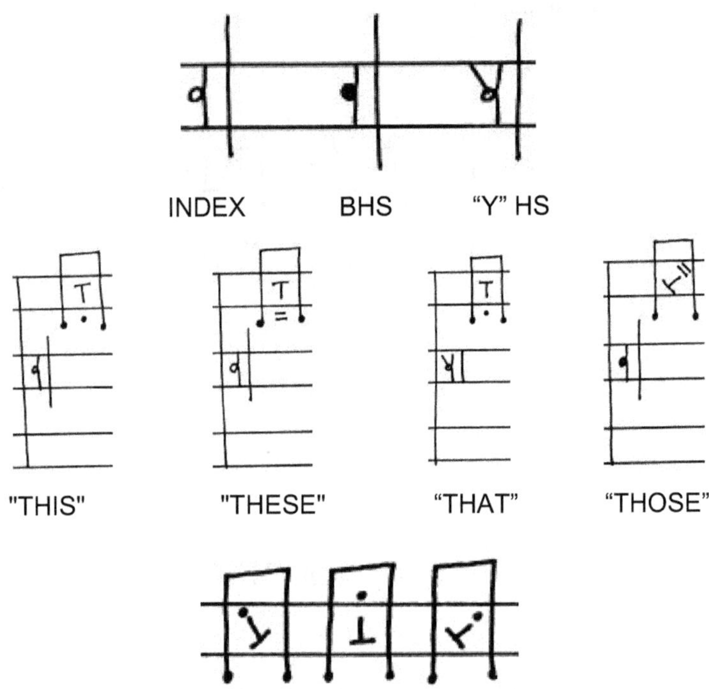

INDEX BHS "Y" HS

"THIS" "THESE" "THAT" "THOSE"

"THIS", "THAT" (SINGULAR,NEAR SPEAKER)

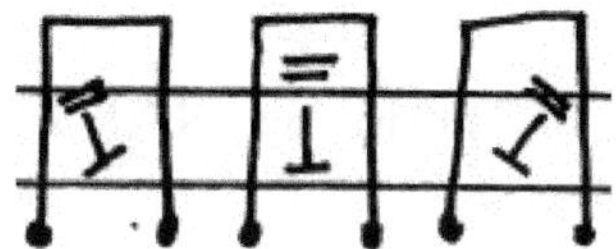

"THESE" "THOSE" (PLURAL, REMOVED FROM SPEAKER)

If the signer uses a base handshape, notate with BHS bracketing:

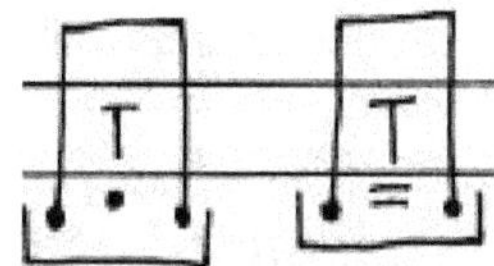

"THIS" AND "THESE" WITH BHS

NOTE: Default for referencing is D HS. If using both hands or ND, that must be notated.

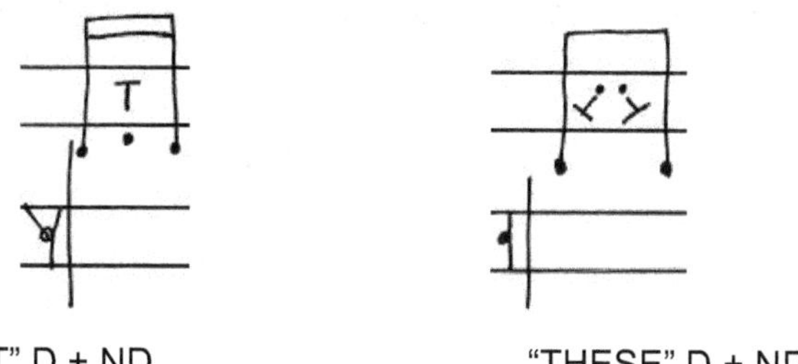

"THAT" D + ND "THESE" D + ND

Another option would be to incorporate them into the "Word Bank" and notate:

TIME SIGNATURE

We need a strategy for adjusting the size or degree of a sign along with the speed or tempo. Many signs are modulated by slight variations in the production of the sign. Borrowing from musical notation, the Time Signature (TSIG) of any particular sign will be noted on the SS in the upper left corner:

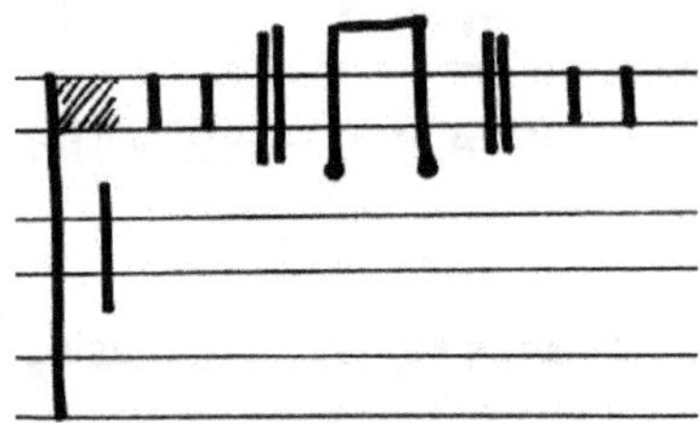

The TSIG will be comprised of both a **degree and tempo**:

$$D/T = \frac{DEGREE}{TEMPO}$$

The normal size and speed or default TSIG is 3/3, and does not need to be recorded for "generic" sign production.

The most common TSIG is 2/4. This is because a slight decrease in the size is usually accompanied by an increase in speed. And the smallest, fastest sign production is 1/5.

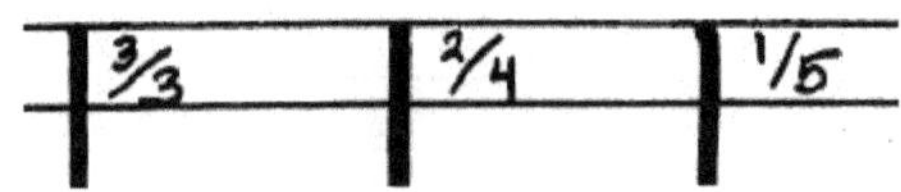

Below is an example of a sign articulation using a 2/4 TSIG:

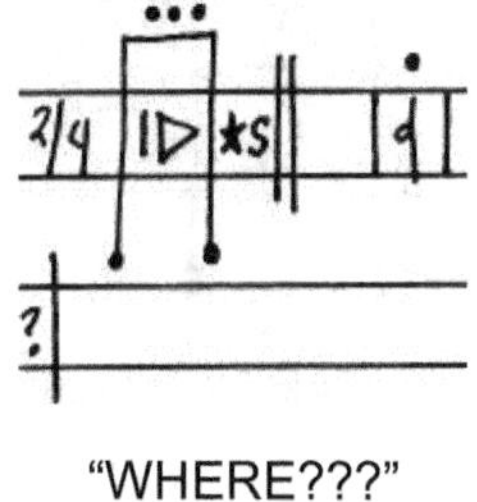

"WHERE???"

One can also notate a sign that is larger and slower such as 4/2 or 5/1.

Below is an example of a large, slow 5/1 TSIG sign:

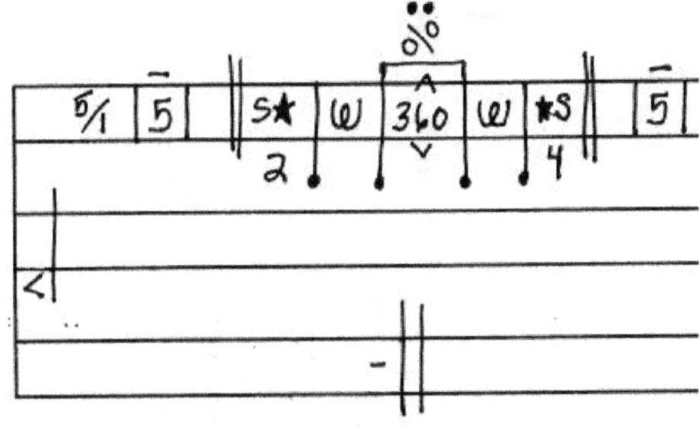

"WAITING A LONG TIME…"

NOTE: This notation includes the NGMS of a head tilt to the left, and narrowed eyes.

YOUR TURN!

See if you can correctly mark the time signature of the following English glossed sign: "hearing" (person). Check your answer in the back section under "YOUR TURN! ANSWERS" (#10)

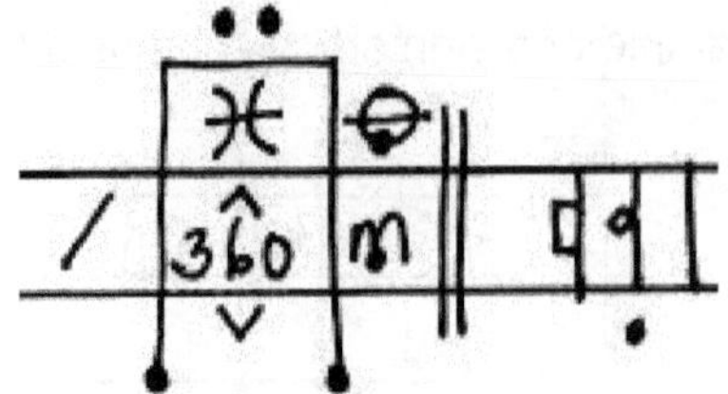

"HEARING" (PERSON)

TORSO SWAY AND ROCK

The signer's side-to side body sway can be notated in the grammar block:

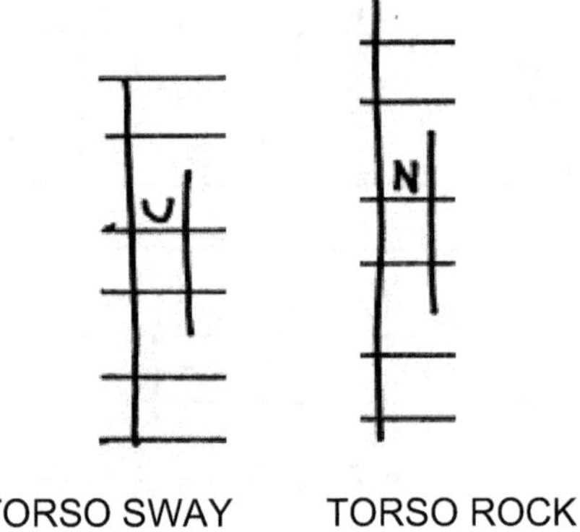

TORSO SWAY TORSO ROCK

TRANSITION TRIPLETS

Transitions between signs that have new grammar information are usually notated in a set of three or triplets. Here are three different sets of triplets. A separation between signs, new grammatical marker and a grammar block divider:

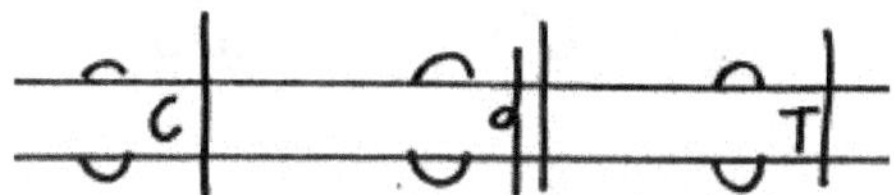

UNIQUE NOTATIONS REPEATED

Within the movement block, occasionally it will be most efficient or accurate to use a notation in a repeated fashion. This is acceptable if the notation is unique and will not be misunderstood. For example there is only one symbol for a contact, or each type of stacked notation:

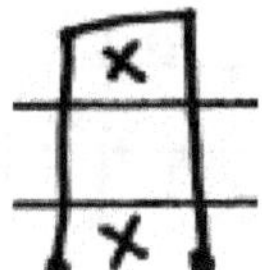

CONTACT, MVT, CONTACT PATTERN

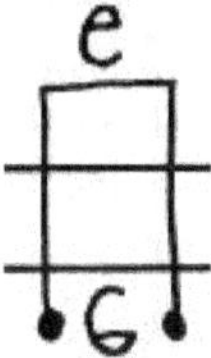

STACKED ORIENTATION FLIPPED DURING SIGN ARTICULATION

An example of this in use is the unusual sign for "become":

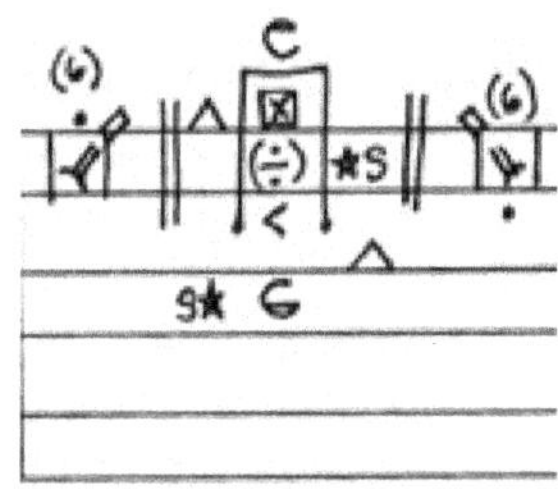

"BECOME"

VARIATIONS IN SIGNS

One of the exciting things about using a system like SN is the potential to show variations in the ways signs are produced. Many signs have more than one or several versions and signs are continually changing to incorporate new content and ways of interacting. Another common factor in sign variants is demographics. Regional sign variations are common as are generational differences in sign articulation. Consider these four sign for "Mother":

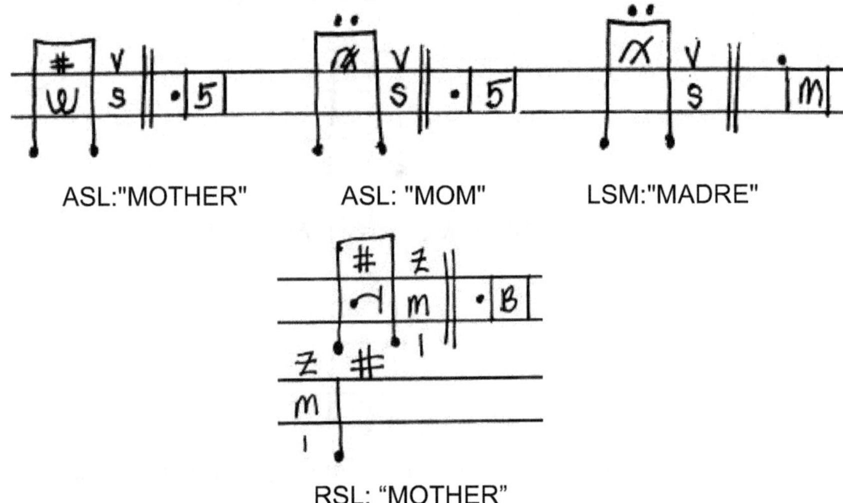

ASL:"MOTHER" ASL: "MOM" LSM:"MADRE"

RSL: “MOTHER”

In the first ASL version "Mother" the fingertips wiggle. In the second the thumb of the open “5” HS taps the chin twice. In Spanish "Madre" is made with an "M" HS, and in Russian an affectionate cheek to cheek touch represents “mother/mama”.

If you'd like a challenge, go to Youtube and watch: **"RJABCstorythanksgiving"** by Ruthie Jordan aka eyepoetic, https://www.youtube.com/watch?v=q5wdkG4BXrA. She lists many versions of the sign for "Thanksgiving". It's fun to explore signs variants!

Try creating SN for some of those she lists...

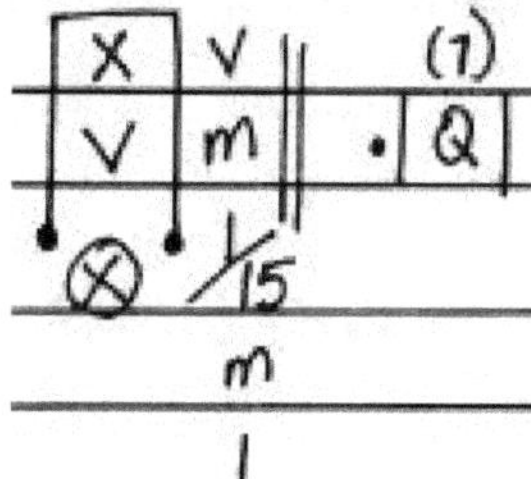

"THANKSGIVING" (1)

Here is that same sign, using a different movement option, however the location details are truncated as a direct vertical downward movement places the sign mid-chest and the contact notation indicates contact with the body:

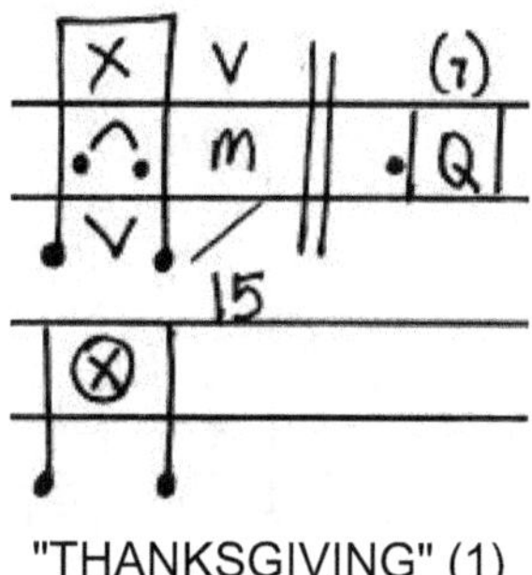

"THANKSGIVING" (1)

Here is a variant she demonstrates:

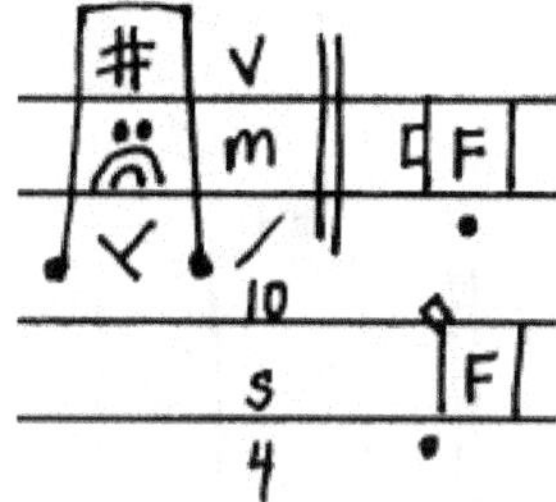

"THANKSGIVING" (2)

Notice the reps for bouncing are notated inside the movement block. This is not an embedded movement because the bouncing movement depends upon a directional notation.

WH? SIGNS

These signs can also be used for RH? and Y/N questions, but we are accustomed to terming these "WH?s". Let's look at the longhand notation for some of the most common WH?s:

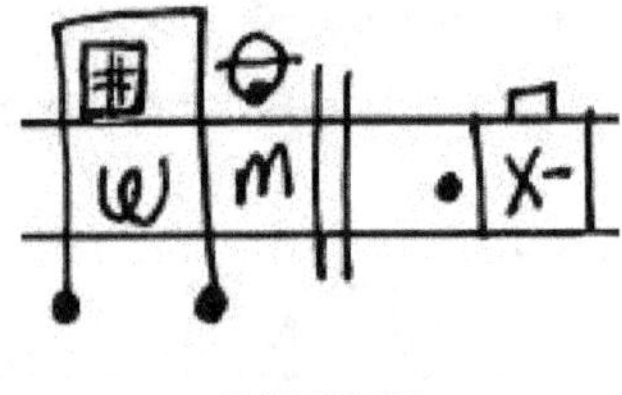

"WHO?"

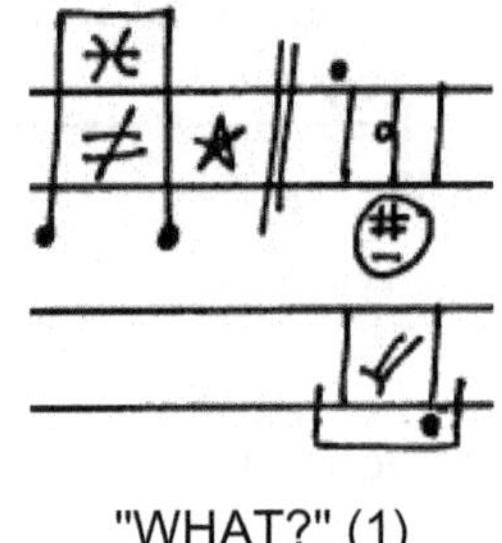

"WHAT?" (1)

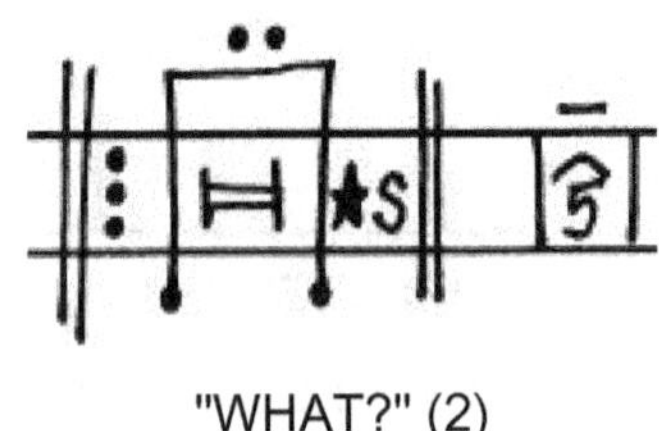

"WHAT?" (2)

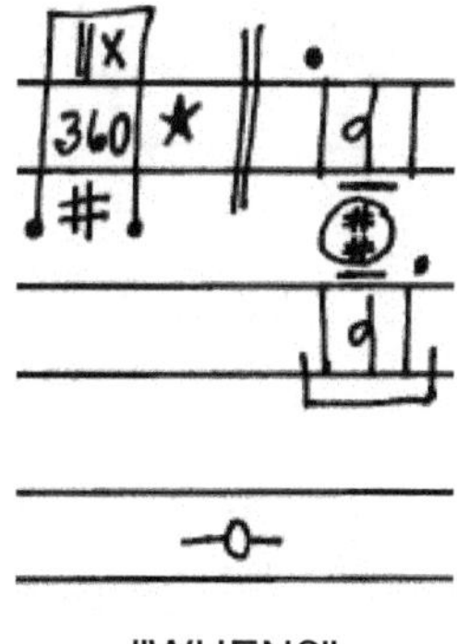

"WHEN?"

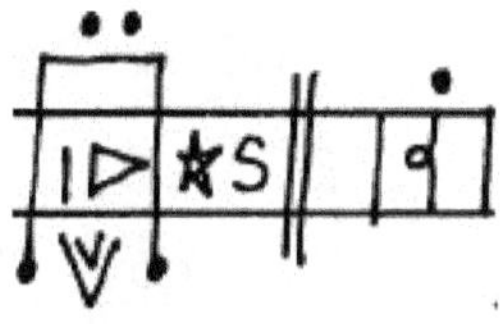

"WHERE?"

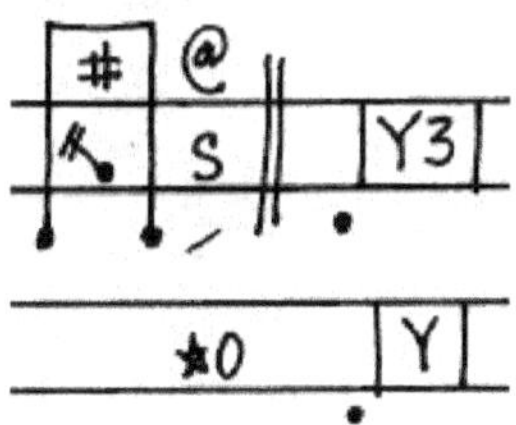

"WHY?" (1)

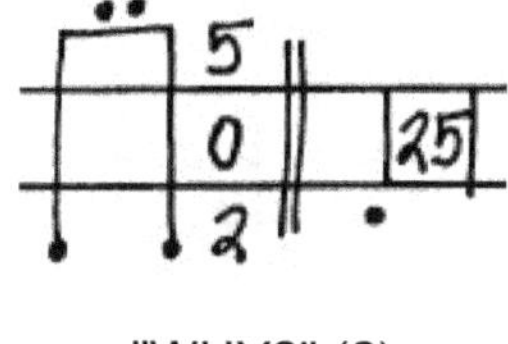

"WHY?" (2)

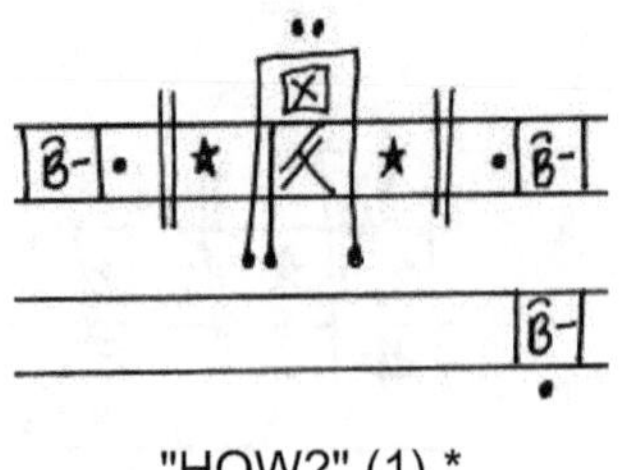

"HOW?" (1) *

"HOW?" (2)

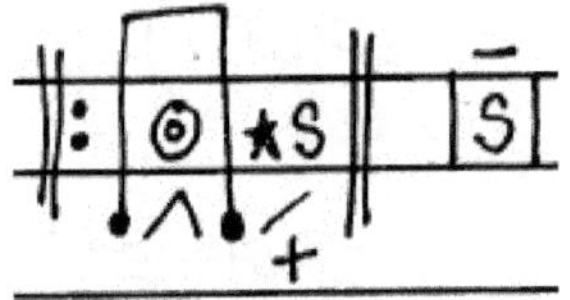

"HOW MANY?"

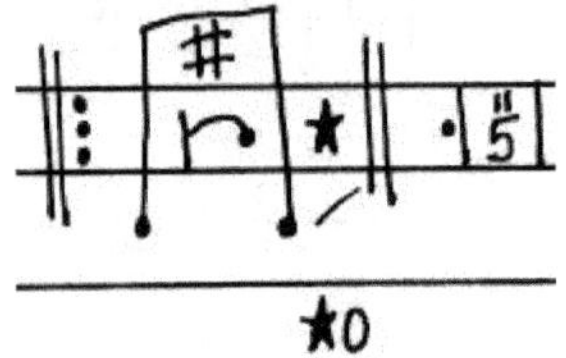

"HOW MUCH?" (QUANTITY)

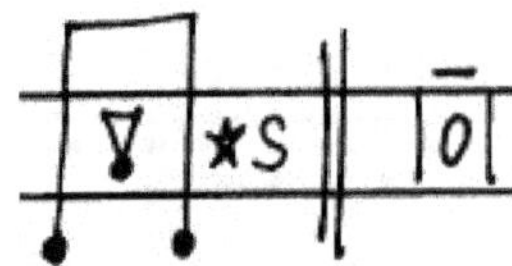

"HOW MUCH?" (COLLOQUIAL: $)

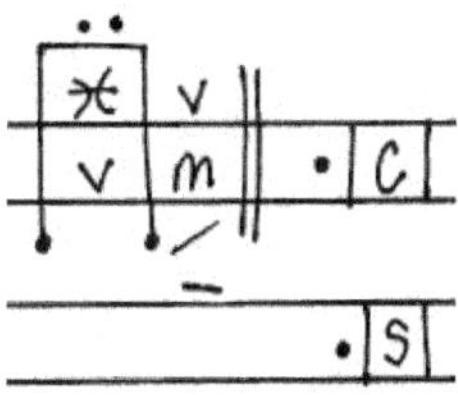

"HOW OLD?"

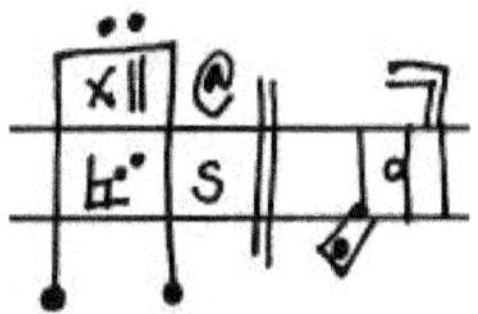

"FOR-FOR?"

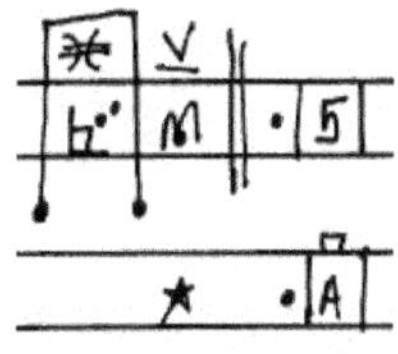

"WHY NOT?"

*This version of "how" is based on Handspeak: "ASL sign for: "how" http://www.handspeak.com/word/list/index.php?abc=hi&id=1067 Retrieved 4/2/16

When constructing a question, the grammar type will be notated in the grammar block, usually in conjunction with a Topic, and then later the actual question (who, what, when, where, why? etc...) will be posed. In ASL, the question comes at the end of the utterance. Using these grammatical notations instructs the signer on the type of FG needed for effective and grammatically correct articulation:

Here is a set of possible shorthand notations for those same signs, to be used with the ? grammar notation. I have included the HS for each to assist the reader, because there are so many:

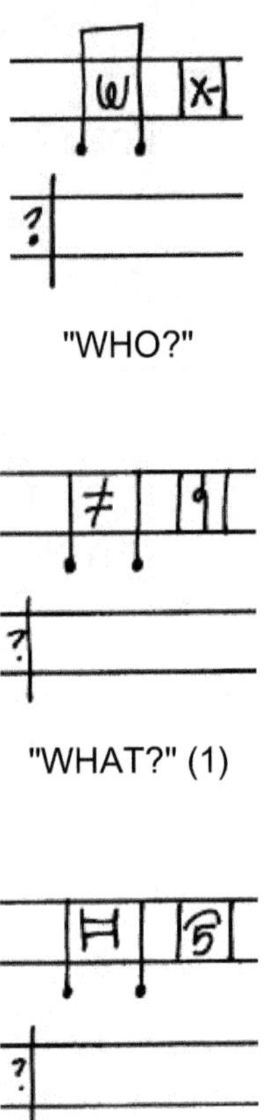

"WHO?"

"WHAT?" (1)

"WHAT?" (2)

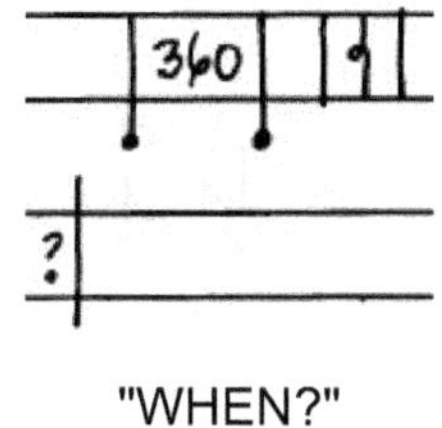

"WHEN?"

"WHERE?"

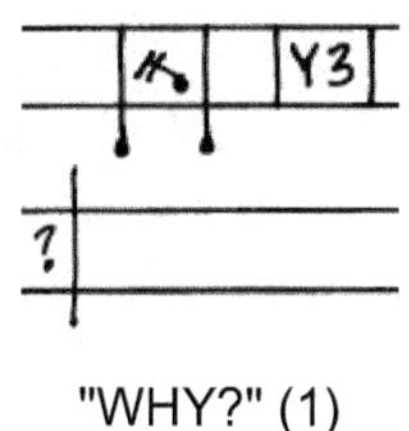

"WHY?" (1)

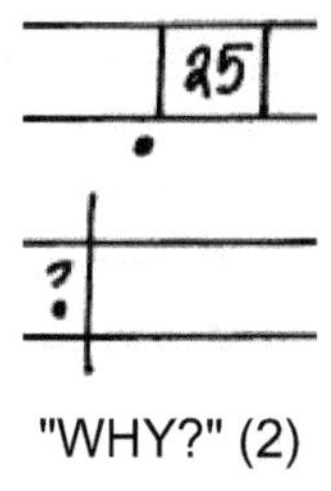

"WHY?" (2)

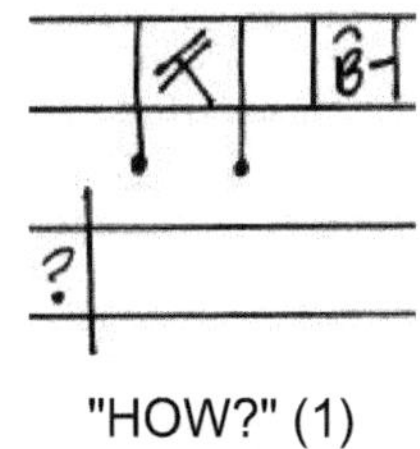

"HOW?" (1)

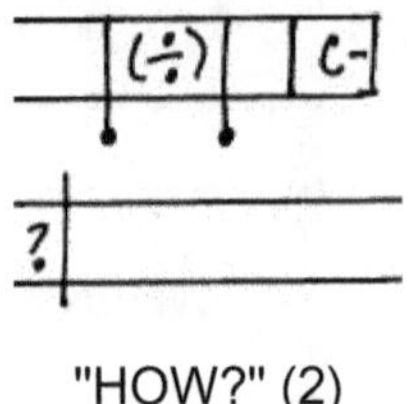

"HOW?" (2)

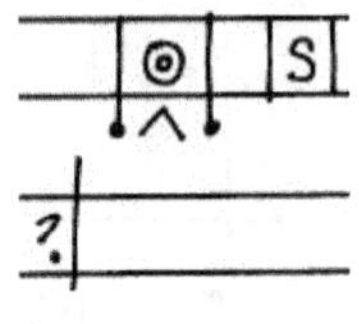

"HOW MANY?"

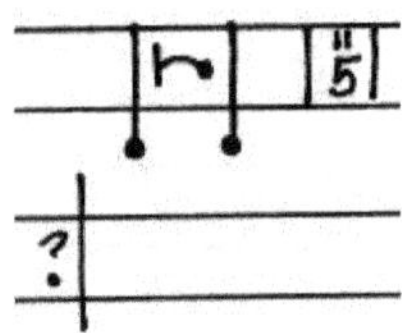

"HOW MUCH?"

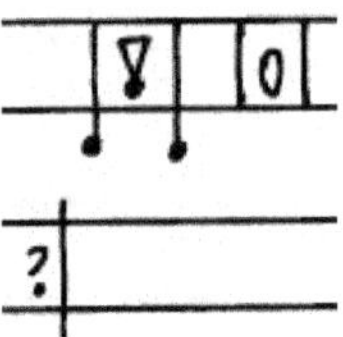

"HOW MUCH?" (COLLOQUIAL $)

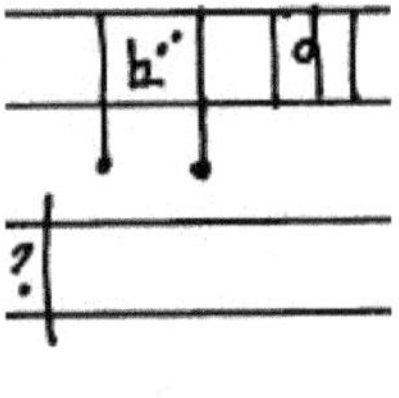

"FOR-FOR?"

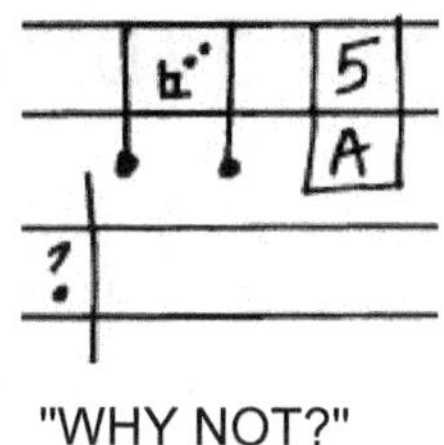

"WHY NOT?"

YES AND NO: SHORTHAND

The shorthand SN for "yes" and "no" is:

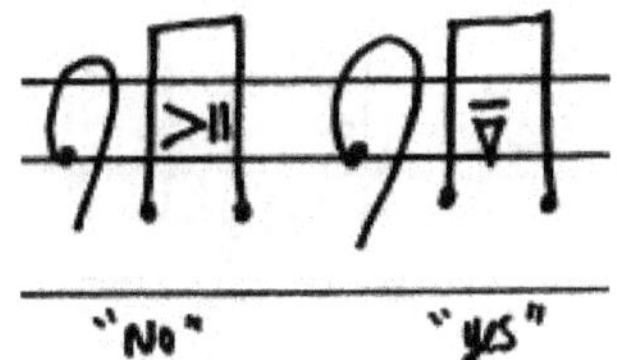

Or how about these?

"YES" "NO"

Because...? No reason...just because…!

SIGNOTATION DICTIONARY

It would be possible to create a dictionary of SN utilizing the parameters. Starting with HS, the notations could be organized by PO, LOC, MVT, and FG to enable a type of Sign to Spoken Language dictionary with synonyms that could be used for Bilingual educational purposes, recognizing the limits of 1:1 translation.

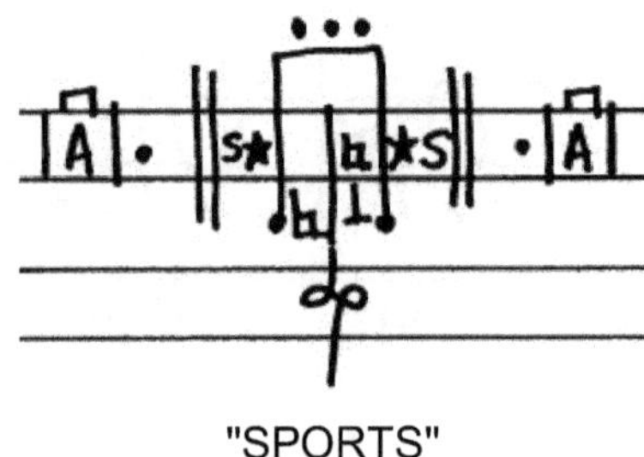

"SPORTS"

"BOOK"

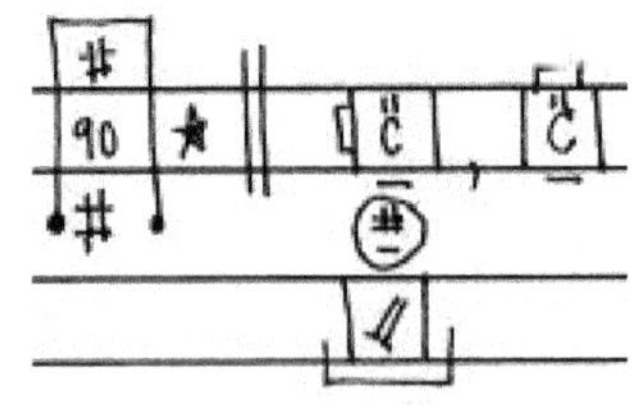

"COOKIE"

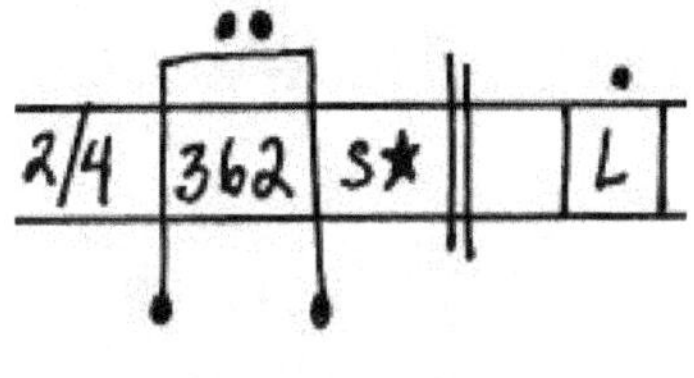

"LIBRARY"

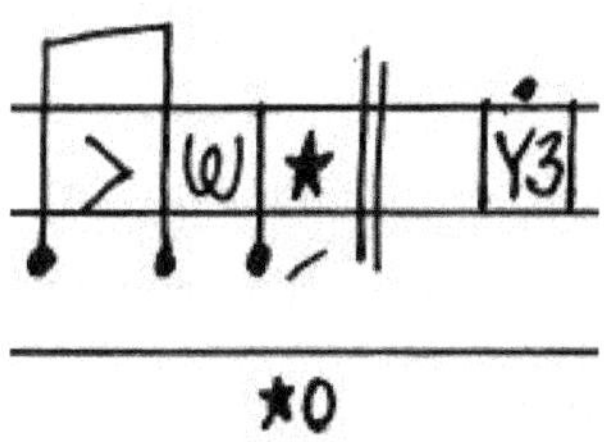

"FINGERSPELLING" (1)

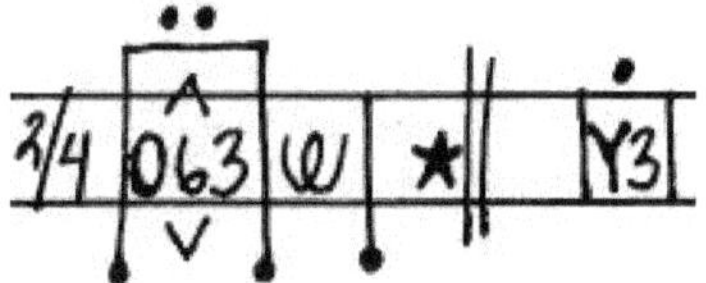

"FINGERSPELLING" (2)

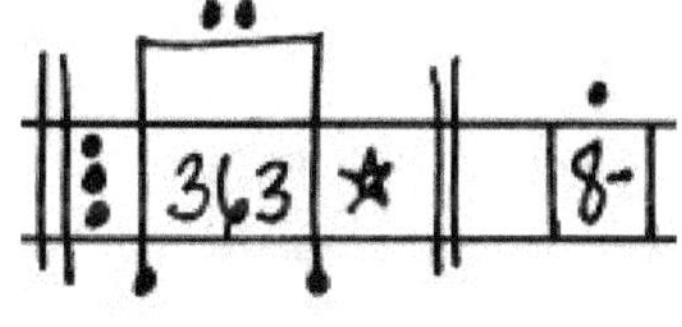

"COMPUTER" (1)

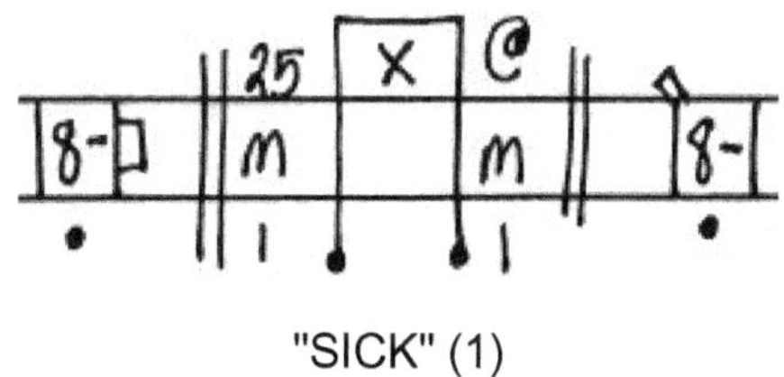

"SICK" (1)

INTERNATIONAL SAMPLES

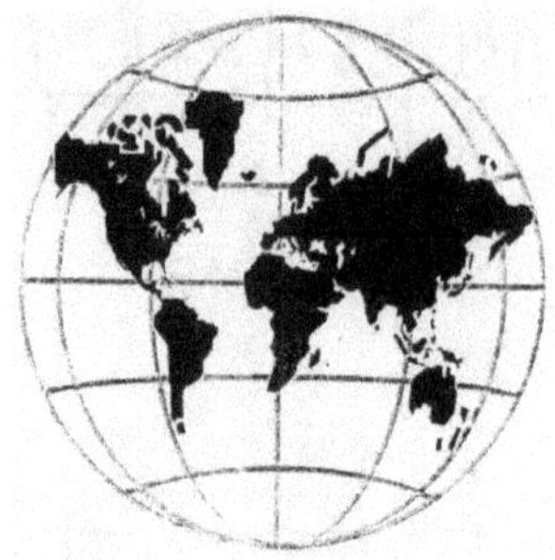

Let's take a look at the SN for some international samples! When researching these, I did a quick online search...and included the Youtube links so you can examine the source material. Whether or not these are "authentic" signs or the "correct" articulation is not our priority for this exercise. Our goal is to experiment with SN based on the available L1 source material.

JSL JAPANESE SIGN LANGUAGE

Nice to meet you!

Lesson 6 My name is .. Nice to meet you / Japanese Sign Language tutorial

https://www.youtube.com/watch?v=ogpCy7poTyg

The notation for an introductory greeting in JSL includes horizontally offset ND/D HS, and a small bob in the entire sign (notated in the MVT block), along with index bobs notated within the HS block.

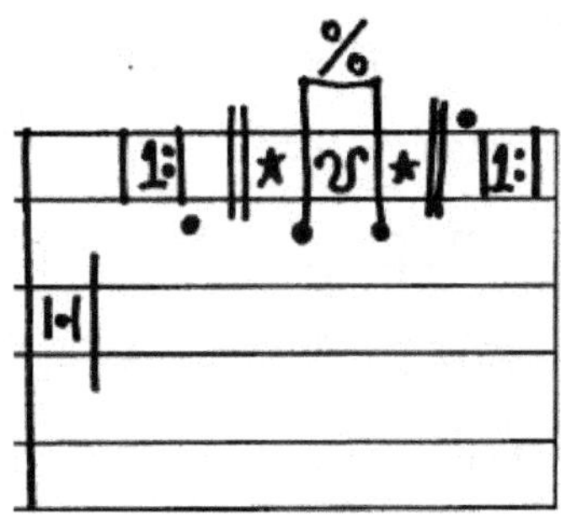

JSL: "GREETINGS"

A fun observation is that this sign is very much like the ASL sign for "to take a photo with a camera", with similar movements but slightly altered HS and LOC:

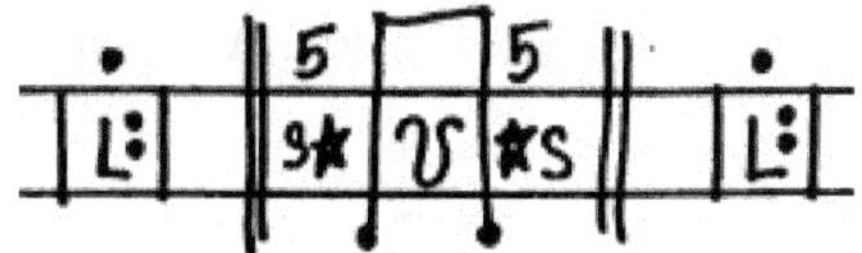

ASL: "TO TAKE A PHOTO WITH A MANUAL CAMERA"

We can insert the spelling of her name in English and add a JLS tag above to notate use of JSL alphabet/fingerspelling norms:

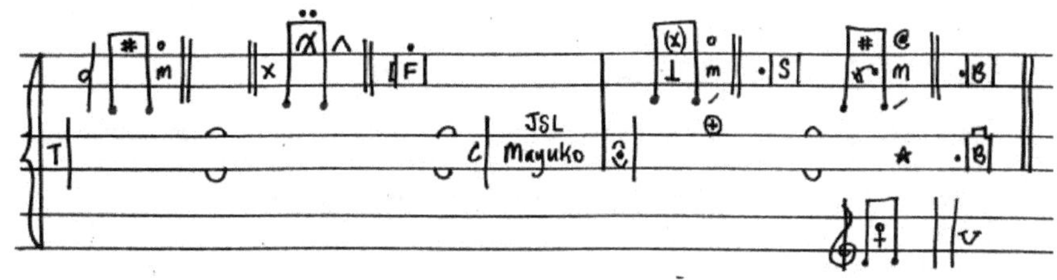

JSL: "MY NAME IS MAYUKO. NICE TO MEET YOU!"

Also, it is so neat to see how SN would need to be expanded to include new notations that reflect unique aspects of each signed language. For example, in Japanese culture, the person does a small bow when being introduced. This is uncommon in ASL, and common in JSL. Therefore a new notation for semi-bow and full-bow are needed:

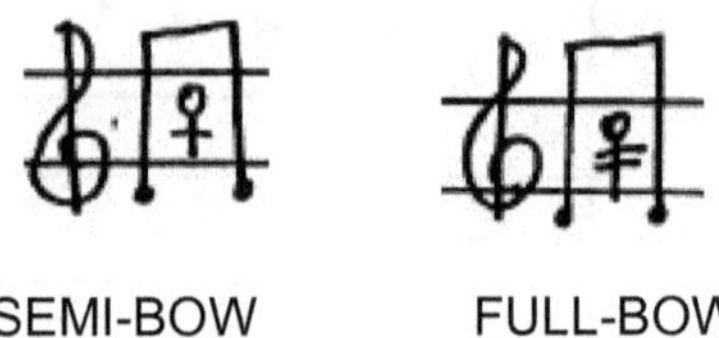

SEMI-BOW FULL-BOW

How awesome is that?!!!

LSM MEXICAN SIGN LANGUAGE

(Lengua de Señas Mexicana)

LSM - 04 - Saludos y otras expresiones en Lengua de Señas Mexicana

https://www.youtube.com/watch?v=VI7aB6ELCcM

Let's explore some common vocabulary in LSM. Working through these prompted me to add a grammar category: Social Courtesies. Terms like "Thank you", "Excuse me", "Sorry", "Good day", "Good morning/afternoon/night" etc...Of course these can be subjective...one person's "social courtesy" is another person's comment or statement, but it would be nice to have the option to alert the reader to anticipate a social courtesy:

SOCIAL GREETING GRAMMATICAL NOTATION

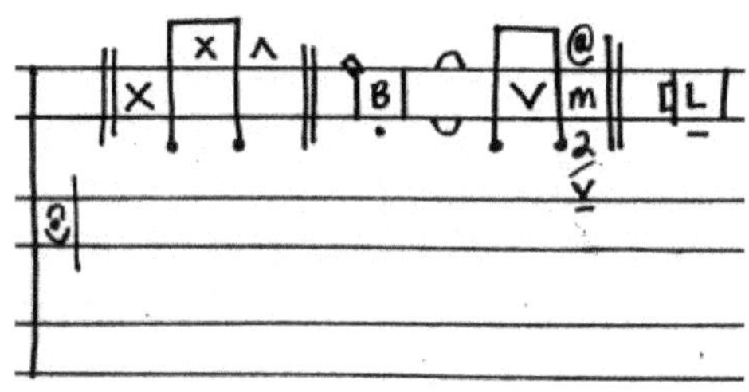

LSM: "BUENAS NOCHES"

In the next sign, you can see usage of locations (8, 12) and (10) above the HS blocks. This could also be notated in the lower section of the LOC block. This flexibility is due to the fact that the only numbers in (parentheses) are in reference to arm/hand locations.

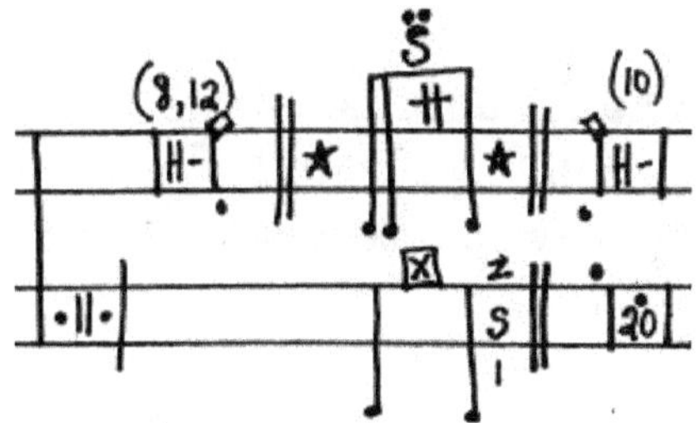

LSM: "HASTA MANANA"

The notation for "Gracias" utilizes a lateral BHS pair and to clarify, I added a repeat symbol below the ND BHS to ensure it remains static during the full sign articulation:

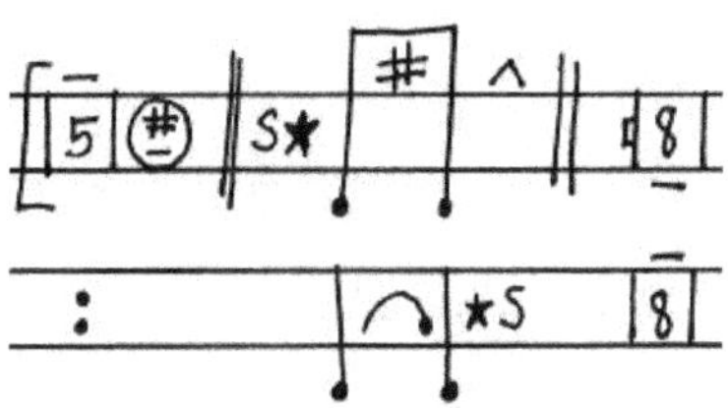

LSM: "GRACIAS"

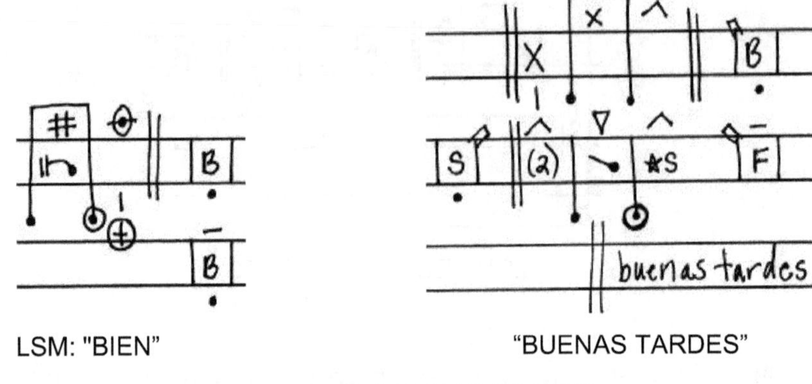

LSM: "BIEN" "BUENAS TARDES"

(WITH AFFIRMATIVE HEAD NOD)

RSL RUSSIAN SIGN LANGUAGE

Russian Sign Language: Lesson 2 - Personal Pronouns, Family, & Around The House

https://www.youtube.com/watch?v=j5C3ipuJrCU

Let's look at some samples from RSL. Each signed language has unique handshapes, locations, movements and cultural framing that impacts language…and notations would need to be developed to fully represent these aspects of each international signed language by those signing communities.

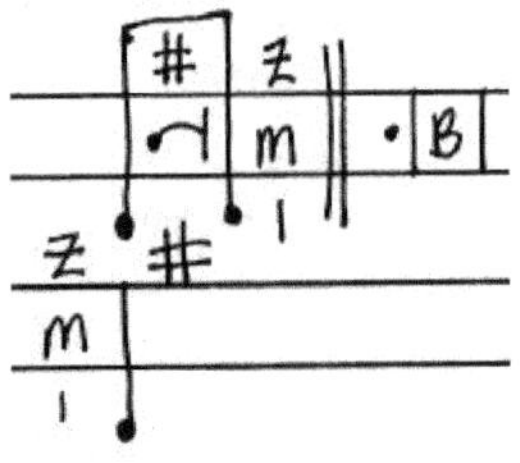

RSL: "MAMA"

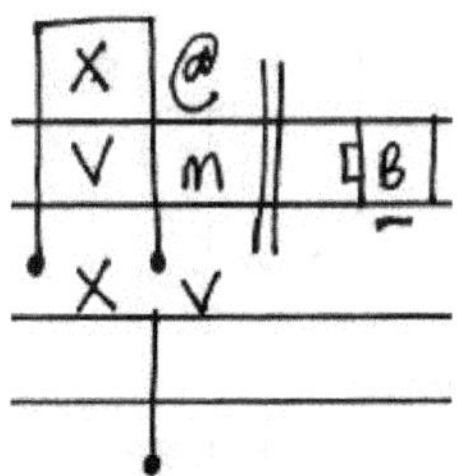

RSL: “PAPA”

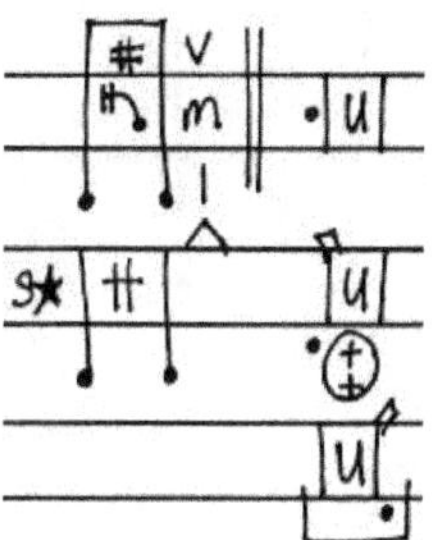

RSL: “SISTER”

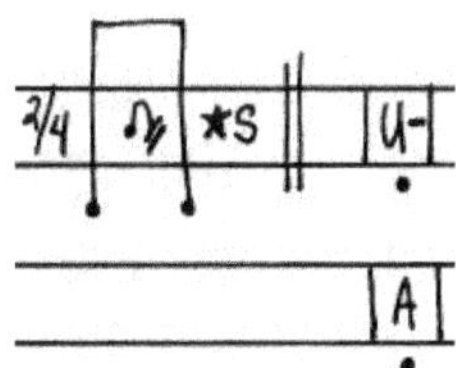

RSL: “YES”

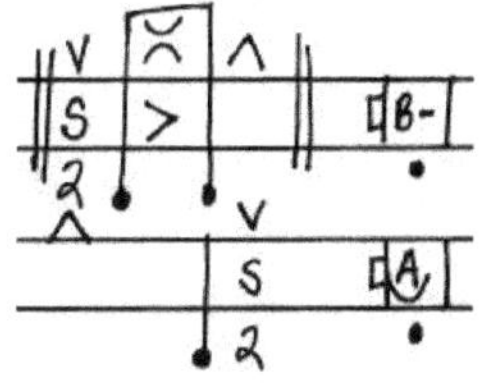

RSL: “NO”

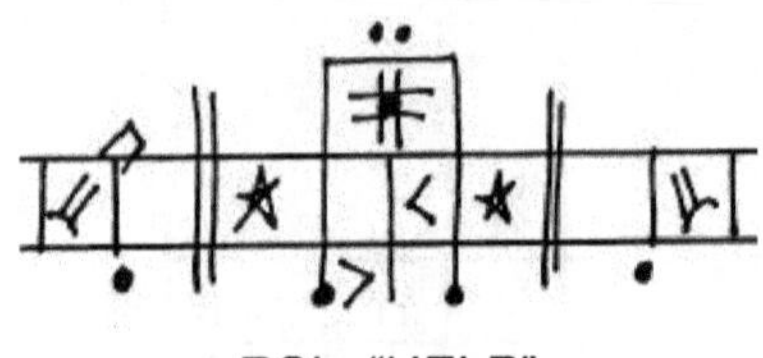

RSL: "HELP"

ASL signers will recognize the Russian sign glossed, "help" to be very similar to the ASL sign glossed: "bother":

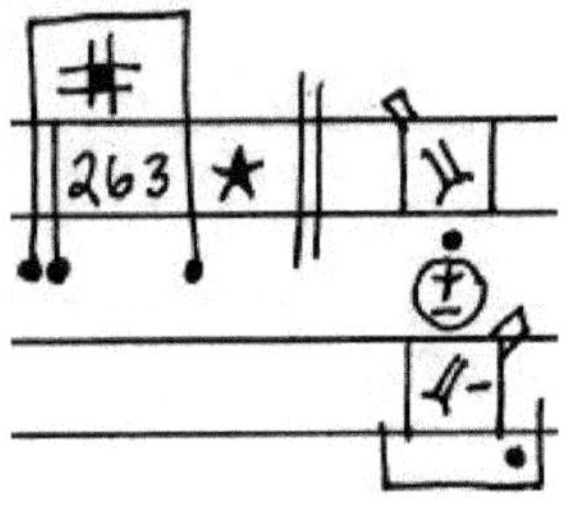

ASL: "BOTHER"

As well as related to the older ASL sign for Germany:

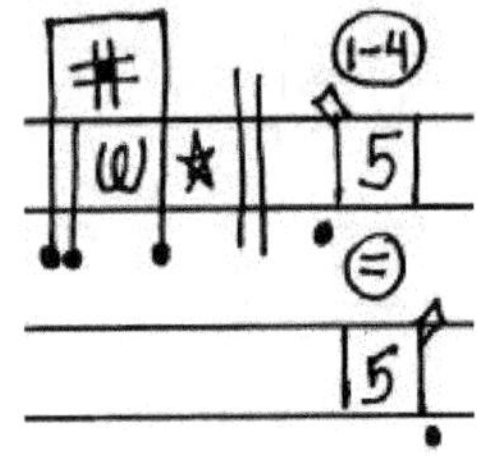

ASL: "GERMANY" (OLD SIGN)

Take a look at this Russian sign for "friend". It's a good example of a unique sign that needs a new movement and "handshape":

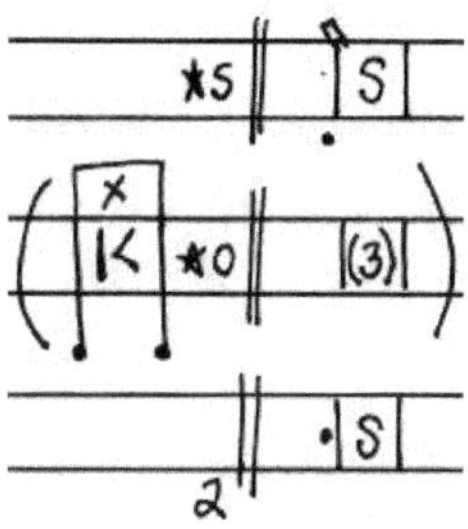

RSL: “FRIEND”

Drawing in the elbow as if tucking someone next to your side is a unique movement. The starting HS **“S”**, with orientation and location are notated on the first tier with no movement. The second tier with stress marks indicates the active phase of the sign with the elbow **(3)** notated in the HS block, its starting location *** O**, and unique movement **| <** . Usually joint locations are not inside the HS block, but in this sign articulation the elbow is functioning as a D HS. The final position of the D HS **“S”** is notated on the third tier to complete the articulation.

BSL BRITISH SIGN LANGUAGE

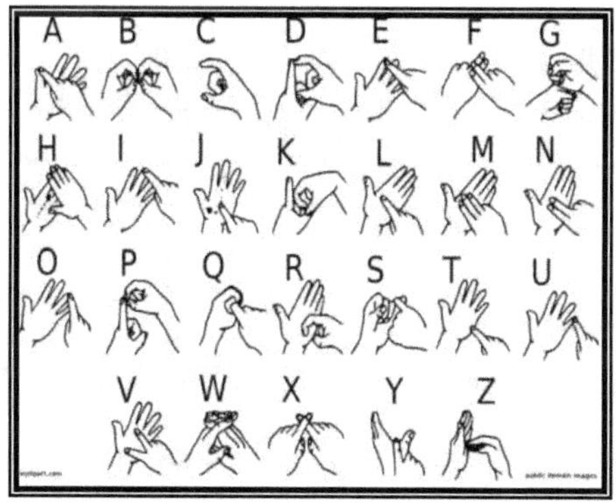

How to sign "My name is... What's your name?" in British Sign Language

https://www.youtube.com/watch?v=WpeGmAqhqQo

Our last foray into the realm of international samples, courtesy of the unbelievably fantastic internet, is from a country with a two-handed alphabet that superimposes the vowels A, E, I, O and U onto the ND “5” HS. I found BSL to be fascinating…as an ASL user there were many recognizable signs with quite different meanings. Let’s look at some of these notations:

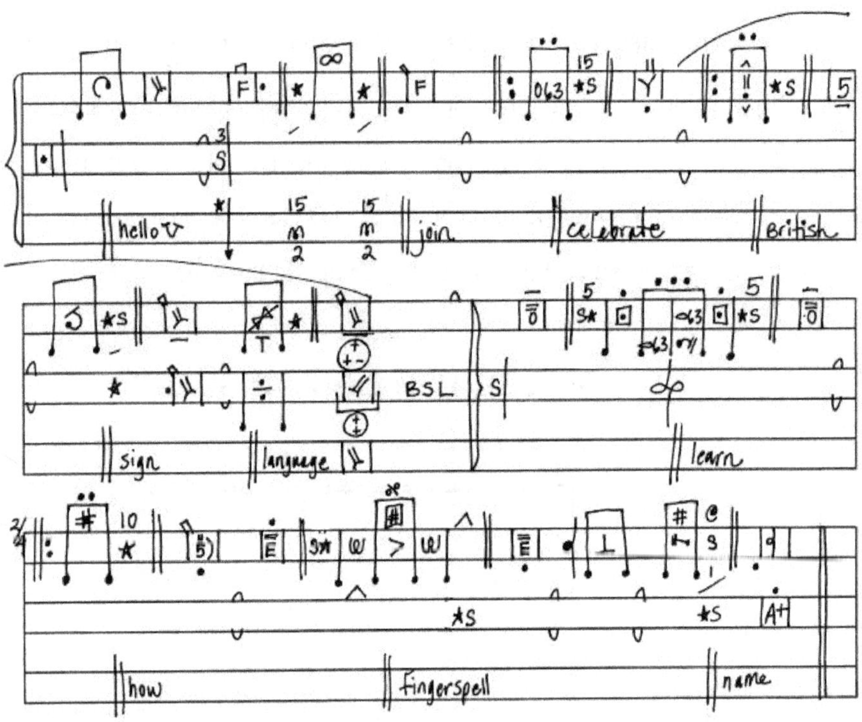

This sample represents just the intro section of the above video. Several interesting things occur in this section. The first is the grammatical content is parallel to the typical English sentence structure, and so is notated as a "statement". On the second tier, the notation for "language" requires two interactions with the BHS and so the second contact is below rather than above the BHS, on the third tier. The movement is only approximate...being similar to the movement "to paint" in ASL. The following sign, "learn" is a unique sign being an alternating and embedded movement sign, and with separate repetition notated for the embedded movement. This would need to be an agreed convention: an open and close movement would occur once during the counterclockwise elliptical movement. The sign for "fingerspell" involves an embedded movement and an off-set stack. The selection of any particular handshape is based on an ASL model and approximation. BSL users would need to determine the handshapes that represent their language for notation. The shorthand notation for the pronoun "your" in between "fingerspell" and "name" draws upon the user to be familiar with the BSL pronoun articulation. And the final sign "name" incorporates a handshape I don't recognize in ASL...a curled A. (Perhaps it is used and I'm overlooking it...) I created a handshape consistent with the "+" handshapes: A+. This is another example of the dependence of notations on the community of users...BSL signers would need to create a handshape set with internal norms. ASL users can of course notate other signed languages using ASL notation symbols, but these would only be approximations unless standardization occurs across signed languages.

BSL SIGN LANGUAGE DICTIONARY

http://www.signbsl.com/sign/hearing

The last tidbit on this topic is the BSL sign for "hearing" (person).

Interestingly, it is the same sign in ASL for one of the most common articulations for “Deaf”:

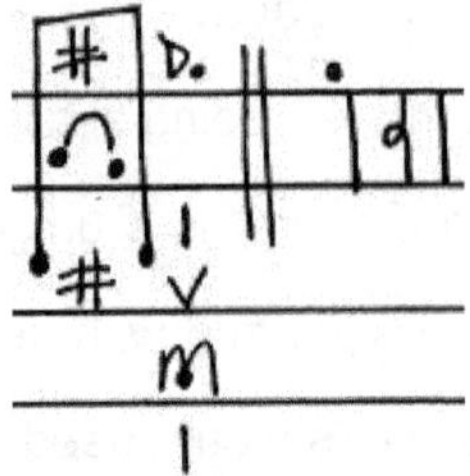

BSL: “HEARING” (PERSON)

ASL: “DEAF” (PERSON)

And one more…the BSL sign for “computer” is so

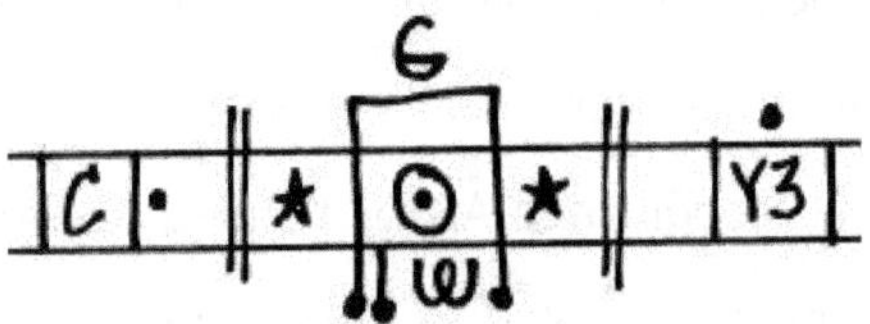

BSL: “COMPUTER”

It is exciting to consider the possibilities of notating native signed languages globally. Brazil has even adopted a sign writing system:

> “In Brazil, during the FENEIS (National Association of the Deaf) annual meeting in 2001, the association voted to accept SignWriting as the preferred method of transcribing Lingua Brasileira de Sinais (Libras) into a written form. The strong recommendation to the Brazilian government from that association was that SignWriting be taught in all Deaf schools. Currently SignWriting is taught on an academic level at the

University Federal de Santa Catarina as part of its Brazilian Sign Language curriculum.

Source: https://en.wikipedia.org/wiki/SignWriting Retrieved 3/14/16.

I personally am unfamiliar with this system for writing sign languages. I have felt in my brief contact with various extant systems via cursory online browsing a lack of visual structure for the reader and have striven to create something that visually represents the process of sign generation by the signer, and specifically deaf or hard of hearing children in bilingual educational programs.

A SAMPLE TEXT NOTATED: ASL NOOK

"ASL NOOK'S INTRODUCTION"

HTTPS://WWW.YOUTUBE.COM/WATCH?V=GISIUMQQBXS&LIST=PLR1YKDVYRSNJAYUWNLVIOG2B_DCDW9GW0&INDEX=36

Wouldn't it be grand to tackle a real text? The sample we will look at doesn't incorporate all the features we've explored, but it does cover many good aspects of SN. For example, it includes listing, body shifting, fingerspelling, numbers, alternating movements, stacked HS, embedded movements, mirror signs, phrase marks, RH?s, greetings, partings, repeats, time signature, eye gaze tracking of signs and even some depicting verbs! I encourage you to view the sample yourself on Youtube and then examine the notations that follow. If you find errors, be merciful and correct them. If you find your notations would be different, that is to be expected and completely fine! There is more than one way for some notations and those adjustments are part of the process of using SN within the signing community. Are you ready?...Here we go!

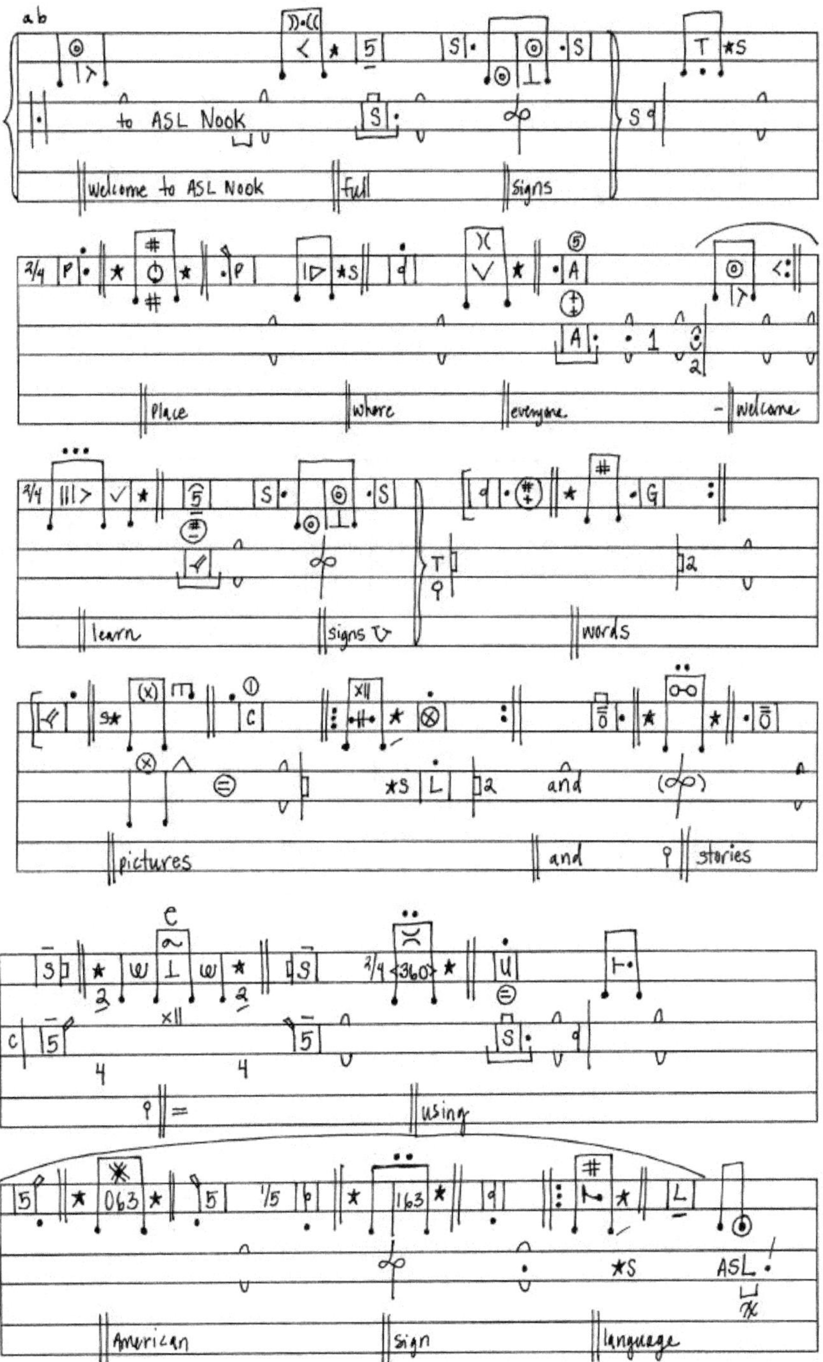
to ASL Nook
welcome to ASL Nook
full
signs
place
where
everyone
welcome
learn
signs
words
and
pictures
and
stories
using
American
sign
language
ASL!

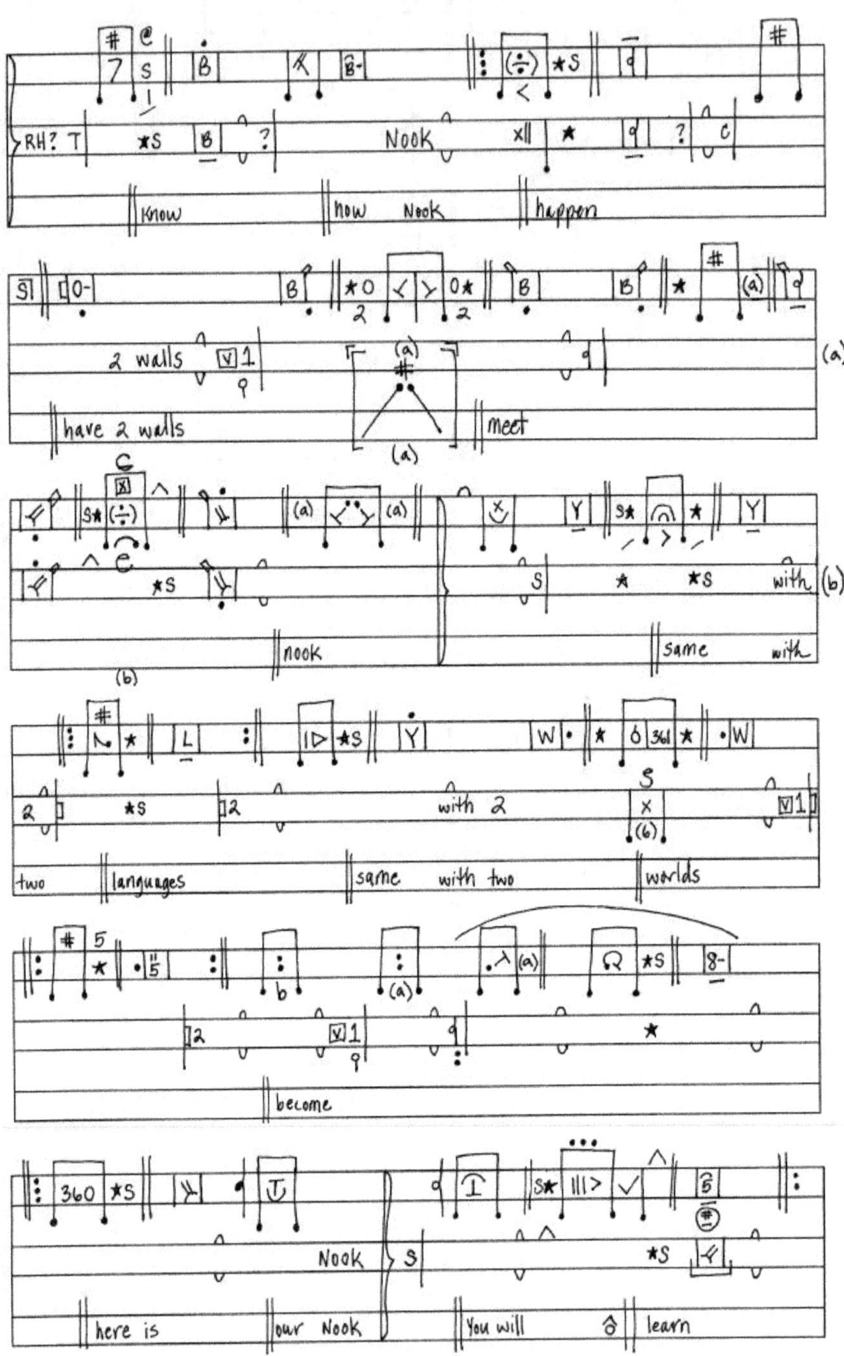
RH? T
Nook
Know
now Nook
happen
2 walls
have 2 walls
meet
nook
with
same with
with 2
two
languages
same with two
worlds
become
Nook
here is
our Nook
You will
learn

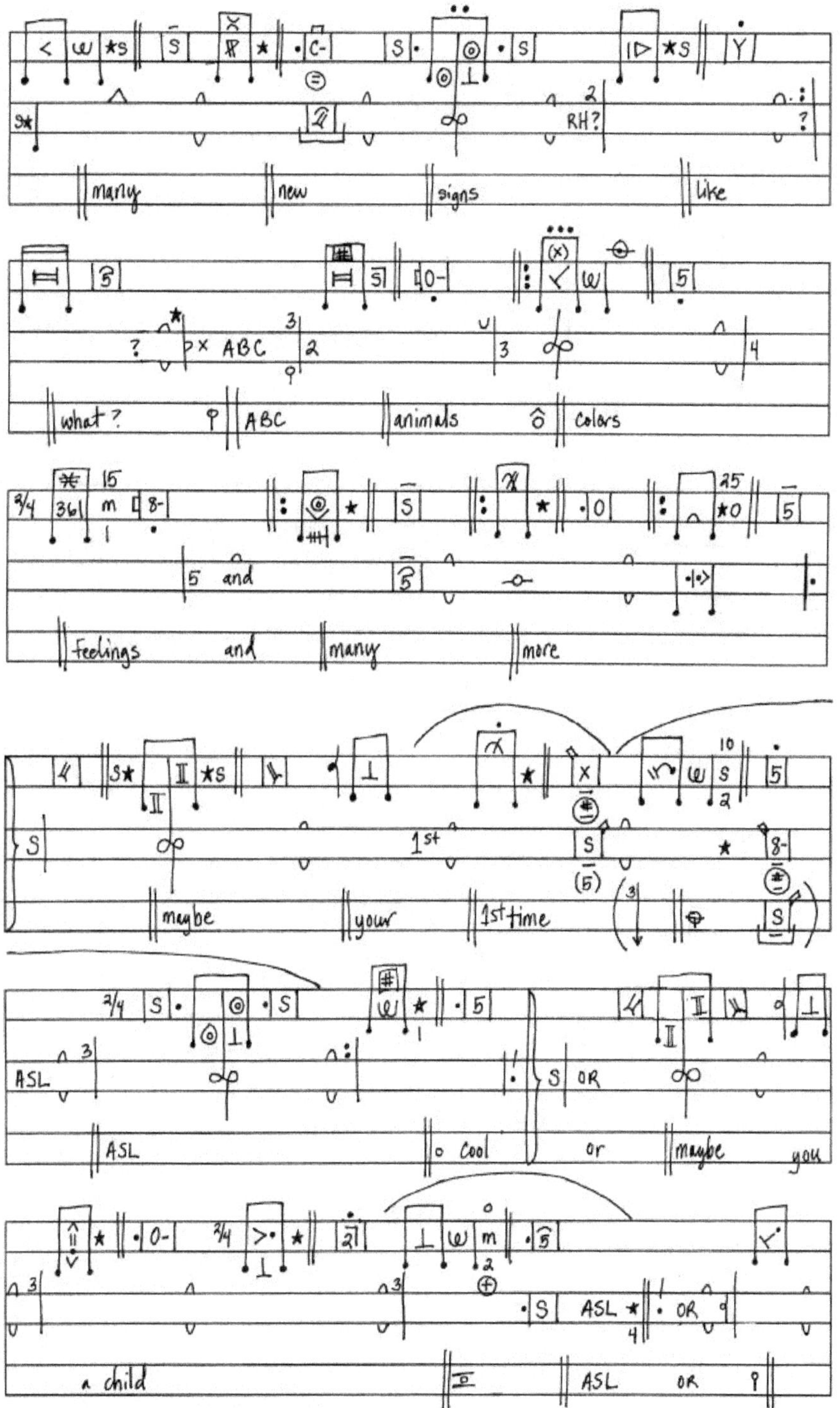
many new signs like
what? ABC animals colors
feelings and many more
maybe your 1st time
ASL cool or maybe you
a child ASL or

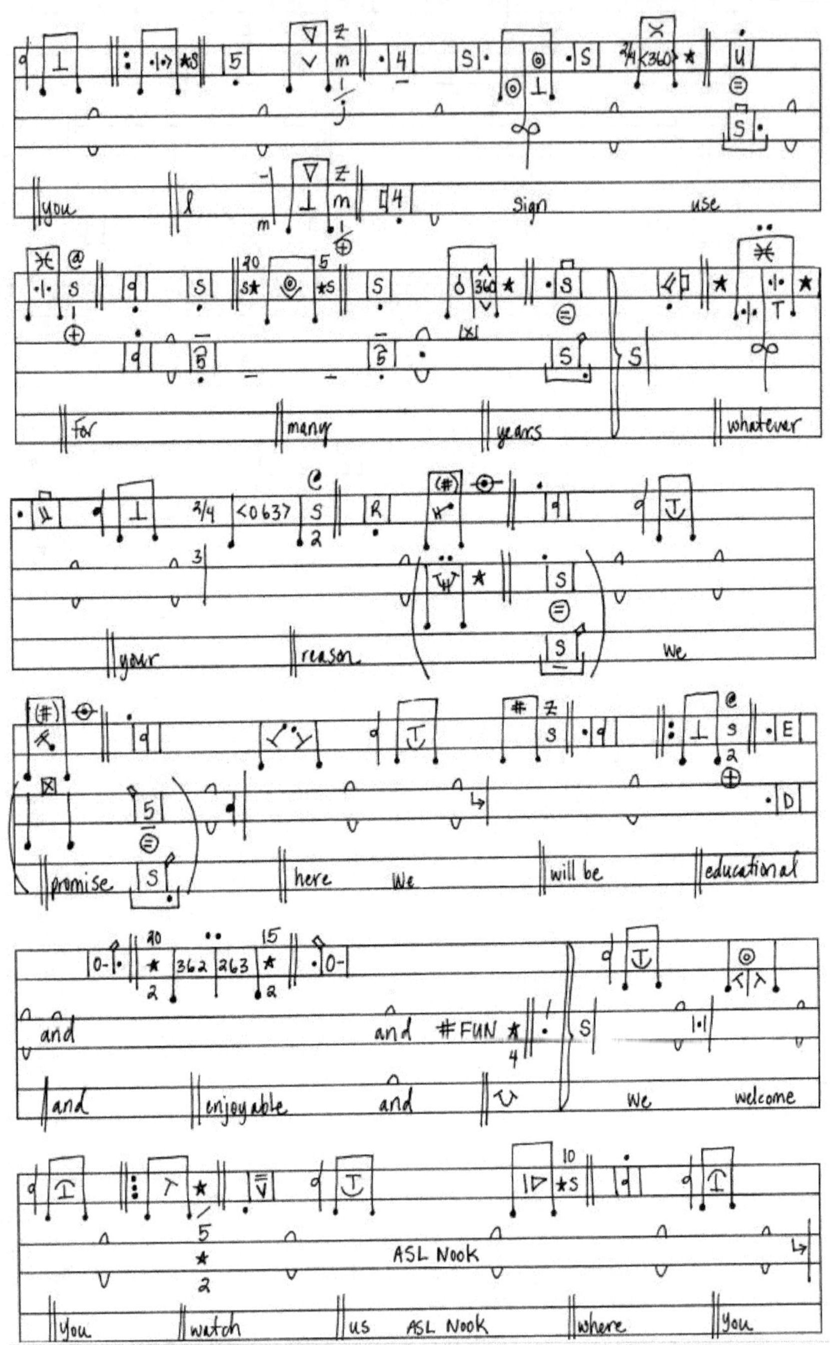
you
sign
use
for
many
years
whatever
your
reason
we
promise
here
we
will be
educational
and
and
#FUN
and
enjoyable
and
we
welcome
ASL Nook
you
watch
us
ASL Nook
where
you

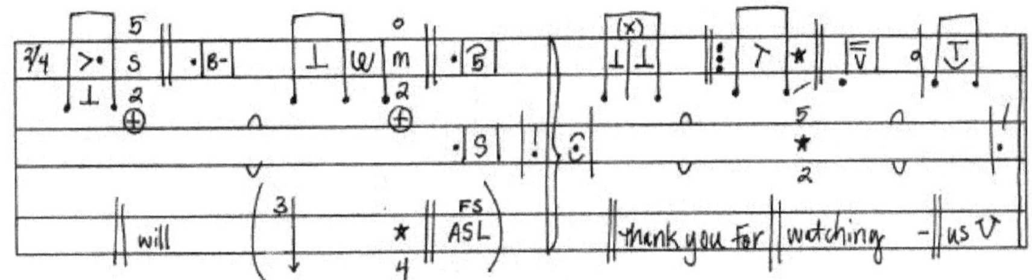

NOTE: In the sample above, mouthing was notated.

REFLECTIONS

IS THIS WHAT ASL LOOKS LIKE ON PAPER?

As this is an exercise in recording what is signed vs. inserting standard notations for specific signs, my goal is to record what was actually articulated. For educational use, creating standard notations would be helpful for evaluating non-standard articulations or changes in language use over time. I found it very challenging to identify specific facial grammar and notate those appropriately. When you are used to how signers communicate, is seems like almost everything they are doing is naturally a part of that sign, given the grammatical type (S, T, C, WH?, Command etc...) or a function of mouthing which is also integral to many signs. It seems redundant to include the double set of facial grammar lines prior to mouthing if there are no other facial grammar notations, so on the cover of this book, you will see those were removed. **Default is terms written on the third tier are mouthing unless otherwise notated, such as when fingerspelling is bumped to the final tier.** I also noticed that it is redundant and therefore unnecessary to mark the midline plane location for signs on the mouth as these locations are incorporated into the mouth notation:

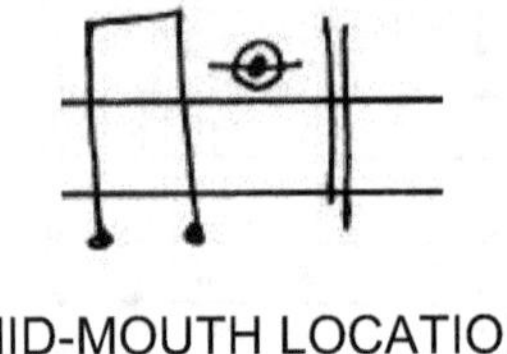

MID-MOUTH LOCATION

Further simplification of mid-locations can be incorporated for the central mid-chest and mid-chin:

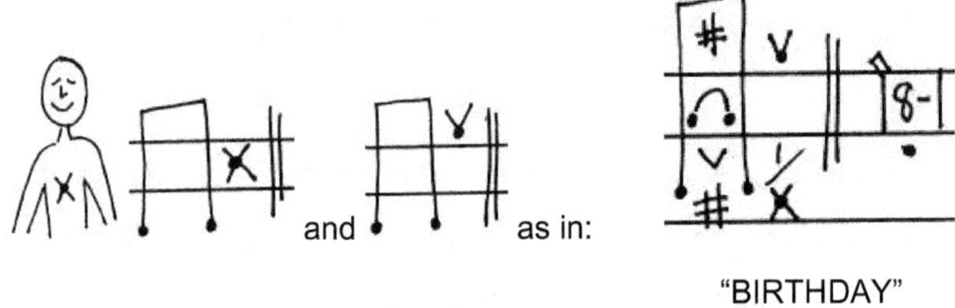

"BIRTHDAY"

I incorporated variety in HS notations, such as the sign glossed, "to watch" which came up twice in this piece, and experimented notating signs that end in fingerspelling such as "fascinated in ASL". If there are any errors in the sample notation above, I apologize. It is a reflection on my own learning process and not the beautiful signing on ASL Nook.

A small revelation occurred regarding the movement for the sign glossed: "sign language". In ASL; a rapid articulation results in a movement that is a counterclockwise "tie" and could be standardized in a shorthand notation that reflects this unique compound sign movement. The "tie" movement has been broken into two phases to accommodate the change in HS and contact mid-articulation:

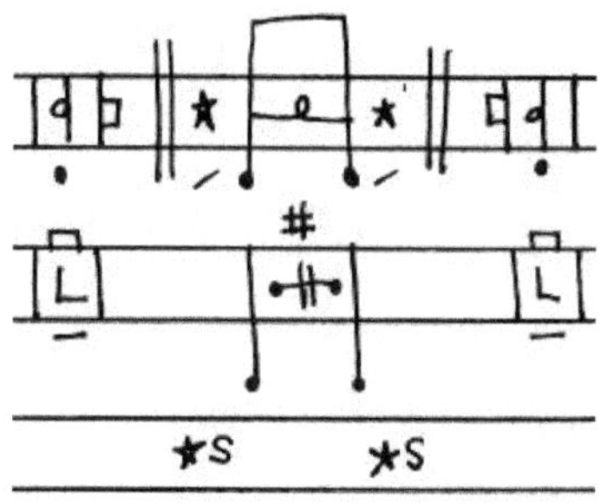

"SIGN LANGUAGE"

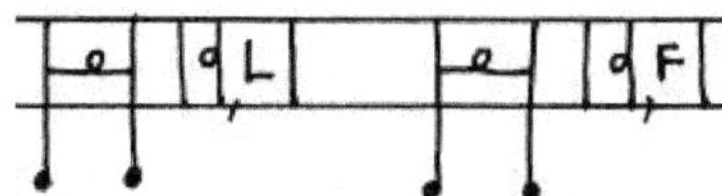

"SIGN LANGUAGE" SHORTHAND ("L" OR "F" HS)

A separate movement for a full tie would include endpoints:

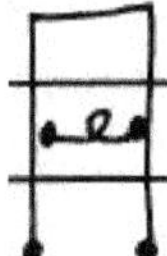

FULL "TIE" MOVEMENT

My final thoughts are how having a written form for a language impacts the way you experience the language. When someone is talking, you can have a simultaneous back-script running…When I'm interpreting, I now see and recognize features of ASL in conjunction with these written forms, can record those if I want, and return later and "read" again what I wrote but have forgotten. I have a deeper appreciation for, understanding of, and love for ASL and its grammatical structure. To all the lovely ASL users I get to chat, chat, chat with…your signs are running in my mind…as notations…!

REVERSE TRANSLATING

The next step is to take a set of notations, and test the accuracy by having a model signer reproduce, based solely on notations, the text and compare that videotaped product to the original sample text. For that to be accomplished, the test signer would need a baseline competence with Signotation. I see this as an important and necessary experiment that would be most appropriately conducted by the Deaf Community if this method of notation is seen as viable.

YOUR TURN!

What common ASL sign is notated below? Check your answer in the back section under "YOUR TURN! ANSWERS" (#11)

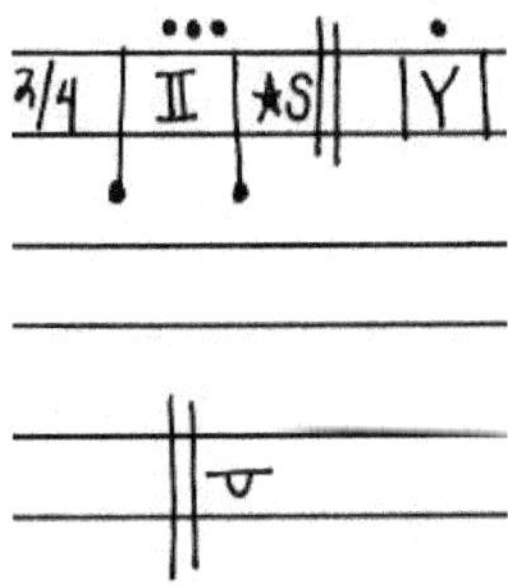

I HOPE YOU ENJOY EXPERIMENTING WITH YOUR OWN SIGNOTATIONS!

YOU TRY! SIGNOTATION STAFF

Download a FREE Sign Staff template, visit: www.Signotation.com

YOUR TURN! ANSWERS

#1 HANDSHAPE:

"SNAKE"

#2 PALM ORIENTATION:

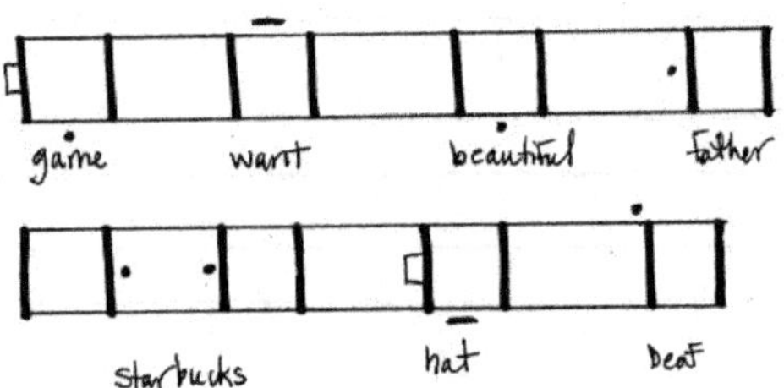

#3 LOCATION:

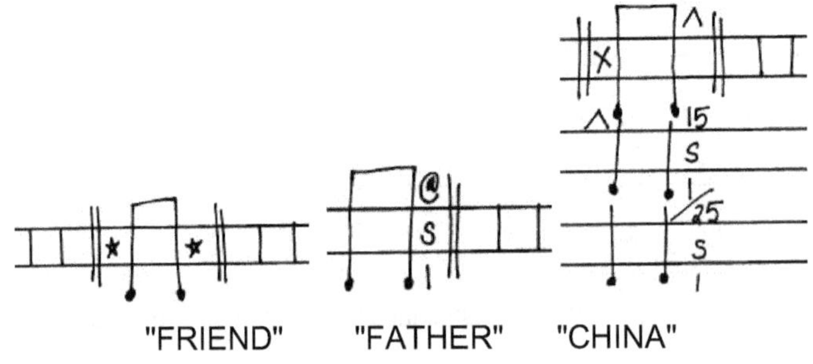

"FRIEND" "FATHER" "CHINA"

#4 MOVEMENT:

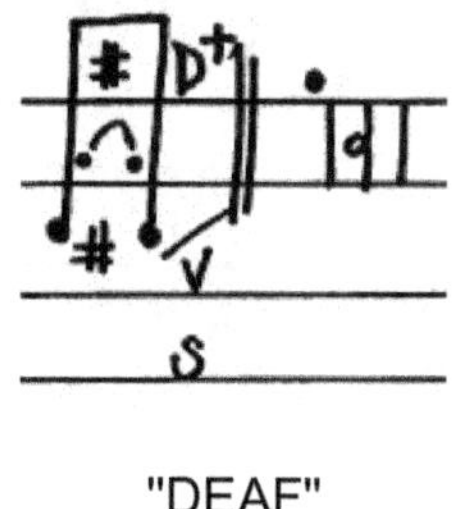

"DEAF"

#5 "CERTIFIED"

#6 DEPICTING VERBS:

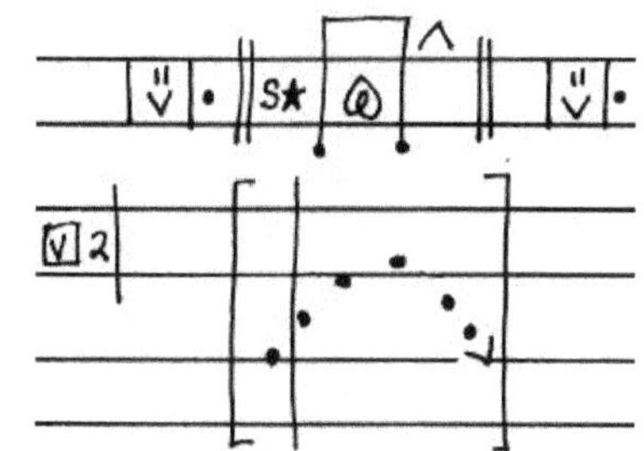

CRITTERS SITTING IN A SEMI-CIRCLE
WITH ND ACTING AS AN "ANCHOR HS"

#7 FINGERSPELLING:

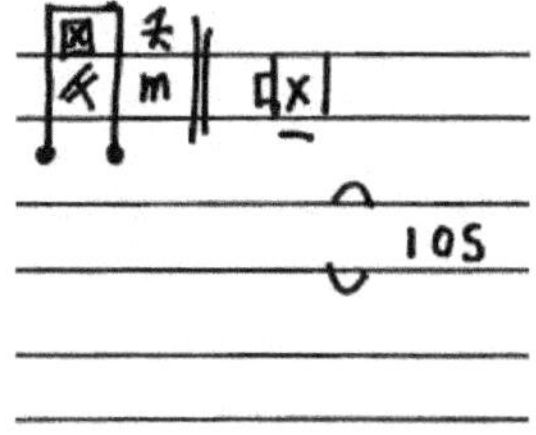

#8 FACIAL GRAMMAR:

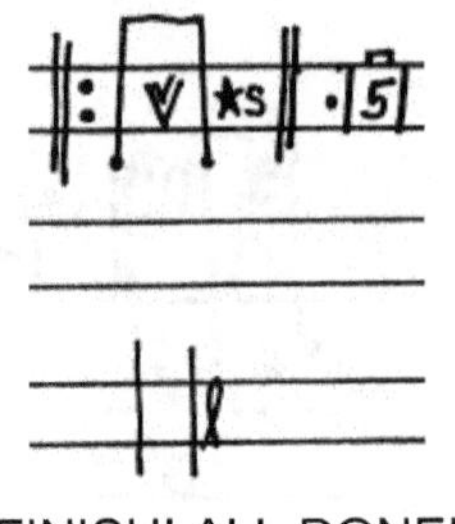

"FINISH! ALL DONE!"

#9 LISTING:

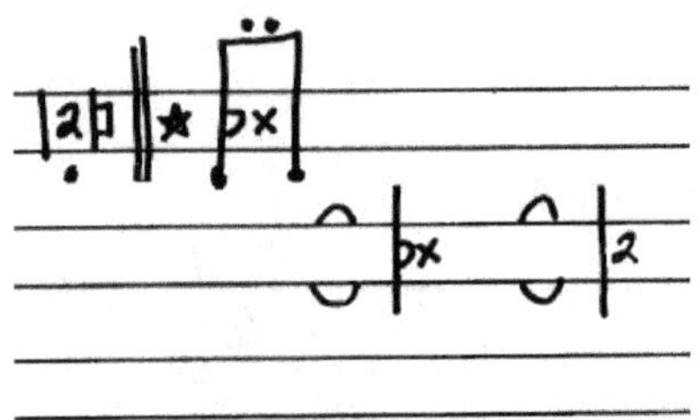

#10 TIME SIGNATURE

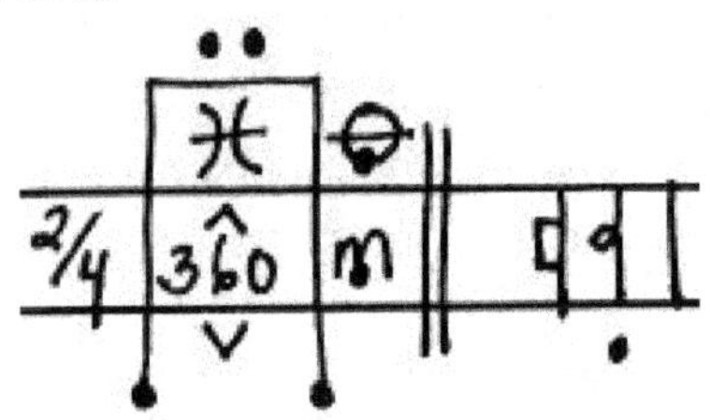

"HEARING" (PERSON)

#11 “OIC”

CONCLUSION

I thought this would be a reasonably quick project...instead it has taken months and years to collect these observations, and is still a work in progress. I have a new appreciation for the work of researchers and linguists who devote significant chunks of their time to an unknown result. I am excited to see if any of this is beneficial or useful to the signing community. Thank you for taking your time to consider this approach to recording signed languages on paper. I look forward to hearing from you! Comments and feedback: Please put "Signotation" in the subject line.

ASLiShansen@gmail.com

www.signotation.com

ARTWORK

The artwork, sketches and notations contained in this text are the product of the author, free clip art, creative commons photos or purchased art.

ABOUT THE AUTHOR

Shelly Hansen, CI/CT/SC:Legal/ED:K-12
has been working as a
RID Certified American Sign Language Interpreter since 1992.
She is an active Community Interpreter, Youtube vlogger
(ASLInterpreter@S.Hansen) and has articles published on
Street Leverage and the RID VIEWS.
She has three beloved children,
Erik, Anna and Josie,
a wonderful husband Paul,
and currently resides in WA state.

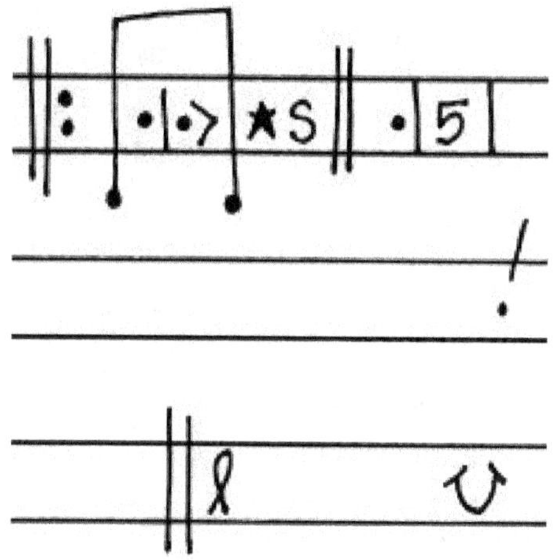

INDEX

D

E

F

G

W

Y

www.ingramcontent.com/pod-product-compliance
Lightning Source LLC
LaVergne TN
LVHW051254080426
835509LV00020B/2968

9780692670187